"With insurgency as an analytical anchor, *Thinking While Black* is an impressive study of how Black intellectual life is generated through hopeful contestations. Offering a deep reading of provocations offered by Paul Gilroy and Armond White, this text beautifully historicizes the soul rebel as a figure of capacious and rigorous critique that seeks out promising and fantastic futures."

KATHERINE MCKITTRICK, author of *Dear Science and Other Stories* and *Demonic Grounds: Black Women and the Cartographies of Struggle*

"*Thinking While Black* provides a critical assessment of two prominent cultural critics. In comparing and contrasting Paul Gilroy and Armond White, McNeil avoids hagiography in his thoughtful, scholarly, and yet accessible appraisal of the two influential intellectuals from two different sides of the 'Black Atlantic.' The result is an insightful reflection on the politics and aesthetics of cultural criticism."

DAVID AUSTIN, author of *Dread Poetry and Freedom: Linton Kwesi Johnson and the Unfinished Revolution* and *Fear of a Black Nation: Race, Sex and Security in Sixties Montreal*

"In *Thinking While Black,* Daniel McNeil explains why the radical approaches inherent in the intellectual journeys of Gilroy and White matter, re/constructs the sociocultural contexts within which each emerged, and examines the processes and consequences of their evolutions from 'young soul rebels' into 'middle-aged mavericks.' His attentive and meticulous analysis of the ambitions, accomplishments, and trajectories of these two Black thinkers complicates any simple categorization of Black intellectualism."

MICHELE A. JOHNSON, professor, Department of History, York University

T0321426

THINKING WHILE BLACK

WORKING WITH BLACK

THINKING WHILE BLACK

TRANSLATING THE POLITICS

AND POPULAR CULTURE

DANIEL McNEIL

OF A REBEL GENERATION

Rutgers University Press
New Brunswick, Camden, and Newark, New Jersey, and London

Rutgers University Press is a department of Rutgers, The State University of New Jersey, one of the leading public research universities in the nation. By publishing worldwide, it furthers the University's mission of dedication to excellence in teaching, scholarship, research, and clinical care.

Library of Congress Cataloging-in-Publication Data
Names: McNeil, Daniel, author.
Title: Thinking while Black : translating the politics and popular culture of a rebel generation / by Daniel McNeil.
Description: New Brunswick : Rutgers University Press, [2022] |
Includes bibliographical references and index. | Identifiers: LCCN 2022010596 |
ISBN 9781978830875 (paperback) | ISBN 9781978830882 (hardback) |
ISBN 9781978830899 (epub) | ISBN 9781978830905 (pdf)
Subjects: LCSH: African Americans—Intellectual life—History—20th century. |
Black people—Great Britain—Intellectual life—History—20th century. | African American film critics. | Popular culture—Political aspects—United States—History—20th century. | Popular culture—Political aspects—Great Britain—History—20th century. | Gilroy, Paul, 1956– | White, Armond.
Classification: LCC E185.89.I56 M37 2022 |
DDC 305.896/073—dc23/eng/20220805
LC record available at https://lccn.loc.gov/2022010596

A British Cataloging-in-Publication record for this book is available from the British Library.

References to internet websites (URLs) were accurate at the time of writing. Neither the author nor Rutgers University Press is responsible for URLs that may have expired or changed since the manuscript was prepared.

∞ The paper used in this publication meets the requirements of the American National Standard for Information Sciences—Permanence of Paper for Printed Library Materials, ANSI Z39.48-1992.

rutgersuniversitypress.org

To Sheila's memory,
and to Alex's future

CONTENTS

PREFACE xi

1.
THEORIES IN MOTION 1
Mapping the Roots and Routes of a Rebel Generation

2.
BLACK AND BRITISH 15
A Lived Contradiction

3.
A MOVIE-STRUCK KID FROM DETROIT 43
Going Deeper into Movies

4.
SLAVE-DESCENDANTS, DIASPORA SUBJECTS,
AND WORLD CITIZENS 61
Paul Gilroy's Historical Sensibility

5.
ENLARGING *THE AMERICAN CINEMA* 77
Armond White vs. the Straight Middle-Class White World
(and the Black Bourgeoisie)

6.
MIDDLE-AGED, GIFTED, AND BLACK 113
Structures of Feeling in the Black Atlantic

CODA 133
Guess Who's Coming to the Awards Dinner

NOTES 149

ACKNOWLEDGMENTS 181

INDEX 185

The capacity to live with difference is, in my view, the coming question of the twenty-first century.

Stuart Hall (1993)

The basic humanistic mission today, whether in music, literature, or any of the arts or the humanities, has to do with the preservation of difference without, at the same time, sinking into the desire to dominate.

Edward Said (2002)

PREFACE

T his book explores the aspirations and achievements of a political and cultural generation that consumed images of rebellion and revolution around the world as young Black teenagers in the late 1960s, and began asserting their ideas about individual self-fashioning and collective liberation in public arenas in North America and Europe during the 1970s and early '80s. The transnational dimensions of this cohort are often overlooked in US-centric discussions about the political struggles and legislative achievements of a civil rights generation, on the one hand, and the individual advancement and digital cultures of a post–civil rights generation, on the other.[1] As a result, I have found it helpful to turn to the insights of Linton Kwesi Johnson, a dub poet and activist born in Jamaica in 1952 and based in the United Kingdom since 1963, who describes his generation as one that asserted their anger, defiance, and resistance in the 1970s and early '80s by working together to fight against racism in general and racist police oppression in particular.[2]

Thinking While Black maps the journeys of intellectual discovery taken by two contemporaries of Johnson whose creative energy, utopian visions, and humanist commitments have made them intriguing agents and avatars of a rebel generation. One is Armond White, a film and culture critic born in Detroit in 1953 who believes that if you cut him open in search of his motivations, ethics, and beliefs, you'll find the Holy Trinity of Motown, Bible verses, and the movies.[3] The other is Paul Gilroy, an intellectual born in London in 1956 who looks back on the 1970s as a time in which an "unusually eloquent, militant and musically rich culture" granted him material and symbolic resources to perceive how Black cultures—in religious, secular and profane spaces—could overflow from the containers that the modern state provides for them.[4]

I did not grow up in the 1950s and '60s listening carefully to Black creative artists translating the legal and bureaucratic discourse of the Universal Declaration of Human Rights, which the United Nations General Assembly adopted in 1948, into lively, radical, and non-sermonizing terms that might resonate with young, multiracial audiences. I was not alive in the 1970s when members of this rebel generation struggled and organized—often outside of conventional politics—for a better future for the planet and all of its peoples. I am, however, painfully aware of the conservative codes for managing minority belonging in the 1980s that they confronted in their political, intellectual, aesthetic, and activist work.

In the accounts of British commentators, which rely on broad, overgeneralized generational labels that obscure as much as they reveal, my date of birth would make me one of "Thatcher's children." Yet as one of the young people who grew up in Merseyside during Margaret Thatcher's tenure as prime minister of the United Kingdom between 1979 and 1990, I felt more like one of Thatcher's bastards. My home community in northwest England was framed as an urban wasteland after its shipping and manufacturing industries collapsed, unemployment rates reached around 20 percent, and multiracial groups of young people targeted discernible local institutions and the everyday networks of local activity in what British opinion leaders described as riots. Cabinet meetings chaired by

Thatcher discussed putting Liverpool, the region's most populous city, into "Detroit-style managed decline,"[5] and journalists portrayed Liverpudlians as "scheming scallies and scousers," "Northern monkeys," and jobless yobs with little or no education. After endorsing Thatcher's Conservative Party in the general elections of 1979, 1983, and 1987, the *Sun* newspaper falsely accused Liverpool supporters of stealing from dead bodies, urinating on police officers, and assaulting front-line workers who were trying to save lives during a fatal human crush at the Hillsborough soccer stadium in 1989.[6] Although the tabloid, owned by Rupert Murdoch's News Corp, dominated the circulation figures for newspapers in the United Kingdom between 1978 and 2018, it was boycotted by news agents in Merseyside and I grew up associating it with toxic waste.

When I migrated south to the University of Oxford in 1998, I encountered a world that treated the tabloid journalism of the *Sun* with similar disdain while tolerating more covert forms of classism and racism. Students being trained to inhabit positions in the British elite found it amusing, for example, to use "the accused" as the collective name for a group of Liverpudlians wearing a suit. When I read Stuart Hall's reflections about the distilled Englishness he navigated at Oxford as a "scholarship boy" from Jamaica almost fifty years earlier, I did not consider them anachronistic. However, I more clearly perceived how the conservative values incubated by London and the southeast had been sold as quintessentially English traits when I moved to Toronto in 2001 as the recipient of a scholarship that funded graduates of Oxford to continue their studies in Canada.

While I was somewhat prepared to navigate the barely concealed Anglophilia among members of a Canadian elite, which considered it common sense to pay homage to the dour cults of Winston Churchill and Oxbridge colleges, I was caught off guard by a Canadian media that sought to achieve recognition from Americans while distancing itself from the unacceptable face of racial capitalism in the United States. I couldn't quite believe the headlines on subway monitors that proudly announced that the Canadian "Nelly Furtado will sit on the front of the American Grammys." I was perturbed by national columnists who asserted that a Black Canadian population was primarily made up of immigrants and "second-generation immigrants" who were unable to claim any historical injustice in the "Great White North."[7] Even when I tuned in to British radio shows, I was taken aback by Canadian luminaries pronouncing that slavery, colonialism, and racial violence had not sullied their home and native land.[8] I couldn't help but wonder if Canadian high schools taught students how to win friends and influence people in the United States in the morning and how to establish some plausible deniability from what they considered the vulgarity and violence of American history and culture in the afternoon.

In conjunction with essays in which Hall expressed how dumbfounded he was by American Cultural Studies, I began to read scholarship that sought to translate his complex and ambiguous writing to address settler-colonial racism in Canada. I discovered that writers who were deemed experts in Canadian "race relations" claimed that many readers found it difficult to comprehend the points Hall and other postcolonial thinkers were trying to make. Rather than think creatively about how they might adapt Hall's striking metaphors about postcolonial subjects being the sugar in the British cup of tea to explore the complexities of identity and culture,[9] prominent scholars and race relations consultants argued that it was "confusing" for Canadian journalists to use metaphors such as "the elephant in the room" in articles that discussed the skin color of victims and perpetrators of gun violence.[10] Hall wrote about irony as a powerful weapon for minority groups striving for liberation and democracy, and permitted scholars of media, culture, and society to bring their research into the broader public realm and make space in the academy for a serious analysis of the politics and poetics of marginalized communities; Canadian social scientists sought to domesticate such radical energy in their reports on racism for "decision-makers" and their textbooks on racism by claiming that it was a problem for museums to muddy the waters of their messages about white colonialism with a "strong use of irony."[11]

Such intolerance for any hidden agendas in language is often deemed necessary in the pursuit of accessible work that introduces, defines, and summarizes the social scientific literature on racism for an "informed general public."[12] Terms such as the informed general public are floating signifiers that point to no actual object and have no agreed-upon meaning. Still, they often accompany public-facing research that considers it "elitist," "overly intellectual," or "impressionistic" to treat people as active, intelligent readers capable of deconstructing systems that position the tastes and values of white, middle-class professionals as universal.[13] They run the risk of patronizing readers rather than trusting them to search out further material to help clarify or deepen their understanding of material that they may, on first reading, have found confusing and challenging. Indeed, Black intellectuals such as Peter James Hudson, Aaron Kamugisha, and Katherine McKittrick have described such approaches as a dominant feature of "sociological plotting" and a condescending liberal discourse that seeks to subsume Black life and livingness within the paternalistic hold of the Canadian nation.[14]

Disgruntled with the patronizing discourses in academic and journalistic institutions, I went searching for writers who contested racial hierarchies with artful, inventive, and compelling prose that I did not find overly didactic or sermonizing. Two of the authors that helped me to navigate the risk-aversion and "multicultural snake oil" that confined and defined a Canadian public sphere were Armond White and Paul Gilroy.[15] I stumbled across White's work when he wrote for the *New York Press*, an alternative weekly with a libertarian and punk rock sensibility. I encountered Gilroy's work when he was a professor of Sociology and African American Studies at Yale University, and had become a well-known (if not always well-read) presence in academic discussions about modernity, hybridity, and double consciousness.

Thinking While Black builds on this initial encounter with White and Gilroy in the early days of the twenty-first century. Chapter one sets out some reasons why the two thinkers matter to anyone who wishes to take academic research out of the classroom and university presses and into the broader public realm for discussion, debate, and examination across multiple media platforms, and push professional, routine, and narrow academic accounts into livelier and more radical directions. It considers what it means to read Gilroy, one of the most-cited Black academics in the arts and social sciences, in relation to White, perhaps the most notorious film critic in the digital age. On the one hand, it outlines some of the differences between writers who appear to be an odd couple to academics accustomed to working within national and disciplinary regimes (and associating evaluative criticism in general, and the polemical journalism of White in particular, with punditry, contrarianism, and unsystematic work rather than serious political and social thought). It engages, for example, with questions posed about the global intellectual history of social movements and how we might read "activist writers whose ideas shift over time and are often written in unclear, fragmented, broken, or partial ways (as opposed to professional idea-havers whose ideas are often published in books with clear reception histories)."[16] On the other hand, it highlights the affinities (discordant or otherwise) between an African American journalist who completed an MFA in Film History, Theory, and Criticism at Columbia University, and an academic with a supplementary career as a journalist exploring the expressive cultures of the African diaspora. In short, I argue that both thinkers provide us with a range of material and symbolic resources to challenge narrow and timid scholasticism as well as oversimplified forms of journalism. I do not just read Gilroy as an academic or confine White to the realm of film criticism.

Chapters two and three provide some formative context for thinkers who came of age in dialogue with the dread ethics of reggae, the do-it-yourself ethos of punk, and the compelling, non-sermonizing work of radical newspapers and magazines. Chapter two considers how Gilroy's approach to "politically-infused acts of pleasure" and "anti-racist, polysexual, democratic aspirations"[17] were directly connected to and organically provoked by historical circumstances in the United Kingdom between 1968 and 1987. In doing so, it draws attention to his oft-overlooked contributions to radical publications such as *Temporary Hoarding*, *Race Today*, *Emergency*, and *City Limits*, which illustrate the interdependence between radical politics and cultural production in Britain in the late

1970s and early '80s. Chapter three interprets White's writings about film and culture for the *South End*, a paper that became an imaginative vessel for the Black radical tradition after the Great Rebellion in Detroit in 1967, as a special and unique archive of American cultural history. As we shall see, the *South End* was transformed from the *Daily Collegian*, a newspaper that focused narrowly on student affairs at Wayne State University, into a paper that boldly expressed its solidarity with the predominantly Black and working-class area that lay to the south of the campus rather than the corporate values of General Motors, whose headquarters lay to the north.[18] Alongside headings that proclaimed "one class conscious worker is worth one hundred students," editorials in the *South End* promised to offer readers a "viable and refreshing alternative to the drivel of the establishment bourgeois press which is the lap-dog of the ruling class."[19]

Chapters four and five reveal how White and Gilroy evolved from young soul rebels who sought to speak to a countercultural public sphere into middle-aged mavericks who sought to smuggle moments of dissidence into academic and journalistic institutions between 1984 and 1996. Chapter four engages with Gilroy's work as a young Black British critic who contributed to intellectual exchange between academics and artists during a period in which there was much discussion and concern about the institutionalization of Cultural Studies and the neoliberalization of academia. It also attends to *The Black Atlantic*, his best-known book, which he wrote in search of a "proper job" as a scholar and which had an "extraordinary influence" among academics in Europe and North America in the early 1990s.[20] Chapter five engages with the thousands of reviews of film, music, art, theater, and other art forms that White produced for the *City Sun*, a Brooklyn-based newspaper that fashioned itself as a political watchdog and New York's most authoritative Black weekly. For much of his tenure at the *City Sun*, White was arts editor of the paper and had considerable leeway to select the topics of his choosing and determine the tone and texture of his published articles. His archive of dissonant, against-the-grain criticism is rarely cited in academic and journalistic discussions about a Black public sphere, a new Black aesthetic, or Black public intellectuals. Excluded from the system of awards and patronage accorded to Black public intellectuals, White anticipated and engaged with the work generated by academic conferences and workshops about Black cinema and a Black public sphere while simultaneously defining himself as a critic who could not be bought in contrast to the "mediocre" and middle-class Black "race hustlers" and "eggheads" who exploited the hard-won victories of a civil rights movement for personal awards, tenure, and prestige.[21] Rather than merely dismiss such language as beyond the boundaries of acceptable discourse, evidence of envious rage, or speculative, armchair psychiatry, I point out that White's trenchant criticism may also be read in relation to the anti-colonial intellectual and activist Frantz Fanon. More specifically, it evokes Fanon's comments about "upstanding intellectuals," often brought up in a strict moral household or community, who not only seek to make the information that they have culled from colonial universities available to the people but also express clear distrust for "smart alecks and profiteers" who race for jobs and handouts in the aftermath of formal declarations of independence or legal victories over racial discrimination.[22]

Chapter six compares the responses of White and Gilroy to a constellation of political, economic, military, and cultural events as they sought to identify and scrutinize the problems of official and corporate multiculturalism, or post-racial "marketing hype," in the twenty-first century. Then, in a coda to the book, I consider their divergent responses to the multi-award-winning film *12 Years a Slave*, which the infamous movie mogul Harvey Weinstein associated with a spate of films about Black slavery and suffering that were distributed shortly after Barack Obama's re-election as president of the United States in 2012. Whereas White interpreted the film as "torture porn" designed to appeal to what he calls "secular progressives," Gilroy described it as a "deadly serious piece of work" about Black suffering, relentless exploitation, and commodification. In the first instance, to my knowledge, of the Black British intellectual citing the African American film and culture critic, Gilroy mused that White's criticism of the film was reflective of cultural insiderism that treated "the bleak history of racial slavery [as] the exclusive property of African Americans."[23] Rather than simply use their contrasting interpretations of the film to reinforce polarities between Black British or Black Atlantic approaches and African American ones—or the narrow, masculinist conceptions of gladiatorial combats and battles between the "father figures" of African American Studies (in which we are asked to declare our preference for Booker T. Washington or W.E.B. Du Bois, Malcolm X or Martin Luther King Jr., Team Cornel West or Team Barack Obama)—I read it as a sign of their ongoing commitment to sustaining a sense of humanist community in which thinkers approach public spheres as sites to learn through disagreement rather than opportunities to promote like-minded souls, pledge allegiance to their political tribes, and castigate mavericks and heretics unable or unwilling to toe the party line.

While attentive to the evolution of the two thinkers' styles, and their attempts to connect with plural reading publics that are often partitioned by age, occupation, political consciousness, cultural politics, and other lines, *Thinking While Black* consistently circles back to the shared sense of purpose that White and Gilroy developed as members of a political and cultural generation that came of age in the late 1960s and early '70s. It reckons with the haunting legacy of the politically infused pleasure they derived from rebel musicians that they considered creative and courageous enough to conquer commodified capitalism, and from long-form journalism that granted them stimulating alternatives to superficial forms of popular culture and dour, timid, and narrow scholarly work. In pursuing such reconstructive intellectual labor, I seek to provide some formative context for their jeremiads against what they consider the "deskilling" of Black music and the "discourteous discourse" of media platforms in the digital age.[24] Rather than dismiss White and Gilroy as curmudgeonly cranks who have failed to move with the times, I seek to clarify their faith in ideas, thinkers, and networks who helped them to perceive that it is possible, and often more productive, to approach disagreement and debate as manifestations of solidarity, collegiality, and love rather than barriers to them.

For the colonized, to be a moralist quite plainly means silencing the arrogance of the colonist, breaking his spiral of violence, in a word ejecting him outright from the picture.

Frantz Fanon (1961)

Fanon's observations on race, culture, and identity . . . do not sound anachronistic in our post–Cold War time. His insights reveal him, quite unexpectedly, to be our contemporary. . . . He can be read as offering a series of difficult and provocative comments on the significance of racism in social life and on the character of postcolonial politics, not only in Africa but also in all the other places where Europe's colonial crimes are vividly remembered, even if Europe itself has contrived to forget them.

Paul Gilroy (2010)

[Jacques] Audiard's Malik is a one-man rationalization of colonialism's flaws, in which France's justice system criminalizes the poor, non-white and immigrant. Tahar Rahim's open-faced, appealing performance doesn't excuse the film's insulting title, *A Prophet*. This is especially offensive when there is no spiritual awakening. Audiard never accounts for Malik's illiteracy, his initial crime or his ignorance of Islamic culture. Even after Malik is coerced by the prison's Corsican gang and forced to spy on and kill other Muslims, *A Prophet* never develops into a St. Paul or Malcolm X or Frantz Fanon story of political or moral conversion. Its title is merely a euphemism for an epithet.

Armond White (2014)

1.
THEORIES IN MOTION
Mapping the Roots and Routes of a Rebel Generation

Why focus on the work of Paul Gilroy *and* Armond White to tell a broader story about art, culture, and politics over the past fifty years? The pairing may seem a bit odd to readers who are securely positioned within the firmaments of academic or media institutions. A book about Gilroy, and how we might read him in relation to other academics, would arguably be more legible to readers accustomed to the conventions of books published by university presses. He is, after all, an eminent professor who, in the words of the committee responsible for the 2019 Holberg Award (a prestigious international prize established by the Norwegian parliament in 2003 for scholars who have made outstanding contributions to research in the humanities, social science, law, or theology), has influenced and reshaped "several fields and sub-fields, including cultural studies, critical race studies, sociology, history, anthropology and African American studies." A book about White, and how we might read him in relation to other journalists, would probably be easier to sell to audiences accustomed to biographies of mavericks and contrarians. He has, after all, been portrayed as the most notorious film critic in the digital age and a "gay African-American fundamentalist-Christian aesthete" consumed by rage who threatens the integrity and significance of film criticism.[1]

In bringing the two thinkers together, I wish to draw attention to the differences in style, speech, and behavior that are evident in a journalist whose ideas are often approached in fragmented, broken, or partial ways via individual film reviews, and an intellectual whose ideas are often discussed in relation to academic books with clear reception histories. White's erasure from the lists of Black public intellectuals and his expulsion from the New York Film Critics Circle in 2014 are often taken for granted because of a belief that his tone—and his opinions—threaten the ability of Black intellectuals and film critics to be taken seriously by broader segments of society. In contrast, Gilroy has playfully described his journey to secure a "proper job" as a scholar and fashioned himself as a "domesticated foe" of British Sociology.[2] He has also invited further reflection about the boundaries of acceptable speech when subjected to personal attacks by African American scholars.[3] In short, this book reflects on the making of two careers that provide us with special insight into the structuring capacities of academic and media institutions in North America and Europe.

While acknowledging some of the significant differences between White and Gilroy, I also wish to draw attention to the connective tissues and discordant affinities between the two thinkers. Although Gilroy has been championed as arguably the most influential intellectual writing in Britain, he is always already ambivalent about narrow academic articles and scholastic papers that seem devoid of irony. More pointedly, he has come to believe that he has been shut out from African American political and social thought in a manner that is not dissimilar to White's exclusion from most lists of serious film critics and Black public intellectuals.[4] In considering the lives and circumstances of two thinkers who are often excluded from dominant and popular understandings of Black public intellectuals, I draw attention to how the term is often used as a euphemism for African Americans with connections to prestigious universities and/or media institutions in the United States. I also argue that the Black

British intellectual and the African American film and culture critic may be understood as sharing a transnational or translocal structure of feeling—the delicate, less tangible forms of activity and mediating structures that facilitate and shape "affective attachment to different objects in the social order"[5]—that is indebted to the autodidacts, mavericks, and iconoclasts who left their mark on their dreams as young Black teenagers.

As Gilroy might say, it bears repetition that the soulful structure of feeling that he and White imbibed during the late 1960s and early '70s was complex and capacious.[6] It includes academics and intellectuals, such as Gilroy, who ended their relationship with Christianity as young soul rebels and have gone on to consider the ethics and aesthetics of Black Atlantic cultures that overflowed from their sacred, secret, and defensive public circles into secular and profane ones.[7] It also includes film and culture critics such as White, who associated Black Consciousness with "belief in God, belief in family, self-trust, growth from the past and loyalty" in the 1970s, and have gone on to identify "secular progressives" as dangers to the art and soul of America and Western civilization.[8] Such significant differences may be amplified in contexts in which we are often encouraged to monetize outrage through social media, and promote or defend our political, institutional, or disciplinary camps rather than find ways to cultivate discussion across them. In reading the lives of White and Gilroy in parallel, I seek to address their personal, idiosyncratic tastes while also paying attention to their similar engagements with elliptical and challenging forms of American, British, and global cultures in the 1960s and '70s, and their shared affiliation to a rebel generation that overflowed from the containers of the modern nation-state. In conjunction with a deep and specific analysis of two thinkers who share an appreciation for nuance and subtlety, are disgruntled by oversimplification and convention, relish learning through debate and disagreement, and are not shy about using polemic and provocation to rouse audiences into some fresh thinking, the book spreads out to tell a broader story that explores the complexities of Black cultural productions and cultural politics across time and space.

Armond White and Global African American Studies

In my previous contributions to books about film criticism in the digital age and about African American aesthetics and activism, I have situated White within an intellectual tradition of iconoclastic African American "race men."[9] I have considered what Pauline Kael described as his "race-based" approach to criticism in dialogue with George Schuyler (one of the most prominent African American journalists of the twentieth century), Albert Murray and Ralph Ellison (who advanced a vision of a "mulatto-minded" America), and James Baldwin, Malcolm X, and Harold Cruse (who, for all their differences, bequeathed a wealth of material and symbolic resources to critique white liberalism).[10]

Such influences also inform other African American contributors to the *Village Voice*, America's first alternative weekly, such as Stanley Crouch, Adolph Reed Jr., Cornel West, and Ishmael Reed, and the tone and texture of their work is analogous to White's resistance aesthetics. Crouch's critique of novels that have, in his estimation, emphasized Black martyrdom and misery and endowed it with special, moral magic resembles White's reviews of critically and commercially acclaimed films that narrowly, condescendingly, or sentimentally focus on abjection and suffering in African American culture.[11] Adolph Reed Jr.'s acid polemics about Black public intellectuals invited to explain Black culture to audiences that are predominantly white and liberal have obvious connections to White's caustic commentary about cautious and compromised Black intellectuals.[12] Cornel West's discussion of what he considers the "sad legacy" of Barack Obama's political career evokes the earlier analysis of the vacuous to repressive neoliberal politics of Obama by Adolph Reed Jr. and White.[13] The Before Columbus Foundation, an organization Ishmael Reed founded in 1976 to promote and disseminate contemporary American multicultural literature, awarded White an "anti-censorship" American Book Award after what it described as his "unfair removal" from the New York Film Critics Circle in 2014.

While cognizant of these linkages, I have chosen in this book to read White out of an African American context dominated by male voices. While appreciating that some of White's political judgments may appear "limited on the question of feminism" to American critics,[14] I do not overlook the impact of his female maîtres à penser such as the African American novelist Toni Morrison and Pauline Kael, a secular Jewish writer who appreciated how the seriousness of American jazz musicians and filmmakers could be aligned with inventiveness, imagination, and artistry rather than pretentiousness and deference to European patterns and rules. Nor do I ignore his engagement with a public sphere of postcolonial, diasporic intellectuals based in the UK such as Paul Gilroy, Stuart Hall, Sonya Madan, and Hanif Kureishi.[15] White's cultural criticism in the 1980s and '90s repeatedly asserted his appreciation for the do-it-yourself ethos of punk and the music and cultural criticism developed by working-class figures from the north of England. In a telling reminder of translocal connections that often trump national affiliations, the published work of the critic from a working-class family in Detroit is more engaged with the work of artists from cities in the north of England—such as Terence Davies and Morrissey—than that of Gilroy and many other journalists based in London. As someone frustrated with media outlets that position the nation as the primary or only frame of meaning and unit of analysis, I have valued reviews in which White introduced readers to humanistic auteurs from around the globe who receive little acclaim within the North American media landscape. As someone uncomfortable with the systems of deference and hierarchy that accompany the British monarchy, I have appreciated his willingness to expose the choices made by producers and artists who ingratiate themselves to royalist sentiment in pursuit of Oscars, BAFTAs, and other film awards. As a writer who is interested in working through the shameful history of the British Empire, I have respected White's sensitive readings of directors who scrutinized British imperialism as well as artists who examined the collective struggles of diverse postcolonial peoples for liberation.

In connecting the two thinkers, this book also speaks to the related yet distinct approaches of Global African American Studies and Diasporic Studies. White's aspirations to be all-American and

internationalist reflect a global form of African American Studies
that rejects parochialism and xenophobia, but does not quite share
Gilroy's critique of a "dogmatic focus on discrete national dynam-
ics" or his desire to subvert the dominant mode of work written on
an "*exclusively* national basis."[16] Put more bluntly, my research for
this book has reminded me that calls to celebrate White as one of
America's least parochial critics are akin to the fabled contests to
discover the world's tallest leprechaun.[17] They seem to say less about
White's global outlook than about the provincialism of writers who
make schoolboy mistakes about British culture and geography[18] or
represent "globally oriented studies" as rather niche because they
are "of less interest to US readers."[19] When I consulted online data-
bases to read the reviews White submitted for *Film Comment* in the
1980s, I found a writer who felt "chauvinist pride" when attending
international film festivals.[20] When I joined him on podcasts to discuss the decolonization of film culture, I listened to him argue that
the imperial adventures of the United States were not necessarily a
bad thing if they meant that the rest of the world could experience
the liveliness and vitality of the best of American culture.[21] When I
consulted the print archive of the *City Sun* in the 1980s and '90s, I
scrutinized reviews in which he expressed doubt that Paul Gilroy
was capable of understanding Black religious language because he
was a "Brit."[22]

Paul Gilroy and the Ambivalence of Community

My reading of Gilroy's wide-ranging work departs from many
attempts to plot his intellectual roots and routes within British
Cultural Studies and African American Studies. Although Gilroy is
often situated in the Marxist humanist tradition of British Cultural
Studies that imaginatively pursued political ends by other than
obviously political means, this is often a prelude to invoking Stuart
Hall, Raymond Williams, and other prominent figures who studied
or taught at Oxbridge.[23] Although biographical accounts emphasize
Gilroy's identity as a protégé of Hall,[24] and Gilroy has acknowledged
his debts to an illuminating and exhilarating teacher who fostered

his curiosity, we should not overlook the fact that Gilroy has also noted that Hall was not a "very good supervisor" and has highlighted the role of other figures at the Centre for Contemporary Cultural Studies (CCCS), such as John Clarke, in providing support and mentorship.[25] Similarly, while Gilroy esteems Williams as a "great critic," he also critiques Williams's failure to develop a sustained, contrapuntal reading of Western and non-Western texts and experiences as belonging together because imperialism connects them.[26] The distinctive energy of Gilroy's writing is fueled by intellectuals who were not academics as well as academics who found important parts to play in cultural climates where the life of the mind is often scorned. Activist-intellectuals who inform Gilroy's language and style that are discussed in this book include David Widgery, a London GP and political journalist who edited the underground magazine *Oz* and was a member of the Rock Against Racism (RAR) central committee and *Temporary Hoarding* editorial collective, and Val Wilmer, the author of *As Serious as Your Life: Black Music and the Free Jazz Revolution, 1957–77*. Like Pauline Kael, Widgery and Wilmer understood that film and Black music were two of the most important popular art forms of the twentieth century, and their writing sought to rescue the energy of Motown, the *Village Voice*, and Jean-Luc Godard "from the galleries, the advertising agencies and the record companies and use them again to change reality."[27] As conscientious writers who refused to erase irony and playfulness from their work, they sought to make popular culture more political and political activism more fun.

Situating Gilroy within the world of countercultural journalism helps us to attend to the distinctive energy—what he has described, with self-deprecating humor, as the "neurotic energy"—of texts that seek to smuggle moments of dissidence into rarefied academic spaces.[28] Even *The Black Atlantic*, the text of his that is most cited by academics and thought to be most weighed down by "forbidding abstraction,"[29] recycled material from his career as a journalist. It repurposed the interviews he'd conducted with Toni Morrison for the British press that discussed her critical distance from an African American middle class that was focused on achieving recognition from the nation-state, and C.L.R. James's belief that ordinary people do not need an intellectual vanguard to help them to speak or tell them what to say.[30] It also included notes of thanks and appreciation to musicians who stimulated his intellectual journey as much as, if not more than, scholars ensconced in academic firmaments and think tanks. As a result, I suggest that it may be productive to read Gilroy's work in connection to the suggestive, provocative, explorative approach of figures such as Widgery, Wilmer, Morrison, and James, who traverse different formats and open up new freedoms, rather than weighing down their work with the weight of evidence that would seem necessary to a professional historian. Whereas White's work engages American libertarians and existentialists who ask how expressive cultures might transcend materialistic values and hold capitalism to account for our spiritual well-being, Gilroy's intellectual projects are stimulated by conversations with radical egalitarians who demonstrate how creative artists construct an anti-capitalist political stance that seeks to overcome capitalist systems of judgment and value.

Living Memory and a "Soulful Style"

While acknowledging the significant differences between White's contributions to Global African American Studies (which demonstrates little engagement with diasporic or Caribbean political thought) and Gilroy's engagement with diasporic theory (which is informed by Caribbean intellectuals such as Sylvia Wynter, Bob Marley, Frantz Fanon, C.L.R. James, and Stuart Hall, among others), *Thinking While Black* also considers how we might read both cultural critics as members of a rebel generation stimulated by a Black Arts Movement in the United States.

Both Gilroy and White sharpened their thinking about the possibilities of Black art by studying Black popular modernism associated with figures such as Amiri Baraka and initiatives that developed jazz mobiles to go into the inner cities, set up study groups to discuss poetry in prisons, and elaborated a concept of a "changing same" ("a tradition in ceaseless motion" that is "invariably promiscuous" and "unsystematically profane" in contradistinction to tradition as closed or simple repetition[31]). Gilroy's frustration with the transformation or recycling of jazz into a classical tradition for corporate patrons of the Lincoln Center in New York, and his suggestion that the success of a Black Audio Film Collective within the international film festival circuit masked a failure to cultivate a "base or context for the type of films they want to make within the black communities in this country,"[32] are two notable examples of his engagement with Black popular modernism and how it provided him with a vision of Black excellence that evaded the domestication of highbrow institutions and corporate multiculturalism. White's role in the *First of the Month* editorial committee, which was described by *Time Out* as one of the few leftist journals that could be read at both Columbia University and Rikers Island jail, demonstrates similar impatience with uncritical celebrations of popular culture and a sheepish adherence to any cultural products bestowed with prestige by prominent institutions such as the Lincoln Center, the *New York Times*, or Ivy League universities. As Black popular modernists who express their distaste for the didactic audiovisual lectures of "European-Marxist" films[33] and the "dour cults of the British Left,"[34] Gilroy and White have been denounced as impressionistic, maverick, and unorthodox threats to professional disciplines and systematic thought.[35] Concurrently, their challenge to mainstream products that they considered "illiterate, insensitive, and unintelligent,"[36] or representative of the vapidness and commercialism of the "worst American product,"[37] has meant that other readers have found them too esoteric or elliptical for their tastes.

To translate the work of critics who have engaged with cultural products deemed highbrow and lowbrow, I have drawn on insightful studies of iconic figures and collective movements that inspired White, Gilroy, and other young Black teenagers in the late 1960s and early '70s to imagine new forms of belonging with time, space, and each other. Books that have transformed and boosted this text include Richard Iton's magisterial discussion of the politics and

popular culture in a post–civil rights era; Michael Denning's reflections on the hopes, aspirations, and failings of a student New Left
cohort that turned twenty "between, say, 1965 and 1975"; and Emily
J. Lordi's reflections on the capaciousness of soulful feelings, practices, and beliefs that cannot be neatly compartmentalized, fixed as
a vague masculinist charisma or some other simple characteristic
(such as irrationality, rhythm, animism, oneness with nature, or sensuality) as an essential and natural feature of Black people, or said
to have been erased from American life and culture in the 1980s by
a constellation of factors (including the AIDS and crack epidemics,
decreased social spending, increased military spending, and market
deregulation).[38]

Working within and against the tendency to treat a rebel generation as a band of soulful brothers and sisters embroiled in a
family romance in which they compete over the memory of icons
of the 1960s and debate, for example, the legacy of Malcolm X,
what Frantz Fanon said, and what Angela Davis meant, *Thinking
While Black* attends to the importance Gilroy and White attach to
forms of belonging outside the family unit. Gilroy claims that the
"uniquely soulful" culture of the 1960s and '70s provided his political and cultural generation with "ideal communicative moment[s]"
that surpassed "anything the structures of the family" could provide.[39] Although White associated Black Consciousness with "belief
in family" in the 1970s, and lived with his parents until he was
twenty-seven, he has similarly argued that a civil rights movement
and "seventies protest ethic" informed his responses to culture as
much as, if not more than, his home, school, and church.[40] Both
Gilroy and White connected these militant cultures and protest
ethics to forms of Black Consciousness that had been defined, by
activist-intellectuals such as Steve Biko, as a commitment to fighting
neocolonialism wherever it may be in the world rather than a matter
of pigmentation or skin tone.[41]

While acknowledging Gilroy's occasional reviews of film and
art exhibits, and White's abiding interest in music and other arts, I
primarily focus on the lives and circumstances of a professor with
a subsidiary career as a journalist who foregrounded music's role in

Black expressive cultures and a journalist who is primarily known as a film critic. A different story could have been told about a rebel generation from the perspective of visual artists such as Sonia Boyce and Lubaina Himid.[42] A more conventional academic approach could also have been pursued by focusing on Henry Louis Gates Jr., bell hooks, or other writers who are better-known representatives of a generation that came of age in the late 1960s and early '70s and were marketed as Black public intellectuals by North American universities and media institutions in the '90s.

Thinking While Black alludes to Gilroy's collegial relationships with prominent African American intellectuals such as Gates and hooks in conversations and conferences on both sides of the Atlantic, and the different tone and register White used to describe Gates as a "mediocre" and middle-class Black "race hustler" and to diagnose hooks as a public figure suffering from "ludicrous arrogance."[43] Yet rather than spend time connecting White and Gilroy to some of their well-known African American contemporaries who have been profiled in articles that draw attention to their ownership of a Mercedes-Benz or some other "elegant" or "fancy" car,[44] this book reassesses the work of two maligned and misunderstood critics who are more likely to be found walking around the city or commuting on public transport than driving a car or using it as a status symbol. It is a study of a Black British professor who often refrained from naming any specific individuals that he associated with the peddling of "squeamish nationalist essentialism and lazy, premature post-modernism" in academic and artistic institutions.[45] It is also an analysis of an African American journalist who believed that an independent Black press needed to confront the "system of privilege and oppression" that constructed middle-class public opinion, and had a responsibility to question the motives of any politicians, artists, and academics that they deemed venal, lazy, or self-serving.[46]

In addition to being a local and deep analysis of two idiosyncratic thinkers, *Thinking While Black* is a translocal and broad study of the ethics and aesthetics of rebel cultures and creative artists that have transformed popular culture over the past fifty years. It is a story about the artists, activists, and intellectuals that have inspired White and Gilroy as much as it is a tale of two critics who have sought to prove, against the odds, that American and British audiences were ready for their contributions. It is a form of reconstructive intellectual labor that documents the engagement of thinkers born in the 1950s with a civil rights cohort associated with the personal sacrifice and commitment to Black liberation of activists, intellectuals, and "Moses figures" such as Muhammad Ali, who actively participated in the revolutionary movements of 1967 and 1968. It is also an account of the humanist declarations of a political and cultural generation that always feels a little different and a little dissatisfied with members of a post–civil rights generation born after 1960 that they associate with the more pragmatic careerism of "Joshua figures" such as Barack Obama. In comparing the late style of White during the "age of Obama" between 2008 and 2016, I draw attention to his identity as the "Kanye West of film criticism" and creative response to peers in the New York media who label him an unserious, intolerant figure who is a threat to the integrity and significance of professional film criticism.[47] Concurrently, I select key works Gilroy published after he came to believe that he was identified as an outsider and "shut out from African American political thought and culture."[48]

In reading the two critics together in the early twenty-first century, I point out the significant differences between Gilroy's mourning for Black expressive cultures that articulated an anticapitalist political stance and White's frustrations with what he considers unthinking, sheepish adherence to spurious forms of resistance. Gilroy's work after the global financial crisis of 2007–8 facilitated and intervened in transatlantic conversations about progressive neoliberalism—which merges entrepreneurial fantasy and managerial technique, identity politics with market-driven policies, and the mystique of meritocracy with the allure of technocratic expertise[49]—in which North American voices do not drown out everyone else. White's work has been more concerned with the tendency to reinforce the privilege of "secular progressives" feted by prominent artistic, cultural, and journalistic institutions rather than to support artists who subvert or circumvent their power.

As befits a study of writers comfortable with irony and ambiguity, I also identify the similarities of their late style—pointing out, for example, that Gilroy and White have both mourned the passing of their peers, lamented the emergence of a Black popular culture that they find less thrilling and pleasurable, and perceived the shiny, multicultural glamour of Obama's campaigns and administrations as a potential distraction from a critical engagement with classism, militarism, and celebrity culture. Whereas Obama talked in a rather condescending manner in his 1995 memoir about "those Communists" who peddle their newspapers on the fringes of college towns, White and Gilroy mourn the demise of radical papers and magazines (and the networks and public spheres that flourished around them) in the 1990s.[50] They remember diverse platforms and movements committed to cultural production, left-wing or countercultural politics, autodidacticism, and working-class self-activity as sites of invention and imagination that helped them and thousands of other members of their rebel generation to approach Black expressive cultures transnationally, "almost placelessly . . . in the utopian key."[51] More pointedly, these publications helped the two thinkers to appreciate artists who manage to do "what politicians pretend to do . . . [speak] to people's deep, unarticulated emotional needs."[52]

Our children can never, will never be able to own all the centuries of history that constitute Britishness, which is more than being "born here." But knowing that they are always on the periphery of class and culture, our children would find the segments of history acceptable to themselves and affirm, "my forebears gave their souls, their spirit, their lives in defence and reconstruction of this green and pleasant land."

Beryl Gilroy (2000)

The most horrific incident was the New Cross fire on January 18 1981, the result of an arson attack on a party which resulted in the deaths of 13 young black people and 26 suffering serious injury.

The response of the black communities to that atrocity and the attempt by the police to cover up the truth and frame some of the party goers for the fire, was the mobilisation of 20,000 people by the New Cross Massacre Action Committee, chaired by John La Rose, for a march from New Cross to Hyde Park to protest the deaths of those young people and to demand justice. It was the most spectacular expression of black political power ever seen in this country; a watershed moment in our struggle for racial equality and social justice. That march, on March 2 1981, known as the Black Peoples' Day of Action, gave black people up and down the country a new sense of our power to resist racial oppression and to fight for change. It became clear for all to see that second and third generation black people—my generation—were no longer prepared to endure what our parents had. We were the rebel generation, a politicised generation and we were fighting back. One month later, in April the uprisings began in Brixton.

Linton Kwesi Johnson (2012)

2.
BLACK AND BRITISH
A Lived Contradiction

Born in the East End of London in 1956, Paul Gilroy was named after Paul Dienes, a Hungarian intellectual and friend of his father, Patrick Gilroy. Patrick was a white English scientist of German descent, a conscientious objector to World War II, and a member of the Communist Party until the vicious repression of the popular revolt against the Communist government of Hungary and its Soviet-imposed policies in the year of Paul's birth.[1] Paul's Guyanese mother, Beryl Gilroy, was part of a cohort of Caribbean students in London universities in the early 1950s that included the novelist, dramatist, critic, philosopher, and essayist Sylvia Wynter. Beryl was the primary caregiver for Paul and his sister, Darla, in a multicultural area of the city in which white English life was only one element, and became London's first Black headteacher, a novelist, and a host to traveling American writers.[2]

In conversations with his family, Paul would ask pointed questions about how a nation that participated in an anti-Nazi war could have graffiti that pledged to keep Britain white, signs on boarding houses that included disclaimers such as "No Coloureds, No Irish, No

Children," and white racists who physically assaulted him and repeatedly forced him and his sister to run for their lives.[3] Concurrently, he would play with Jewish migrants and South African exiles,[4] and find a sense of solace and security as a choirboy in the Church of England.[5] Although Paul would attend an independent day school founded by University College London that inherited many of that institution's progressive and secular views, and would end his relationship with Christianity as a teenager, he would continue to relish "ideal communicative moment[s]" between performer and crowd—which he believed surpassed anything the structures of the family can provide—when he started going out to experience live music in London in the late 1960s and early '70s.[6]

This chapter addresses some of the significant events and experiences after 1968 that informed and inspired his journey of intellectual discovery from "Paul" to "Dr. Gilroy," and helped him to perceive how Black musicians from America and the Caribbean communicated their rebel spirit to audiences in the United Kingdom and were "lovingly borrowed, respectfully stolen and brazenly hijacked" to meet the needs of young Black Britons.[7] The first section, "How Does It Feel to Be a Problem?," outlines the political language that constructed immigrants and "immigrant-descended populations" as alien wedges that threatened the integrity and maintenance of British institutions. This language was transmitted with intensity and urgency in the notorious speech Enoch Powell delivered to a Conservative Association meeting in 1968, which laid down the political codes for managing issues of minority citizenship and Black belonging that would dominate British political culture for at least twenty-five years.[8] The second, Militancy, Boldness, and Despair, documents some of the politically infused acts of pleasure of a Rock Against Racism movement that granted Gilroy and his rebel generation a range of material and symbolic resources to critique the "unwholesome power of nationalism."[9] Section three, Media, Culture, and Sport, focuses on the lessons Gilroy learned from seminars and soccer stadiums in the West Midlands when he pursued graduate studies at the Centre for Contemporary Cultural Studies at the University of Birmingham. Section four, What Is This

"Black" in the Union Jack?, engages with the struggles to build a
Black British political identity that brought together members of
African, Caribbean, and Asian diasporic communities in the late
1970s and early '80s. Section five, Diaspora, Utopia, and the Critique
of Capitalism, draws on the countercultural outlets that Gilroy
contributed to while working as a research officer for the militant
Greater London Council between 1982 and 1985. These left-wing
publications included *Race Today*, a leading organ of radical Black
politics in Britain that featured contributions from intellectuals
such as Darcus Howe, Linton Kwesi Johnson, C.L.R. James, and
Toni Morrison, and advertisements about studies of mugging and
the Race and Politics Group at the CCCS; *City Limits*, an arts and
events listing magazine that broke away from *Time Out* magazine
when its owner abandoned the publication's original co-operative
principles and imposed changes to its collective working practices;
and *Emergency*, a short-lived journal of the radical imagination that
aspired to challenge morbid forms of conservativism as well as the
rigor mortis of the British left. Finally, Denounced as a Heretic
reveals how Gilroy's commitment to the analysis of Black vernacular
cultures was not always deemed serious by revolutionaries committed to the development of a strategy to achieve Black and Third
World Liberation or consultants hired to produce reports and quan-
titative data about race relations to guide public policy.

"How Does It Feel to Be a Problem?"

In conjunction with its acquiescence to the winds of change bringing an end to formal British political rule in Asia, Africa, and the
Caribbean, the British Conservative Party debated the merits of an
immigration policy that offered a quasi-open door for subjects of
the British Commonwealth. On January 17, 1961, the Conservative
MP Cyril Osborne, a member of the far-right Monday Club, noted
that non-white immigrants were a "problem" because "this is a
white man's country and I wish it to remain so."[10] Such pressure
from the Monday Club and other right-wing groups informed the
1962 Immigration Act, which specified that all Commonwealth

citizens without a relevant connection to the UK would be subject to immigration control. The Conservative Party leader, Edward Heath, also delivered a statement on immigration and race relations in 1966 that emphasized the need for "tight control on entry" and "voluntary repatriation" of non-white immigrants to Africa, Asia, and the Caribbean. He was, however, concerned that inflammatory statements and an incendiary tone about non-white immigration would damage race relations, lead to civil strife, and prevent the Conservative Party from picking up support from ethnic minorities and moderate members of the electorate.[11] Tighter controls and repatriation policies were to be combined with calls for "equal treatment for all" and "more support for local authorities facing pressures arising from immigration."

As the Shadow Secretary of State for Defence, Enoch Powell had little time for the niceties of Heath's managerial approach and often took a line that was embarrassing or contrary to the Shadow Cabinet. Even sympathetic biographers of Powell admit that he could not, in any ordinary sense of the word, be considered a "good" colleague.[12] In early 1968, Powell became convinced that the 1962 Immigration Act was inadequate when more than one thousand Asians fleeing persecution from Kenya were arriving in Britain per month. He was also determined to disrupt the Labour government's plans to extend their 1965 Race Relations Act with further anti-discriminatory legislation. Powell communicated his firm belief that "the integration of races of totally disparate origins and cultures is one of the great myths of our time. It has never worked throughout history. The United States lost its only real opportunity of solving its racial problem when it failed after the Civil War to partition the old Confederacy into a 'South Africa' and a 'Liberia.'"[13]

The civil disturbances in the United States following the assassination of Martin Luther King Jr. on April 4, 1968, further added to Powell's determination to convey his concerns that 1) assimilation and integration were not possible; 2) this lack of assimilation and integration would lead to violence; 3) the real victims of attempts to assimilate and integrate were ordinary, decent English people; 4) the English people were not consulted about immigration; and finally,

5) the answer to these problems must lie in a reduction in the size of the "immigrant and immigrant-descended population."[14] On April 20, 1968, Powell delivered a speech to a Conservative Association meeting in Birmingham that he hoped would "fizz like a rocket; but whereas all rockets fall to earth, this one is going to stay up."[15]

Drawing on his rhetorical training and expertise as a classical scholar, author, linguist, soldier, philologist, and poet—as well as anecdotal evidence that he claimed to have culled from his constituents in Wolverhampton—Powell sought to evoke and exploit a range of emotions in his audience. He began by claiming that he felt compelled to repeat a conversation in which an ordinary, white, middle-aged constituent had told him, "in fifteen or twenty years, the black man will have the whip hand over the white man." Powell then expressed concern for the well-being of (ordinary, decent, and white) English people if immigrants and "immigrant-descended" people were permitted to increase to around six million, or approximately 10 percent of the total population, and *occupy* "whole areas, towns and parts of towns across England." From among the many letters of anguish about immigration Powell claimed to have received from constituents, he discussed one that described the plight of a pensioner who found herself the only white homeowner and resident on a once-respectable street, besieged by noisy "Negroes" and "wide-grinning piccaninnies" from families that rented their accommodation. He was aghast that the United Kingdom was sleepwalking toward a situation like the United States, where African Americans comprised over 10 percent of the national population and racial violence was a "tragic and intractable problem."[16]

The day after Powell delivered his speech, Heath sacked him from his post as the Shadow Secretary of State for Defence. The following day, on April 22, the *Times* newspaper supported Heath's decision as the right and courageous thing to do in response to a carefully planned and scripted speech by a "serious British politician" who "appealed to racial hatred, in a direct way."[17] On April 23, many MPs referred to Powell's Birmingham speech during the second reading of the Race Relations Bill. Outside of the House of Commons, a thousand dockers marched on Westminster to protest against what they considered Powell's victimization. The next day, there were other mass demonstrations of working-class support in London and Wolverhampton. By the end of April, Powell had received almost 120,000 predominantly positive letters and over 70 percent of the respondents of a Gallup poll indicated that they agreed with Powell's position on immigration. As Stuart Hall commented in the Eurocommunist monthly *Marxism Today* a decade later, Powellism dominated the national discourse about immigration and established magical connections and short circuits "between the themes of race and immigration control and the images of the nation, the British people and the destruction of 'our culture, our way of life.'"[18]

Three years after Powell delivered one of the most influential political speeches in twentieth-century British history, Gilroy attended the infamous trial of Richard Neville, Felix Dennis, and Jim Anderson, the young editors of the underground magazine *Oz*. After publishing lewd cartoons and articles by teenagers, Neville, Dennis, and Anderson were accused with "intent to debauch and corrupt the morals of children and other young persons and to arouse and implant in their minds lustful and perverted desires." In the gallery of the court, Gilroy witnessed the disjunctures between the young editors of the magazine and members of a jury from a different political and cultural generation that found the editors guilty of publishing an obscene article, sending obscene articles in the mail, and two counts of having obscene articles for publication for gain. Outside the court, Gilroy encountered protesters who clashed with police, burned an effigy of the judge, and set off smoke bombs, and would be described in the conservative *Daily Express* as "The Wailing Wall of Weirdies." Despite the guilty verdict, the editors of *Oz* would serve less than two weeks in prison after a successful appeal found that the judge had misdirected the jury.

To transcend what he considered the "sclerotic confines" of British nationalism in the late 1960s and early '70s,[19] Gilroy turned to American and Caribbean sources as well as the underground press in London. He would read *Rolling Stone* to learn about a similar trial of anti–Vietnam War and countercultural protesters charged with conspiracy and incitement to riot during the 1968 Democratic National

Convention in Chicago. From W.E.B. Du Bois's *Souls of Black Folk*, a book his mother had given him as a teenager, Gilroy studied how African American intellectuals had drawn on music and sorrow songs to transcend the parochialism of their fellow countrymen who wondered, *How does it feel to be a problem?*[20] From the prologue of Ralph Ellison's *Invisible Man* and jazz recordings by Fats Waller and Louis Armstrong, he reckoned with the "autobiographical writing, special and uniquely creative ways of manipulating spoken language and, above all, the music" that engaged with the fateful, heroic question, *What did I do to be so black and blue?*[21]

In 1970, Gilroy attended the Isle of Wight Festival, one of the largest music festivals of its time, where he listened to performers such as the Voices of East Harlem and Jimi Hendrix, one of his musical heroes. Later in the year, he went to see the Voices of East Harlem in orchestra seats behind the stage at the Royal Albert Hall and fell, irrevocably, into the music of an African American vocal ensemble. The group of singers, aged between twelve and twenty-one, conveyed "the power of the people" and a "soulful feel" to the British teenager.[22] They also helped him to mourn the loss of Hendrix, who had died shortly after performing at the Isle of Wight. As part of recovering and commemorating the experience of watching Hendrix's uneven performance at the festival, Gilroy has described him as a "shamanic pastor" of an electric church—"a collective social body of musical celebrants that gathered periodically to engage the amplified offshoots of the Mississippi Delta and harness them in the causes of human creativity and liberation."[23] He draws attention to Hendrix's rejection of military codes and repeated affirmation of itinerancy, which he connects to the secularized faith of modern subjects who wish to separate their belief that a change is going to come from "God-terms" such as militarism and nationalism as well as religious institutions.[24]

Aside from Hendrix, Curtis Mayfield and Bob Marley are the musicians referenced most extensively, and most affectionately, in Gilroy's oeuvre. Gilroy's memories of bearing witness to Mayfield's "shamanic January 1972 shows at the Rainbow Theatre in London's Finsbury Park" inform his determination to resist "ethnic brokers and project-managing pimps of corporate multiculturalism" who threaten to turn such thrilling memories into something less alive and pleasurable.[25] Seeing and listening to Bob Marley perform in the Greyhound Pub on Fulham Road in 1973 further stimulated Gilroy's desire to translate the cosmopolitan commitments of diasporic artists. He recalls the magical evening in which he heard Marley sing "Get Up, Stand Up" as a moment in which a vernacular intellectual appropriated the legalistic and bureaucratic language of the Declaration of Human Rights and put it into the hands of ordinary people.[26] When Gilroy moved to Birmingham to join the Race and Politics Group at the Centre for Contemporary Cultural Studies in 1978, he continued to engage with Marley's rebel spirit by locking his hair and delving more deeply into the communitarian elements of livity, which refers to dietary habits, personal aesthetics, and/or the various Rastafari beliefs, whether secular or metaphysical, that may guide our actions in the world and our relationship with nature and other human beings.[27]

Militancy, Boldness, and Despair

A week after Gilroy had started life as an undergraduate at the University of Sussex in the autumn of 1975, he learned that his father had died. Responding to the trauma of this event, and to his general frustrations with lectures and approaches to teaching that were in many ways antithetical to his interest in self-directed study, Gilroy gave serious consideration to dropping out of university and pursuing music full-time. He went to see Donald Wood, a historian of the Caribbean at Sussex, who counseled him to go away and read *The Black Jacobins* by C.L.R. James and *The Wretched of the Earth* by Frantz Fanon before he abandoned academia.

This intervention was critical to Gilroy's decision to stay at Sussex and combine his engagement with Caribbean intellectuals such as James and Fanon with undergraduate dissertations on the sociology of Afro-American music and modes of masculinity in the radical novelists of the early twentieth century.[28] He would pursue the Caribbean political and social thought expressed in *The*

Black Jacobins, The Wretched of the Earth, and journals such as the *Black Liberator*—which contained contributions such as Linton Kwesi Johnson's "Five Nights of Bleeding (for Leroy Harris)," Colin Prescod's "Revolution of the Caribbean Peoples," and Claudia Jones's "The Caribbean Community in Britain"—and academic work that grappled with the ideas of Amiri Baraka, W.E.B. Du Bois, Ralph Ellison, and other African American luminaries. In conjunction with those writings, Gilroy also sharpened his ideas about Black cultural politics in dialogue with a Rock Against Racism movement that, in the late 1970s, forced race onto the consciousness of "the most mainstream people."[29]

In the late 1970s, the far-right National Front organization had a paid-up membership of around 17,000 and was producing five or six million items of printed propaganda per year. Its poisonous rhetoric was amplified on August 5, 1976, when Eric Clapton drunkenly told an audience at a concert in Birmingham that Britain should "get the foreigners out, get the wogs out, get the coons out," and repeatedly shouted the National Front slogan "Keep Britain White." In response, the photographer and activist Red Saunders and his friends Roger Huddle, Jo Wreford, and Pete Bruno signed a letter voicing their disgust with the hypocrisy of a white musician who'd had his first hit with Bob Marley's "I Shot the Sheriff." Within a few days of the publication of their letter in *Sounds*, *Melody Maker*, the *New Musical Express*, and the *Socialist Worker*, they received 140 letters enthusiastically supporting their intention to start a rank and file movement to "Rock against Racism (RAR)." On November 12, 1976, the first RAR gig took place at the Princess Alice pub in London's East End. Headlined by the blues singer Carol Grimes, the night ended with Black and white musicians performing in a jam. Such multiracial collaboration would become a signature of RAR's gigs at a time in which it remained relatively rare to see Black and white performers on stage together.

Cultural autodidacts working in photography, theater, music, graphic design, and fashion launched a revolutionary fanzine called *Temporary Hoarding* that same year to support the RAR movement. David Widgery, a political writer and doctor, authored the fanzine's first editorial, which called for "Rebel music, street music. Music that breaks down people's fear of one another. Crisis music. Now music. Music that knows who the real enemy is. Rock against Racism. Love Music Hate Racism." During his medical studies in 1971, Widgery had acted as a lay representative for the editors of *Oz* magazine when they were accused of "conspiracy to corrupt public morals," and he was the co-editor of the magazine when it closed in 1973. However, he had also made it clear that he had his own vision of rebellion, which went beyond the narrow masculine sexual radicalism that *Oz* championed,[30] and believed that the underground press in London had failed to do enough to push cultural radicalism into the working classes.[31]

As a member of the *Temporary Hoarding* editorial collective, Widgery sought to purge the fanzine of "hippyism" and develop a propaganda machine that would effectively compete with the far-right National Front for the hearts and minds of disenfranchised and disenchanted working-class people. *Temporary Hoarding* "wasn't just an art object but contained information, lots of music, political comment and the practical experience of organizing against the NF" and the violent racist attacks on immigrants and racial minorities in England.[32] Widgery was determined to tap the immense creativity and imaginative ability of working people and an "off-the-wall bunch of left-wing artists outside the leadership of the established organization," and to prevent *Temporary Hoarding* from descending into the expression of duller voices and rather lifeless question and answer sessions. Without being sermonizing, the magazine was educational about trade union movements, sexual and gender politics, and anti-racism.[33] It would develop an expansive musical, literary, and visual style, which drew from French surrealism, a "dubbed version of Marxism" shaped by encounters with C.L.R. James and W.E.B. Du Bois, and punk's do-it-yourself ethos.[34] It circulated among local RAR groups that had been established in London, Leeds, Birmingham, Manchester, Hull, Newcastle, Edinburgh, Glasgow, Belfast, Sheffield, Cardiff, Swansea, and Bristol in 1977 and 1978. By 1979, RAR offices were also established in the United States, France, Belgium, Sweden, Holland, Germany, Norway, South

Africa, and Australia, and the movement would sell around twelve thousand copies of each issue of *Temporary Hoarding*.[35]

Gilroy wrote for *Temporary Hoarding* under the nom de guerre G-Roy, and was well aware that many Marxist theoreticians and left-wing organizers were not convinced that the people who read (or contributed to) the magazine were any more sympathetic to the Socialist Workers Party than to the National Front or the Labour or Conservative parties. Many also suspected that the mere presence of white and Black bands such as the Clash, Jimmy Pursey, X-Ray Spex, and Steel Pulse playing together at RAR concerts was no guaranteed antidote to racism among the audience. Once they entered the public domain, RAR's symbols became just another signifier, ripe for appropriation—as demonstrated by punks wearing RAR pins alongside buttons for the racist National Front. Placed side by side, the only meaning that remained intact was the assertion of subcultural affiliation through carefully composed clothes, accessories, hairstyles, make-up, and body language.

There were, however, notable alliances between anarchic artists and Socialist Workers Party activists. Street battles in Lewisham in August 1977 featured Bob Marley's "Get Up, Stand Up" blaring out of a window above violent clashes between approximately 500 members of the National Front, 5,000 police in riot gear, and a coalition of 4,000 anti-racists. Joint Rock Against Racism and Anti-Nazi League carnivals sought to make the politics more fun and the music more political. In April 1978, over 80,000 people attended the first Rock Against Racism / Anti-Nazi League Carnival in Victoria Park, providing a striking response to Margaret Thatcher's expression of solidarity with ordinary, decent English people who feared that they might be "swamped" by people from a different culture.[36]

Media, Culture, and Sport

In the spring of 1978, as Gilroy prepared to graduate from the University of Sussex, he spent time puttering around a university bookstore that carried *Resistance through Rituals: Youth Subcultures in Post-War Britain*.[37] Much like *The Black Jacobins* and *The Wretched of the Earth* influenced his decision to continue his undergraduate career, this text would inform his decision to move to Birmingham and pursue a journey of intellectual discovery as a graduate student at the Centre for Contemporary Cultural Studies.[38]

Resistance through Rituals was co-edited by Tony Jefferson and Stuart Hall, the director of the CCCS from 1968 to 1979, and it included a chapter collectively authored by the CCCS Mugging Group that built on its direct involvement in defense campaigns for two Black men charged with a mugging in Handsworth. The chapter's discussion of the relationship between culture, the news media, and the construction of law and order would be revised and published as part of *Policing the Crisis: Mugging, the State and Law and Order*, a seminal text that considered how "mugging," a term previously reserved for extreme US crime, swept the British media in 1972–73 and was described as a new crime. What was new, of course, was not the crime itself but the labeling and the set of associated images of violent crime, Black youth, and an overly permissive society that were condensed in law and order ideology. Hall and his colleagues famously used their analysis to point out that race was the modality in which class is "lived," the medium through which class relations are experienced, the form in which it is appropriated and "fought through."[39]

Put slightly differently, *Policing the Crisis* exemplified how the work of the CCCS connected the insights of European Marxism, particularly Antonio Gramsci's ideas on hegemony, to those of a Black radical tradition. Other chapters in *Resistance through Rituals* examined how individual self-fashioning and collective protest came together in music and youth cultures. Dick Hebdige's "Reggae, Rastas and Rudies" analyzed the polymorphous nature of reggae—"the call and response patterns of the Pentecostal Church, the devious scansion of Jamaican street talk, the sex and the cool of US R. and B., the insistent percussion of the locksmen's jam-sessions."[40] Iain Chambers argued that Black radical traditions and revolutionary politics were retained more in the realm of Black music than in Black literature, entertainment, and sports.[41] John Clarke demonstrated how a sense of grievance informed the violent attacks of Mods, Teds, skinheads, and punks on perceived threats to their communities.[42] The collection also examined how Cultural Studies might attend to reading publics fractured by gender and generation as well as class and race. Angela McRobbie and Jenny Garber challenged the overwhelmingly male and masculinist focus of the collection in a chapter on girls and subcultures;[43] Graham Murdock and Robin McCron showed the difficulties of generational analysis when there exist several "differentiated, antagonistic generation-units" within each generation;[44] and Paul Corrigan and Simon Frith discussed the need for studies of youth culture that did not assume that institutional incorporation (which has been the experience of the British working class over the last 150 years) necessarily meant ideological incorporation.[45]

Gilroy also learned about stylish resistance to racism when he moved to the West Midlands and followed the exploits of the dancer, fashion icon, and sublime soccer player Laurie Cunningham. Cunningham was born one month after Gilroy, grew up nearby in the Archway neighborhood of London, and shared his desire to disarticulate the richness of cultural and moral resources from capitalist systems of judgment and value. As noted by Nikki Hare-Brown, Cunningham's partner, "if Laurie touched something it turned to gold with a different richness, not a financial richness. . . . Even if something cost nothing or was genuine and he liked it, he'd say, 'That's different class.'"[46] Along with the Black British players Cyrille Regis and Brendon Batson, Cunningham regularly featured in West Bromwich Albion's soccer team in the 1978–79 season. They encountered a hostile environment in an area that bordered the constituency Enoch Powell represented between 1950 and 1974. On Saturday afternoons, the three men would play through a barrage of abuse and monkey chants from the stands. Then, when they returned home, they would screen hate mail and abusive phone calls from people who did not believe that the proverb "an Englishman's home is his castle" extended to non-white subjects. When it became known that Cunningham was in a romantic relationship with a white woman, the volume of hateful letters and phone calls increased.

The British media rarely commented on such racist abuse or

communicated its toll on the players. It tended, instead, to write about the three men's athletic and sexual prowess, and called Regis, Batson, and Cunningham the Three Degrees after the trio of African American female vocalists that achieved thirteen top 50 singles in the UK between 1974 and 1985. Shortly after West Brom had ended a successful campaign in which they finished third in the first division, a testimonial match pitched a White XI composed of current and former members of the West Brom squad against a Black XI (or "Regis and Cunningham XI") that consisted of an invitational side of Black players from across the professional leagues. In this game, one of the last he played at West Brom's Hawthorns ground before becoming the first English player to sign for Real Madrid, the most decorated team in the history of the European Cup, Cunningham did not hear the monkey chants and boos that he had become accustomed to as a professional athlete. In contrast, he was cheered on by a multiracial crowd of around seven thousand people that included the twenty-three-year-old graduate student Paul Gilroy.

What Is This "Black" in the Union Jack?

In anticipation that the Labour Prime Minister James Callaghan would call a general election in 1978, the Conservative Party ran an advertising campaign that announced "Labour isn't working" above an image of an endless line of people waiting to sign on at the unemployment office. Below the long, snaking line (which was obtained by repeatedly photographing a group of twenty young Conservatives and then striping them together) was the tagline "Britain's better off with the Conservatives." The campaign, designed by the advertising agency Saatchi & Saatchi, was revived for the 1979 general election and garnered considerable media attention when Denis Healey, the Labour Chancellor of the Exchequer, complained that it was an example of the Americanization of British politics in which parties were sold "like soap-powder."[47]

After ousting the incumbent Labour government with a parliamentary majority of forty-three in 1979, the Conservative Party re-enlisted Saatchi & Saatchi to bolster its 1983 election campaign.

One of the advertisements, using the tagline "Labour says he's black. Tories say he's British," was strategically located in ethnic minority newspapers and public transport routes. It included a long note that claimed that the Conservatives delivered on their promises to unite the country, recruit more police officers from minority ethnic backgrounds, and abolish the SUS law (this law permitted police to stop, search, and potentially arrest people on suspicion of them being in breach of section 4 of the Vagrancy Act, and led to almost a thousand predominantly Black people being stopped and searched by the police over a period of five days in 1981). The advertisement did not mention that the SUS law had been abolished in August 1981 after a cross-party House of Commons Sub-committee on Race

"Labour Isn't Working." Source: Conservative Party Archive, Bodleian Library POSTER 1978/9-01

Relations and Immigration heard evidence that it was believed to be a contributory factor to the so-called race riots in London, Liverpool, Bristol, and other English cities in 1980 and 1981. Nor that campaigns to scrap the SUS law received legal advice from Paul Boateng, chair of the Greater London Council's police committee, vice-chair of its ethnic minorities committee, and a future Labour MP and member of the first cohort of Black Britons elected to parliament in 1987.

Paul Gilroy's book *There Ain't No Black in the Union Jack* was published by Routledge in 1987. Based on Gilroy's doctoral dissertation on racism, class, and the contemporary cultural politics of "race" and "nation," it included an illustration of the "Labour says he's Black. Tories say he's British" poster that featured a man of African descent wearing a suit. This illustration accompanied

LABOUR SAYS HE'S BLACK.
TORIES SAY HE'S BRITISH.

CONSERVATIVE

"Labour says he's Black. Tories say he's British (African)." Source: Conservative Party Archive, Bodleian Library 1978/9-34b

Gilroy's analysis of the advertisement, which drew attention to its depiction of a solitary Black male subject in an unfashionably cut suit, interpreted as a way for the Conservatives to avoid the "hidden threat of excessive fertility which is a constant presence in the representation of black women."[48] Such visual discourse analysis was attentive to the cultural or new right racism of a Conservative Party that siphoned off votes from the far-right National Front. Rather than limit their definition of racism to overt forms of "biological or scientific racism," cultural theorists such as Gilroy called for critical analysis of new right discourse that fixed certain cultures as lesser breeds outside the law who needed to be sent back to their ancestral homelands or strictly controlled and managed if they were to coexist in British society and be prevented from swamping "us." These critics were also attentive to the capacity of such discourse to incorporate isolated individuals from other cultures who carefully constructed an image contrary to the stereotype of Black criminality, reinforcing the idea that the British national culture was, at its core, welcoming and tolerant. While hooligans sang "There Ain't no Black in the Union Jack," politicians strategically used non-white individuals who achieved musical or sporting success for Great Britain to project "real" or "serious" racism onto other countries, the past, and the odd bad apple.

There Ain't No Black in the Union Jack did not mention that the Conservative Party developed two advertisements in its "Labour says he's Black. Tories say he's British" series. One is labeled "African" in the Conservative Party Archive; the other, which features a solitary man of Asian descent, is labeled "Indian." Such reluctance to attend to the range of Conservative advertisements that asked individuals to choose between a British or Black identity reflect some of the tensions in Gilroy's hopes for a politically Black identity—which included a diverse set of radical, postcolonial peoples from Asian, Caribbean, and African diasporic communities—and the content of his work—which focused on young radicals of Afro-Caribbean ethnicity and the impact of Afro-Caribbean and Afro-American expressive cultures on British society.

In 1981, twelve members of the United Black Youth League, an anti-fascist and anti-racist organization primarily composed of Asian- and Caribbean-descended young people, were arrested on charges of

**LABOUR SAYS HE'S BLACK.
TORIES SAY HE'S BRITISH.**

CONSERVATIVE

"Labour says he's Black. Tories say he's British (Indian)." Source: Conservative Party Archive, Bodleian Library 1978/9-34a

manufacturing explosives in anticipation of a large-scale attack by fascist groups that year. One of the young men arrested was Tariq Mehmood, an activist born in Pakistan and raised in the United Black Youth League's headquarters in Bradford, a city in the north of England. While in prison he started writing his first novel, *Hand on the Sun*, about young people's resistance to racism in 1970s Britain. In his review of the young adult novel for *Race Today* in 1984, Paul Gilroy critiqued its sloganeering and claimed that its political efficacy was dulled when it failed to show young Asians engaging with the politics of Afro-Caribbean people who shared their class, their street, and their predicament.[49] Yet Gilroy's deconstruction of such political failures did not mean that his writings on Black British culture demonstrated how Afro-Caribbean young people engaged with the politics of young Asian people who shared their class, their street, and their predicament.

As Gilroy elaborated in the preface to *The Empire Strikes Back:*

Race and Racism in 70s Britain, members of the CCCS Race and Politics Group "opted to remain within the bounds of our own historical resources rather than make pronouncements of things that were unfamiliar. Only one of us has roots in the Indian subcontinent whereas four are of Afro-Caribbean origin. This accounts for the unevenness of our text," which focused on African and Caribbean experiences and devoted only one chapter to Asian women in resistance.[50] Gilroy's report on Channel 4's Black television programs is another intriguing example of this "unevenness." On the one hand, Gilroy's review expressed his commitment to a political definition of Blackness that African, Asian, and Caribbean communities had struggled so hard to create in opposition to white supremacy.[51] It showed how the new Channel 4 show, *Black on Black*, which was aimed at the Caribbean community, failed to reveal that Blacks in Britain were excluded from public services regardless of their ethnicity.[52] On the other, such abstract declarations of faith in a Black political identity were not accompanied with any specific reflections about *Eastern Eye*, which was developed at the same time as *Black on Black* to provide news for the British Asian community. Consequently, scholars such as Tariq Modood have claimed that Blacks of Asian ethnicity were merely granted a "walk-on part" in Gilroy's analysis of racism in Britain when they expressed solidarity with Afro-Caribbean communities or appeared, like Afro-Caribbean communities, to borrow, recycle, and repurpose the music of African America and the Caribbean.[53]

Diaspora, Utopia, and the Critique of Capitalism

After becoming the leader of the Greater London Council in 1981, Ken Livingstone told *Marxism Today* that his victory symbolized the post-1968 generation in politics.[54] "During the Brixton riots of 1981—a mass protest against aggressive racist policing—Livingstone was seen, as the *Times* noted with horror, on the streets of Brixton at the height of the rioting. He publicly defended the rioters and refused an invitation to the Royal Wedding taking place elsewhere in the capital so that he could be in Brixton on the 'front line.'"[55]

Although the radical economic projects of the council are often overlooked, such political propaganda and its expressions of solidarity with explicitly anti-racist, anti-homophobic, anti-imperialist, anti-sexist movements have received sustained attention.[56]

In the early 1980s, Gilroy combined his work as a research officer for the Greater London Council with his contributions to editorial collectives such as *Emergency*, a journal of the radical imagination that examined the cultural politics of race and nation.[57] Other founding members of *Emergency*'s editorial collective included Max Farrar, a white scholar-activist whose article on "Love and Dread in Modern Times" in the journal's second issue asserted that pop music had something profound and honest to say about the complexities and contradictions of modern existence, but had to fight for survival amid the banality of commercial radio. Farrar also contended that cultural critics needed to challenge the presumption that serious discussions of modern subjecthood could solely revolve around European thinkers who had been legitimated by academic institutions. His article repeated an encounter in which the African American novelist Richard Wright pointed to the writings of European existentialists on his bookshelf before telling C.L.R. James that he knew every word of their philosophical accounts before he read them.[58] Gilroy would later repeat this exchange between Wright and James in *Small Acts* and *The Black Atlantic*, and highlight James's conclusion that the lived experiences of Black people in the United States provided them with an insight into "what today is the universal opinion and attitude of the *modern* personality."[59]

Gilroy's meditations on modernity and double consciousness in Black Atlantic cultures would also be inspired and boosted by Val Wilmer, the first white British journalist to describe jazz music as Black music. In her cultural criticism, Wilmer consistently wrote against the exploitation of Black music and the expectation that Black artists should be content to play a minstrel role, and she unsentimentally described the potent mix of racism and sexism that informed the precarity of Black male jazz artists in Europe who were often reliant on the financial support of white female romantic partners.[60] According to Gilroy, she should be recognized as a world figure in the history of African American musical culture and an ethical advocate of Black music who refused to separate her appetite for the music from her anti-racist advocacy.[61]

Wilmer helped Gilroy to break into the somewhat insular world of music journalism in the early 1980s as a contributing editor to *City Limits*. His record reviews and concert previews for *City Limits* would be published alongside studies of filmmaking, advertisements for Irish freedom festivals, conferences on socialist economics, forums on workers' education, and other initiatives that demonstrated the interrelationship and interdependence of cultural production and radical politics.[62] In these works, Gilroy would interpret Black musical cultures as integral parts of the political opposition to Thatcher's "Caesarist regime"[63] and lament those who would soften and dull the creative spirit of the rebel music to try and make it more palatable for the tastes of commercial audiences.[64] He looked beyond the national charts and radio stations to welcome Black Atlantic musicians who toured London's concerts and underground venues.

Front cover of *City Limits*, August 27– September 2, 1982. Photo: Paul Trevor; design: David King

In his 1982 review of Afrika Bambaataa, an American DJ whose parents were born in Jamaica and Barbados, Gilroy communicated the show's expression of Black self-reliance and survival with its fusion of cultural and political elements found in Rastafarianism.[65] Shortly before the birth of his first child in 1983, who would be named after the legendary bass guitarist Marcus Miller, Gilroy praised the power of music that took an uncompromisingly critical view of domestic violence and male contempt for child-rearing.[66] Cognizant that some readers may confuse moral seriousness with humorlessness as well as masculinist politics, Gilroy championed records as serious when they expressed a Black, bitter, and radical humor that sought to capture the spirit of Black working-class communities, develop their struggles, and add to their power.[67] He also expressed concern that the wit and dexterity of lyricists could be drowned out by computerized, synthesized, and programmed drum technology,[68] and acknowledged that some records could combine powerful beats with an unquestioning attitude toward heteronormative values.[69] When he imagined historians of the future working through the musical archive of hip hop in the early 1980s, Gilroy hoped that they would focus on the ability of lyricists to carve something precious out of a conjuncture in which Black people in racially segregated and economically disadvantaged communities were infected with Reaganomics, crack cocaine, and aggressive policing rather than the quality of their backbeat.[70]

There Ain't No Black in the Union Jack translated such journalistic work about serious, humorous, and imaginative musical cultures for readers who may not have ventured into an underground rave or spent time listening carefully to hip hop records. It identified three elements of anti-capitalist resistance in Black expressive cultures: a politics around work and its overcoming, a politics around law and its dissociation from racial domination, and a folk historicism that sets special store by the recovery of historical sensibility. The first element evoked Hannah Arendt's distinction between creative work and labor by focusing on the aspects of Black creative expression that critiqued dispiriting or alienating labor.[71] Gilroy repeatedly emphasized the lyrics and performances of Black musicians who celebrated Black bodies as sites of pleasure and autonomy rather than mere instruments of productivism.

He also challenged the idea that DJs who removed the labels of records that they played were merely seeking to keep the information secret to support their role as cultural gatekeepers. Somewhat impressionistically, Gilroy suggested that the DJs who concealed the origins of the records they played were creatively fashioning underground spaces that were in opposition to a commercialized and almost exclusively white pop world.[72] By inviting audiences to enjoy the music without knowing who it was by or where it was in a chart, Gilroy portrayed DJs as facilitators of spaces in which the uplifting and intoxicating blend of music, dance, and atmosphere was separated from the information essential to purchase it. What may otherwise have been a passive or individual act of buying a record was, as a result, turned into a procedure of collective affirmation and protest in which "authentic public spheres" were brought into being.[73]

There Ain't No Black in the Union Jack did not provide an extended definition of what might constitute an "authentic" public sphere but, like his later allusions to "real, principled multiculturalism,"[74] it was informed by his unwillingness to partition off where we see and act as a collective (as, for example, abstract citizens of the state) from where we see and act as individuals (as, for example, everyday participants in economic and civil life, members of social and political movements, and users of music who refuse to inflate or minimize the things that divide us). It is also possible to unpack the concepts such as an "authentic public sphere" and "real, principled multiculturalism" by connecting them to Gilroy's contributions to *Temporary Hoarding*, *Emergency*, and the Race and Politics Group at the CCCS, in which he expressed his aspiration to develop networks for diverse people to come together to discuss and debate racism and fascism as something internal to Britain—not just as an external threat to it—and courageously build anti-racist and anti-fascist movements that communicated the pleasure of encountering difference and figuring out what we share.

In discussing the second element of this anti-capitalist stance in Black musical cultures—which contested racial domination and state brutality in legal and political discourses—Gilroy connected the guilt and fear of Powellite discourse about the Black man holding the whip hand over the white man to similar panics about the Black man controlling the dance floor.[75] Extending his earlier contributions to *Emergency*—which suggested that, underneath their "narcissistic self-discipline," the fury of dancers could be aligned with the commitment to collective liberation by people who took to the streets to protest state violence in 1980 and 1981—he argued that the pleasure taken in the exercise of individual power on the dance floor was connected to the pleasures of collectively defeating the police.[76]

If Gilroy associated the first two elements of Black music's anti-capitalist political stance to "dem a shuv an shuffle dem feet / sockin in di sweet musical beat" without necessarily worrying about the origins of the music,[77] the third discernible element of Black music's anti-capitalist stance drew attention to its resistance to the suppression of historical and temporal consciousness under capitalism. Gilroy emphasized, for example, how dancers and DJs who participated in nighttime raves in underground spaces could go blinking into the daylight to trace the origins of the music in libraries, record stores, and "specialist publication devoted to black music and in the community's own news and political weeklies."[78] He wished to remind scholars and policy workers that it was possible and necessary to attend to daring, lively protest in the dance floor and the careful recovery of historical sensibility if they were seriously committed to the production of richer histories about the ambivalent mainstreaming of Black culture in Britain.[79]

Denounced as a Heretic

Gilroy was a long-standing critic of the routine brutality and machismo in policing evident in governments led by the Labour Party as well as by the Conservatives. His essays and articles consistently asked pointed questions of Black professionals—largely dependent on the Labour Party or the Greater London Council for material support in the media, social work, academia, and elsewhere—who claimed to represent the causes of the working-class Black communities but so rarely managed to advance them.[80] Gilroy identified the failings of "community bureaucrats" who depicted the poor as inert, criminal, or passive figures who needed to be told how to conduct their affairs by some form of elite. He called for more ambitious work that seriously considered the possibility that protesters burning a police car, for example, were attacking discernible local institutions and the everyday networks of local activity.[81] The tone and texture of such interventions were closer to the spirit of *Temporary Hoarding* than left-liberal policy advisers and scholars who were consulted and hired to generate evidence-based work on race relations.

Activist-intellectuals devoted to Black and Third World liberation may have articulated similar concerns to Gilroy about "race relations" being a euphemism for "maintaining inequality, division and an acceptable level of racism."[82] In 1972, A. Sivanandan and fellow activists participated in an internal struggle at the Institute of Race Relations (IRR) that led to Sivanandan being appointed its new director and reorientating the IRR away from advising the government and toward servicing community organizations. However, Gilroy's emphasis on the creative and pleasurable elements of social and political movements also led members of the new IRR and its journal, *Race & Class*, to label him a "romantic," "utopian," or "heretical" figure unable or unwilling to do the hard work of organizing and developing revolutionary strategy.[83]

At the end of his chapter on "Police and Thieves" in *The Empire Strikes Back*, Gilroy thanked people outside of the Race and Politics Group at the CCCS who had provided him with comments and criticism. The list of names in the acknowledgments included Stuart Hall, his dissertation supervisor; Vron Ware, his partner, editor of the anti-racist and anti-fascist magazine *Searchlight,* and a founding member of the editorial collective of *Emergency*; A. Sivanandan; and Lee Bridges, who had co-authored an article in 1982 with Gilroy for *Marxism Today* about the police use of race in crime statistics.[84] Bridges would review *The Empire Strikes Back* twice for *Race & Class*. In his first review, he associated a Cultural Studies approach with impenetrable language, idealism, and a failure to ground its work in the lived experiences of Black communities.[85] In the subsequent issue of *Race & Class*, the journal took the unusual step of publishing a corrective comment from Bridges. The second review noted the "political error" of reviews that treated "comrades like enemies" and acknowledged that *The Empire Strikes Back* had unsettled the dominant sociology of race relations in Britain as well as a white British left that was, at best, aggressively indifferent to racism.[86] Although

Bridges did not specifically mention it, Gilroy's contributions to the book included critiques of E.P. Thompson for endorsing the dominant view of a relation between race and crime and implying that Black settlement precipitated an increase in sexual assault in "parts of our cities where women are afraid to walk alone."[87] Gilroy's work in the late 1980s and early '90s would also combine respect for the interventionist work of Raymond Williams with critical readings of the "sage of the Black Mountains borderland" that claimed that the pictures he drew of the relationship between "race," national identity, and citizenship were analogous to Powell's.[88]

In 1988, *Race & Class* published a review by Colin Prescod of *There Ain't No Black in the Union Jack*. Prescod had made the journey from the *Black Liberator* journal to the Institute of Race Relations because he felt that *Race & Class* had made its language and analysis intelligible to the people it was struggling with and for. He argued that Gilroy appropriated the political struggles of others for theorizing that was too enamored with the "self-consciously difficult language of the new sociology." To go further, Prescod claimed that there was "something very European" about a book that did not explicitly recognize non-European thinkers such as Mao and Amílcar Cabral.[89] One year after Prescod's review, Sivanandan crystallized such disjunctures between the CCCS and the IRR by accusing the New Times project of Stuart Hall and Martin Jacques of retreating from Black working-class struggles against racism and neocolonialism into culturalism, discourse analysis, deconstruction, and "Thatcherism in drag."[90]

Chapter four considers how Gilroy responded to such arguments, which he considered "alternately spiteful and insightful," by pursuing Black Atlantic exchanges that did not seek to expunge all traces of irony, ambiguity, poetry, or postmodern theory from the writing of Black cultural history or revolutionary ethics.[91] As we shall see, he drew on intellectual sources, often in the United States and the Caribbean, that revealed new forms of struggle "beyond any corporatist definition of 'the political.'"[92] Influenced by the ethical work of June Jordan, Toni Morrison, and other kindred spirits, for example, he would examine cultural work in which "autopoiesis articulates with poetics to form a stance, a style and a philosophical mood" that disrupts masculinist and heteronormative approaches to race and class.[93]

Before we turn to Gilroy's contributions to transatlantic dialogue in the 1980s and '90s, however, we will attend to the self-fashioning of an ambitious and acerbic writer from Detroit who concocted a distinctive blend of all-American humanism in the 1970s. In counterpoint to Gilroy's reviews of music and Black cultural politics—written in conversation with activist-oriented papers in London such as *Race Today*, which connected the collective struggles for liberation developed in cities such as Detroit and Toronto by Asian, African, and Caribbean diasporic communities— Armond White's cultural criticism was written in dialogue with Marxist-Leninist revolutionaries and countercultural dissidents at the *South End* newspaper in Detroit who focused on getting news from Africa and America to their audiences. To go further, chapter three reveals how White's ability to contest the prestige attached to English culture in America (as part of a broader campaign to unsettle stereotypes that fixed African Americans as violent threats to the production of healthy, self-regulating, and self-fashioning citizens) intersected with Gilroy's attempts to disrupt the dominant political language in Britain, which used racial violence in the United States to construct non-white immigrants as alien wedges that would bring bloodshed to its "green and pleasant land."

As one of the instructors of the film history course at Wayne State, I'd like to congratulate Armond White on his film reviews. Long may he write.

James L. Limbacher, letter to the *South End*, February 14, 1974

Even before her retirement . . . acolytes had reduced Pauline [Kael]'s ideas and phrases to a simplistic pleasure esthetic. I prefer to recall the principles within her criticism—not watching films exactly as she did, nor repeating her vivid, ardent phrases or corrupting her personal esthetic, but appreciating aspects of movies to which she more than any other critic was sensitive. She changed the way people watched film by exciting them to respond in fresh, openhearted ways. It was her true erudition that made Bertolucci's career as surely as it made Morgan Freeman's, Brian De Palma's and inspired a movie-struck kid from Detroit . . .

Armond White (2001)

3.
A MOVIE-STRUCK KID FROM DETROIT
Going Deeper into Movies

Much has been written about the range of cultural, economic, and religious institutions with which African Americans exercised their political aspirations and achievements in Detroit during the twentieth century. As noted by Suzanne E. Smith in her historical account of Motown, Detroit was home to cultural institutions such as the Broadside Press, one of America's first Black-owned publishing houses; the Concept East Theater, the first African American theater company in the urban north; and WCHB, the first radio station built, owned, and operated by African Americans. Detroit was also the birthplace of economic organizations such as the Booker T. Washington Trade Association, one of the largest chapters of the National Negro Business League, and religious communities such as the Nation of Islam and the Shrine of the Black Madonna.[1]

The cultural, economic, religious, and political realms often intersected. The first Black Arts Convention was held at the Central United Church in Detroit in 1966; it featured Grace Lee Boggs, a candidate for the Freedom Now Party, who called for

Black independent political action that added moral and spiritual dimensions to the materialist struggle for power and resources. For activists such as Grace Lee Boggs and James Boggs (whose thinking and formation of the Freedom Now Party developed in relation to, and in conflict with, C.L.R. James's vision of the revolutionary agency of the American working classes and the Black struggle[2]), a Black cultural worker at Motown might have as much need to strike as a Black autoworker at Detroit's Dodge Main plant, and a Black political activist might spend as much time, if not more, bringing young people together to plant gardens, rehabilitating homes, and creating murals as constructing speeches and facilitating reading groups.[3] Similarly, the second Black Arts Convention, held at the Central United Church in 1967, would bring together speakers affirming Black culture, success, and entrepreneurship and showcase the church's new mural of the Black Madonna to demonstrate the different realms of Black struggle and cultural politics that were often connected under a concept, symbol, and structure of feeling called "soul."

One year after the Great Rebellion in Detroit in 1967, one of the largest periods of mass unrest in US history, a multiracial group of four thousand workers participated in a wildcat strike to protest working conditions at Dodge's Hamtramck assembly plant. Subsequently, the plant's management disproportionately targeted Black workers for punishment and only fired participants in the strike who were associated with the network that published the *Inner City Voice*, a newspaper subtitled both *Detroit's Black Community Newspaper* and the *Voice of Revolution*. Undeterred, the *Inner City Voice* network would form a caucus to represent the needs of Black workers called the Dodge Revolutionary Union Movement (DRUM), which inspired the creation of several new organizations over the summer of 1968 (including UPRUM for United Parcel Service workers, HRUM for health workers, and NEWRUM for workers at the *Detroit News*). In such revolutionary movements and publications, activists might scrutinize the vague declarations of Black pride by Motown founder Berry Gordy and other Black

business owners and ask if they were willing and able to demonstrate substantive material and concrete commitments to the health
and well-being of their workers or the Black communities that had
produced them.[4]

Despite such diverse sources of political authority in Detroit (to
paraphrase the Black social and political theorist Richard Iton, Black
Detroiters would forge the general rules under which they lived in
the pulpit, the concert stage, the dance floor, and the political rally,
among other venues[5]), relatively little attention has been paid to the
relationship between culture, politics, and a Black radical tradition
in Detroit after the 1970 release of the League of Revolutionary
Black Workers' (LRBW) documentary film *Finally Got the News*.[6]
While alluding to the *Inner City Voice* as a catalyst of Black political activity, and to the revolutionary commitments of its editor
John Watson, historians have often failed to convey the richness
of Detroit's underground media as imaginative vessels of the Black
radical tradition. Smith's wide-ranging discussion of the complex
set of historical forces that produced Motown Record Company and
its music, for example, does not mention the *South End*, the student
paper of Wayne State University that Watson and the *Inner City Voice*
network used to communicate the political messages of DRUM and
the LRBW in Detroit during the late 1960s.

In this chapter, we will consider the impact of the revolutionary ideas and movements in Detroit in the late 1960s by examining
Armond White's reviews of film, music, theater, books, and other
forms of expressive culture for the *South End* between 1972 and 1977.
His cultural criticism called on Black businesses to be relevant to the
communities that helped them to grow and that they purported to
serve, and was wary of Black entrepreneurs "selling out," particularly after Motown officially moved to Los Angeles in June 1972 to
expand into television and filmmaking and was accused of betrayal
by some members of Detroit's Black community.[7] Yet it rarely
engaged explicitly with the Marxism-Leninism of Watson (who had
been removed from the paper by a Wayne State University administration concerned about the *South End*'s explicit commitment to

Black liberation in 1973), European critical theory, and neo-Marxist critiques of the culture industry. It was far more engaged by White's ideas about Black Consciousness (which he associated with belief in God, belief in family, self-trust, growth from the past, and loyalty), and his reading of journalists such as Pauline Kael, who believed that the charms of a lively, jazzy American culture were irresistible to talented individuals around the world who refused to be boxed in by their class, race, or gender.

In the four sections of this chapter, I will discuss these diverse influences on White's personal and political expression. The first, "One Class Conscious Worker Is Worth One Hundred Students," provides a brief introduction to the struggles of Marxist-Leninists to turn the *South End* into an imaginative vessel for DRUM and the LRBW. The second part, An *American* American at the Movies, outlines Pauline Kael's development of a writing style that was original, personal, and intellectual rather than stuffy, academic, and dour. The third section, Portrait of the Critic as a Young Man, reveals how White's cultural criticism for the *South End* sought to interpret politically conscious, aesthetically advanced, multicultural, popular culture during the 1970s by synthesizing Black cultural politics with Kael's language and style as a secular *American* American. Finally, in American Existentialism, I note how White's self-fashioning as a lone, dogged figure who ventured behind the veil of a segregated America to sit with Black thinkers such as W.E.B Du Bois as well as white journalists such as Pauline Kael emerged decades before New York film critics suggested that he may be unable to keep his identities as a "gay African-American fundamentalist-Christian aesthete" from tearing him asunder.[8]

"One Class Conscious Worker Is Worth One Hundred Students"

In their landmark study of urban revolution in Detroit, Dan Georgakas and Marvin Surkin describe John Watson as a "hardcore revolutionary."[9] He was dismissed by the Congress of Racial Equality for being too radical and expelled from the Student Nonviolent

Coordinating Committee as part of a Detroit chapter that advo-
cated for direct action in northern states as well as southern ones.
He considered Marxism-Leninism to be the theory that related
most closely to the lives of production workers and participated
in reading groups—often on or around the Wayne State University
campus—that discussed the work of Marx, Lenin, and anti-colonial
activists such as Frantz Fanon, Che Guevara, Fidel Castro, Amílcar
Cabral, Malcolm X, and C.L.R. James.[10] As the editor of the *Inner
City Voice*, he published local poetry, cartoons, original artwork, and
photography and sought to connect militant struggles on the factory
floor to the scrutiny of the police and other institutions.

In addition to its investigative journalism about the failure of
the United Auto Workers union to promote a significant number of
Black workers into positions of senior management (in Chrysler's
Dodge Main plant in the early 1960s, 99 percent of the general fore-
men and 100 percent of the superintendents were white[11]), the *Inner
City Voice* would report on the acquittals of police officers charged
with murdering three teenagers at the Algiers Motel. It would accuse
Black liberals in city politics of being "Uncle Toms" or "Sambos"
if they appeared too cautious and compromised to move against
police harassment and US Senate surveillance of Black radicals,[12]
and express solidarity with fifteen thousand Detroit high school
students who made Malcolm X's birthday a holiday by conducting
a successful walkout.[13] FBI agents made publication of the newspaper difficult by visiting local print shops that produced the paper
and questioning the owners about their participation in subversive
activities. As a result of such policing, the *Inner City Voice* was never
printed in the same location twice and copy was eventually shipped
to Chicago to be published by the firm that produced the Nation of
Islam's *Muhammad Speaks*.

In the 1968–69 school year, Watson became editor of the *South
End*, which had a significantly higher circulation and printing budget
than the *Inner City Voice*. While nominally the student newspaper
of Wayne State University, it had changed its name from the *Daily
Collegian* to the *South End*. It did so to express solidarity with the

Front page of the *South End*, January 23, 1969. Source: Walter P. Reuther Library, Archives of Labor and Urban Affairs, Wayne State University

predominantly Black neighborhoods that lay to the south of the university campus, and convey its critical opposition to the values of the headquarters of General Motors—one of "the wealthiest corporations in the world, an international symbol of the Power of America, and the validity of American economic values"—which lay to the north.[14] With trenchant language that named and shamed political leaders, the *South End*'s editorial team sought to recruit workers dissatisfied with the reformist, pragmatic approach of Black leaders who were incorporated within the political machinery of government and unions. Watson and his colleagues would, for example, develop an exposure series on the Detroit General Hospital that it distributed free to hospital workers and give out thousands of copies of its special issue on DRUM to factory workers.[15]

On February 13, 1969, the Wayne State University's board of governors announced its deep concern about the tone and content of the university-sponsored newspaper. The university administrators considered the paper's "vulgar expression" and "hate-mongering verbiage" to be reasons why it needed to be shut down. For a brief moment in July 1969, the president of the university officially suspended the paper "until the Student Newspapers Publications Board can review and investigate the entire problem of [its] vulgarity and obscenity and lack of reference to the student community."[16] Well-known histories of the period, such as Heather Thompson's study of politics, labor, and race in Detroit, similarly describe the language used by Black radicals in the American city to denounce white privilege in the 1960s and '70s as divisive, "vitriolic," "off-putting," "racist and anti-democratic."[17]

An *American* American at the Movies

Born in 1953 in Detroit, Armond White was raised in a large working-class family who became the first African Americans to move to a predominantly Jewish neighborhood in the northwest of the city.[18] His family attended the neighborhood cinema on Saturdays until his parents converted to Pentecostalism and came to associate movie theaters with vice. With his trips to the cinema curtailed, Armond would vicariously consume film culture via profiles of Hollywood movies and celebrities in magazines such as *Time* and *Life*, lavish illustrations and original stories of American life and culture in the *Saturday Evening Post*, and the films of Italian auteurs such as Federico Fellini, Vittorio De Sica, and Luchino Visconti that he could watch at home with his mother and siblings on Canadian television stations.

When teachers at Central High, the oldest public secondary school in Detroit, organized a school trip to the cinema, Armond sensed an opportunity to argue that the cinema was one site, among others, in which he might explore truths about communal obligation and personal autonomy that others seek in churches. After his parents acceded to his request (on the understanding that the trip had educational value), he would join his classmates in experiencing *Camelot*, an American musical drama fantasy film. It would, however, take a serendipitous encounter with Pauline Kael's writing for him to envision film criticism as an art form in which he might put into practice some of the values his parents had taught him about the importance of being of worth to other people and the value of thinking for himself.

As a teenager, White would spot a copy of Kael's *Kiss Kiss Bang Bang: Film Writings, 1965–1967* in a drugstore twirling in a rack next to the shelves of magazines he enjoyed browsing. The book would quickly become one of White's most treasured possessions, and it would help him to perceive how film critics might convert passive consumers of movies into active users and producers of culture. He was enthralled by a writer who had joined the *New Yorker* after reviewing films for *Film Quarterly* and KPFA radio in the Bay Area, and fashioned herself as a "common person with common feelings" by extolling the virtues of enjoyable "bad" American movies and exposing the pretentiousness and dullness in movies from Europe and Japan that other film critics hailed as "good," "serious," and "powerful."[19] He identified with a critic who leaned into the personal and subjective nature of her responses to film in contradistinction to the work of her predominantly white, male, middle-class peers. He would follow the path of a journalist who, when asked if she would consider writing a memoir, responded that her personal tastes and history could already be gleaned from her film reviews.

Like Kael, White believed that objectivity was often used as a cover for obtuseness. He was unconvinced that the mask of journalistic objectivity could hide white, male, middle-class identity politics or permit writers to communicate the depth of feeling and emotion that they witnessed on screen with robustness or elegance. White was also in agreement with Kael's belief that conscientious critics could, with courage and integrity, offer their audience an independent point of view that was distinct to the shilling of movie studios. Even before her brief stint as a consultant at Paramount Pictures, Kael was unimpressed by films made for adolescent boys who lived vicariously through the computer-generated special effects of galaxies far, far away.[20] Her prominence coincided with the golden age of American cinema in the 1970s, and in 1974, she was recognized with a National Book Award for *Deeper into Movies*, a collection of her movie reviews in the *New Yorker* between 1969 and 1972. By 1980, she was concerned that publicists' and media executives' power and obsessions with ratings and box-office returns had tipped the delicate balance between art and commerce in film culture decisively toward commercial interests.[21]

Kael advanced a vision of an *American* American identity with which she sought to escape the pitfalls of ghettoization as "merely" a "Jewish American" writer, and differentiate her vision of an open-minded and open-hearted American culture from the state of closure and security granted to American citizenship, a United States passport, and the assumption that the only or most authentic way to be all-American was to be a blond, blue-eyed white person.

As a child of Jewish immigrants, Kael creatively adapted the "New Colossus" poem mounted on the Statue of Liberty to insist that American pop culture offered poor, huddled masses around the world the opportunity to escape the loneliness, moroseness, and depression of Old Europe.[22] Her highest praise was reserved for emotional and thrilling work that conveyed the complexity, self-awareness, and ambition of an American culture that was a melting pot of creative artists and thinkers from around the world.[23] Such jazzy American art was, on the one hand, defined against people with American citizenship that she found too parochial or pretentious to appreciate the liveliness and vitality of ethnically diverse and working-class American cultures in a non-condescending manner. It was open to people without American citizenship such as the Spanish director Pedro Almodóvar, whom Kael associated with the originality and "crazy energy" of *American* art.[24] With that said, Kael's defense of an American melting pot that did not trap individuals in ethnic camps (whether they were oppressed minorities or Euro-American political and cultural elites) could also descend into overgeneralized attacks against European cultures that she deemed stifling and collectivist. Her reviews would, for example, poke fun at the moroseness of Eastern European folk culture, lampoon the sophistication of European intellectuals such as Milan Kundera, and recycle stereotypes about Jewish refugees who waxed nostalgic about a European culture in which they had servants and a "stuffier, more middle-class materialism than they could afford in the New World."[25]

Portrait of the Critic as a Young Man

After graduating from Central High, White enrolled in Wayne State University and in 1972 began reviewing film, music, theater, books, and art exhibits for the *South End*. He started writing for the paper when editorials in the paper promised to offer readers a "viable and refreshing alternative to the drivel of the establishment bourgeois press which is the lap-dog of the ruling class,"[26] but shortly after his arrival John Watson and his successor Gene Cunningham were

Portrait of the Journalism I class of Central High School, 1971–72. This class
published the *Central Student* newspaper four times a semester. It was taught
by Nacretia Judkins (seated, bottom left) and its editor-in-chief was Armond
White (standing, top right). Source: Walter P. Reuther Library, Archives of Labor
and Urban Affairs, Wayne State University

removed from the *South End*'s staff after the newspaper published
a graphic of the Star of David with a swastika in the center and was
the subject of sustained opposition from the Jewish community in
Detroit. After the departures of Watson and Cunningham, the paper
would adopt a less stridently militant tone and no longer aspire to
educate the workers of Detroit about unionization or the struggles
of oppressed peoples against neocolonialism. When White signed
off from Detroit's third-largest daily newspaper in 1977, he was
praised by his colleague Sweet T Williams for his refusal to submit to
the demands of "consumer or entertainment conglomerates" or the
blandishments of white liberals.[27]

Such praise may suggest that there were overlaps between
White's jeremiads against a mass audience that had "lost their
sensitivity to subtlety" and a neo-Marxist critique of the culture
industry.[28] However, he would also denounce "audio-visual lectures"
in films that he deemed "*too* political" or "European-Marxist."[29]
White's writing was always more informed by Kael's writings about

America and film culture than by the critical commentary about a culture industry circulated by Theodor Adorno and other European transplants in America. His dismissive comments about juvenile posturing and arrested development, a "kindergarten mentality," and "insultingly childish" movies written for adolescents who "haven't really learned to think yet" were influenced by Kael's tendency to blame television and other critics for their failure to build awareness and appreciation for the elegance and visual wit of "deeply felt films."[30] White's distaste for the strained seriousness of "purposefully abstruse movies" from Europe also reflected Kael's aspirations for cultural productions that artfully engaged with high levels of social tension, the prominent place of social minorities in popular culture, and the right to free speech.[31] He would excoriate unimaginative and dull histories of European monarchs that revolved around "stiff upper lip limeys,"[32] and confront anything that reeked of condescension about the "fickleness," "sham," and "vulgar liveliness" in American life.[33] He feared that *American* Americans who were irreverent, unpretentious, and shallow (in a good way) might feel pressured into producing overly pretentious films so that they might be taken seriously by a critical establishment enthralled by art-house cinema from Europe and Japan.[34]

Kael and White both considered Robert Altman to be one of the leading exponents of *American* American art. Kael was delighted by the "pure emotional highs" that Altman delivered with *Nashville*, which brought together a dazzling array of performers to explore American history, politics, religion, and culture and expose the racist, colonial outlook of a visiting reporter from the BBC during the bicentennial celebration of the United States.[35] White celebrated *Nashville* as a film that avoided the "pre-digested, spelled out, moviemaking styles" of American trash as well as the solipsism of dreamlike European films.[36] Revealingly, he deemed it a virtuosic example of "complexity and control" on a par with the best *American* American jazz,[37] and felt deflated and betrayed when Altman directed *3 Women* and seemed to be enthralled to "hushed, portentous, schematic and obscure . . . artsy-fartsy bullshit" rather than staying true to his "American heart."[38]

American Existentialism

In the run-up to the US presidential election of 1972, which had the lowest voter turnout since 1948, Kael expressed her surprise that *Sounder*, an "inspirational movie about black strength and pride ... based on a prize-winning children's book, by a white author ... could transcend its cautious, mealy genre to become the first movie about black experiences in America which can stir people of all colors." Although she often poured scorn on historical films that felt sentimental and anachronistic, Kael believed that the family drama about Black sharecroppers during the Great Depression "earns every emotion we feel" by putting "modern consciousness on screen" and dispensing with tired stereotypes like the "conventional movie trust-in-the-Lord black mother."[39] Five issues later, the *New Yorker* published Kael's review of the simple pleasures and tawdry electricity of a "Black blockbuster" produced by Motown Productions for Paramount about the life of Billie Holiday. Kael did not believe that *Lady Sings the Blues* represented the subtler and more lasting pleasures of jazz. Nor was she convinced that it came close to honoring the complexity of its protagonist's life. However, she was willing to tolerate its artificiality and "immediate emotional gratifications" as the price of Black film's entrance into the consciousness of mainstream America.[40]

Just over a month after Kael's reviews of *Sounder* and *Lady Sings the Blues*, White submitted his first article for the *South End*. In it, he reported on the activities of the coalition against Blaxploitation in its campaign to resist "shallow, unreal, one-dimensional portrayal of black people without, or with little responsible co-operation from blacks themselves."[41] During the rest of the fall term, White consistently lamented that "Black people working in movies have yet to do anything magnificent, consequential or historically important," and debunked the assumption that the inclusion of more non-whites in prominent onscreen roles meant that film culture was actively engaging and demonstrating Black Consciousness.[42]

When he returned to his writing duties after the Christmas holidays, White was proud to champion *Sounder* as a credit to the conscientiousness of the Jewish director Martin Ritt, the Black screenwriter Lonne Elder III, the stirring musical score by Taj Mahal, and the honest, affecting performances of the predominantly Black cast. While Kael encouraged her mostly white audience to reconsider a movie that they may have associated with weeping violins and sentimental trash, White implored his multiracial audience to buy tickets for a film that had the potential to transform American culture. He testified that *Sounder* "may be the finest motion picture made in American movie history! There's not another film in the world like it, some foreign films have the same feelings, but not nearly so . . . effective."[43] White clarified why it was emotionally and intellectually thrilling to witness a film that dramatized the beauty and necessity of learning from African American culture, history, and memory. He paid particular attention to scenes in which W.E.B. Du Bois's famous concept of double consciousness—"the sense of always looking at oneself through the eyes of others, of measuring one's soul by the tape of a world that looks on in amused contempt and pity"[44]—was dramatized by characters who revealed Black folks' distinctive awareness of their personal and social identities in a white supremacist country.[45]

Aside from *Sounder*, White reviewed motion pictures that featured athletes and comedians who demonstrated Black excellence. He drew attention to the artistry, discipline, and self-respect worthy of Muhammad Ali,[46] and the confessional comedy of Richard Pryor that was "relevant to the way we live our lives."[47] He found *Sounder*, Ali, and Pryor an inspiration to earnest Black filmmakers who wished to succeed by "doing the right thing" in response to Jesse Jackson's calls to move from ethnicity to ethicalness to excellence.[48] In contrast, he considered the attempts to transfer the music of Motown to Hollywood in *Lady Sings the Blues* a gaudy attempt to achieve economic success that represented its disconnection from the local community that supported its growth.[49] Although it did not directly mention the fact that Motown formally announced that its general headquarters would move from Detroit to Los Angeles, White's review was haunted by what many Detroiters considered a betrayal.

In subsequent years White would use films by the Italian American director Martin Scorsese, made with a fraction of the budget of *Lady Sings the Blues*, to claim that quality films about ethnic minorities in America required dedication, imagination, and talent—not money.[50] White also aligned Scorsese with Altman as an artist who expressed the practical values of *American* Americans who were "not too erudite" or "staunchly intellectual,"[51] and claimed that the power of American existentialism in Scorsese's *Taxi Driver* lay "in the way it goes past where European existentialism stops. The film's point is not just alienation, but the violent reality and consequences of it."[52] Whereas White associated European existentialism with an excessively personal and autobiographical approach that he found repugnant and unintelligible,[53] he praised the American existentialism of filmmakers who dramatized the psychology and violence of isolated figures in a manner that he found thrilling and relatable.[54] Indeed, he would celebrate the "American existentialism" of Scorsese's *Mean Streets* because it managed to convey "the excitement of contemporary life better than anything bar Stevie Wonder's 'Living for the City,'" which was inspired by the critical and commercial success of Marvin Gaye's *What's Going On?* album and spoke to the political aspirations of a Black community in Detroit on the verge of electing Coleman Young, an African American state senator and former member of the United Auto Workers union.[55]

In his reviews of film, music, and culture for the *South End*, White reminded his readers to vote for Coleman Young, and scolded Detroit's suburban-controlled, backward-looking media for romanticizing the 1950s rather than examining the human impact of its racial segregation.[56] He complained about journalists, filmmakers, and audiences who were "distressed when movies aren't as complacent, clichéd and infantile as television" or "banal soap operas" that glamorized suburban lives as the epitome of the American Dream.[57] However, such critical sorties about the myths and platitudes propagated in American media, culture, and society were expressed by an existentialist and libertarian who was interested in art that demonstrated how racism and nationalism were experienced by individuals rather than forces that drove people. He responded to the myopia and obtuseness of political and cultural institutions by drawing attention to individual artists who transcended them.

An interview with White in *New York* magazine in 2009 ably illustrates his self-fashioning as a lone, dogged figure who ventures behind the veil of a segregated America in search of truth in cinemas as well as churches. In it, White recalls a period in which he was assigned to cover a local screening of Steven Spielberg's *Close Encounters of the Third Kind* and had to travel to Southfield, then a nearly all-white suburb, because Detroit's status as "Murder city" in the late 1970s meant that there were no theaters downtown deemed suitable to show the picture.

> White took the bus out there and walked several blocks to the theater. The film, needless to say, blew him away, especially the climactic descent of the giant mother ship, a moment White took to be nothing less than a revelation of the "face of God." During the time White had spent in the theatre, a heavy snow came down, nearly a foot.
>
> "There I was, having seen that film, *a truly great film*, and I was walking through this blanket of pristine snow in the suburbs. I was the only one around. I'd never experienced a moment of such purity; perhaps I never will again."[58]

Armond White's story is not one that has been used by journalists to delve beyond their statistics about white flight from Detroit. Readers of evidence-based stories that discuss the shift in Detroit's population from Coleman Young's inauguration as mayor in 1974 (when 50 percent of Detroit's population was classified as Black) to the time he left office in 1994 (when approximately 75 percent of Detroit's population was racialized as Black and the city had lost around one-third of its population) are not informed about White's attempts to translate how such systemic crises were lived and felt. Historians have also overlooked the dissidence and defiance of White in their accounts of Black representation and inclusion in formal politics in Detroit, which can, of course, coexist with structures that discriminate against African Americans by intensifying the policing and incarceration of African Americans in the illegal economy and boosting the political power of predominantly white suburbs.[59]

In the next chapter, I consider Paul Gilroy's distinct yet related challenge to what he describes as the "totalizing schemes of macropolitical narratives,"[60] and the tendency of materialist historians to place labor—rather than a politics around the overcoming of dispiriting and alienating labor—as the centerpiece of emancipatory hopes. Whereas White asserted a soulful vision of American existentialism that defined itself, in part, against dour Marxist lectures, Gilroy influenced a range of academic disciplines in the 1990s by taking the political aspirations and achievements of Black Atlantic cultures seriously and exploring how they were "expressed in autobiographical writing, special and uniquely creative ways of manipulating spoken language, and, above all, the music" that had overflowed from religious and national containers into secular and profane venues.[61] Although Gilroy's work has not been repressed or marginalized in scholarly communities to the extent of White's, it has also run up against academics who deem it too idiosyncratic and maverick for a serious analysis of Black history and culture.

One does not wish to romanticize the historian by belaboring his aloneness, but in the final analysis he is probably the least able of all scholars to work for a team, the least willing to collaborate, to co-author, to engage in public testimony and debate. . . . The historian remains a private person, unwilling to reveal much of himself in his written word. His individuality is to be discovered, rather, in the range of topics on which he chooses to write, in the way in which he gathers evidence, in his conception of peripheral as opposed to central questions, in the very style of his expression. In history perhaps more than in any other discipline, the book is the man, the medium is the message, and the understanding of evidence and how to employ it is one's closest approach to that truth others seek in churches.

Robin Winks (1968)

[John Berger] is not an academic historian and his historical method is radically illuminating rather than systematic. He sifts through historical raw material to find confirming evidence for a thesis he seeks to prove. His historical generalizations are not supported by the weight of evidence that would seem necessary to a professional historian. Berger's work is investigative, exploratory and provocative rather than definitive. . . . While lacking in procedural rigor . . . his concern is with opening up new freedoms, clearing new paths.

Geoff Dyer (1986)

4.

SLAVE-DESCENDANTS, DIASPORA SUBJECTS, AND WORLD CITIZENS

Paul Gilroy's Historical Sensibility

O n January 24, 1988, forty-eight African American critics and writers published a statement in the *New York Times Book Review* lamenting that Toni Morrison had not been the recipient of a Pulitzer Prize or a National Book Award.[1] Shortly after this affirmation of her work, and shortly before she was awarded Pulitzer Prize for Fiction that same year, Paul Gilroy interviewed the author of *Beloved* for an alternative arts magazine in London.[2] In this interview, Gilroy noted that Morrison appreciated the expression of love, appreciation, and respect from her peers in the "hallowed, mainstream pages of the *New York Times Book Review*." Yet he also recorded how she felt estranged from Black Americans who merely wished to declare, "I have made it."[3] Such alienation from a Black bourgeoisie in the United States resonated with Gilroy's concerns that a proto-Black middle class in the United Kingdom was so rarely able to advance the interests of the communities that its members purported to serve. Morrison's assertion that she "found more to share with Third World peoples in the diaspora" also reflected his belief that national approaches were insufficient to analyze Black expressive cultures.

Gilroy's portrait of Morrison as a diasporic artist who consistently refused to "identify herself as an American" was republished in chapter twelve of *Small Acts*, a collection of his essays and interviews about Black cultural production in the United Kingdom and the United States in the late 1980s and early '90s. In chapter thirteen of this collection, Gilroy critiqued Spike Lee for an affiliation to America and Americanism that meant his films took the "easy, lazy options that reduce race politics to the simple binary code of black and white."[4] While acknowledging that Lee's earlier films drew attention to misogyny, homophobia, and color caste divisions within the African American community, Gilroy argued that the filmmaker had increasingly capitulated to the "populist demand that black life be revealed sentimentally, therapeutically and without criticism"; developed films that portrayed pathological family forms being ruled by women and the healthy Black family being headed by a patriarch; and didactically told audiences to cleave "to those who share our own phenotypes if the integrity of our cultures is to be preserved."[5] Such cultural politics stood in stark contrast to Gilroy's appreciation of Morrison (who had identified the pitfalls of therapeutic and nostalgic approaches to Black art in an interview with *Race Today*, the activist-oriented journal in London that communicated and connected the collective struggles for liberation in cities such as Detroit and Toronto by Asian, African, and Caribbean diasporic communities[6]), and Isaac Julien, who had portrayed "transgressive phenotypically asymmetrical desire, through music, affirmation, celebration and play" in films such as *Looking for Langston* and *Young Soul Rebels*.[7]

The first part of this chapter, Threatening Pleasures, focuses on Gilroy's contribution to the production and dissemination of *Young Soul Rebels*, a film directed by Julien that drew on the political and cultural resources of Gilroy's *There Ain't No Black in the Union Jack* to assert an identity that was Black and British.[8] The second part, *Small Acts: Thoughts on the Politics of Black Cultures*, considers Gilroy's approach to cultural criticism and the calculation of political choices in essays, reviews, and interviews that straddled academia and journalism. The third section, *The Black Atlantic: Modernity and Double Consciousness*, turns to Gilroy's most-cited book, which delves beneath the surface of African American writers to unearth "important" and "carefully deployed" clues about their "own struggles,"[9] and interprets what it tells us about his struggles to navigate an academic career he had formerly considered out of reach.

Threatening Pleasures

In 1983, Isaac Julien, Martina Attille, Maureen Blackwood, Nadine Marsh-Edwards, Robert Crusz, and other art school graduates founded Sankofa Film and Video Collective. They were supported with funding by the Greater London Council as well as the British Film Institute (BFI) and Channel 4, and aspired to develop an independent Black film culture. Gilroy has described Julien's early work, such as *Who Killed Colin Roach?* (a film that reflects upon the death of a twenty-three-year-old who was shot at the entrance of a police station in East London in 1982) and *Territories* (a film that examines how identities of race, class, gender, and sexuality intersect at work, and how mainstream British culture reduces the complexity of the Notting Hill Carnival by labeling it as a remainder or reminder of an ancient retrogressive custom) as among the best documents with which we can explain why the conflicts of the 1980s arose and why they must be examined again.

Young Soul Rebels is credited as a BFI production with Film Four, Sankofa, and television and film production companies in France, Spain, and Germany. It had a budget of £1.2 million, substantially more than Julien's previous films with Sankofa, which permitted an extended cast, shooting locations, special effects, and crowd scenes. This budget was secured, in part, by pitching the film as viable commercial property that would appeal to young cinema-goers and successfully recoup its budget at the box office and in the sales of CD soundtracks and other media tie-ins.[10] Much like other British films of the 1990s such as *Babymother* and *Rage, Young Soul Rebels* would borrow the portrayal of sound system culture, police racism, and Black disillusionment from the 1980 British drama *Babylon* and follow a group of young protagonists expressing personal ideas and forging their identities through the creation of music and social and sexual activity. When Julien and his co-writer Derrick Saldaan McClintock found it challenging to write a more mainstream script, Colin MacCabe, the head of production at BFI, suggested that the film might include narrative elements drawn from their own lives. McClintock's experience as a young mixed-race individual wrongfully suspected of murder in 1977 informed a revised script (written with Paul Hallam, a white, gay screenwriter), which also included the trappings of a generic detective thriller.

The plot of *Young Soul Rebels* follows two friends, Chris and Caz, who run a pirate radio station called Soul Patrol from a tower block in East London. The script describes Chris as a "nineteen-year-old light-skinned youth." Caz is depicted as "darker-skinned and a bit older." After their friend TJ is killed while cruising for sex in the local park at night, Chris begins a relationship with Tracy and Caz begins a relationship with Billibud. The film's screenwriters imagined Tracy as a female production assistant on the one show on a Metro radio station that plays soul music, and a Black woman with "South Molton Street style . . . a bit older, a bit classier, less street." They introduced Billibud as a young white rebel selling the *Socialist Worker* newspaper who expressed his cultural politics by carefully curating his clothes, music, and a room that was a "shrine" to punk.

Although *Young Soul Rebels* does not include the formalized tableaux and montages that Julien used to stunning effect in his earlier films and art projects, it would be a mistake to overlook the visual symbolism that accompanied its portrayal of distinct social groups. It juxtaposes the pristine Union Jacks that loyal subjects unfurled during street celebrations in honor of the Queen's Jubilee with ripped-up Union Jacks in the bars of underground venues that pledged allegiance to the Sex Pistols and other "space traitors" who declared patriotism to be dead. The camera lingers on images of support for the National Front as well as Pan-African icons on the walls of barbershops. Dialogue about the "patriotic listeners" of mainstream radio stations complaining that that one hour of Black music was "too much" serves as a wry counterpoint to a soundtrack that featured one hour of Black music for outernational listeners. The film features mixed-race characters such as Chris, a DJ who translates American music for London revelers while wearing the shirts of baseball teams from San Francisco and Kansas City, and Kelly, a "mixed-race skinhead" who belongs to a working-class tribe decked out in the shirts of the British designer Fred Perry.

Gilroy worked as a freelance researcher and consultant for the film, made a cameo appearance in it with his family, and wrote the sleeve notes for its exhilarating soundtrack. In post-screening discussions, he warned audiences against overly literal readings of the film and suggested that it should be read as an allegory of the British Empire that featured Black and white characters who were residues of postcolonial Britain. Such contributions to the production and dissemination of *Young Soul Rebels* were illustrative of solidarity between academics, critics, and artists in the 1980s and early '90s that was evidenced in collectively authored projects and collaborative work with and for a Black public sphere (in contrast to the exaggerated individualism with which figures were often marketed as Black public intellectuals in, for example, the hallowed, mainstream pages of the *New York Times Book Review*).

Shortly after *Young Soul Rebels* received a Société des auteurs et compositeurs dramatiques (SACD) award during the 1991 Cannes Film Festival, Gilroy shared his reflections on the film's music, sexuality, politics, and pleasure with Stuart Hall and Homi Bhabha. Then a faculty member at the University of Sussex, Gilroy's alma mater, Bhabha had contributed to public debate and discussion about the representations of Muslims in the Western media after Ayatollah Ruhollah Khomeini issued a fatwa calling for the assassination of the British Indian novelist Salman Rushdie. Gilroy was a lecturer in Sociology at the University of Essex who had also written articles for magazines that compared the British media's portrayal of the muscular Black English athlete Frank Bruno with the esoteric and scholastic image of Rushdie.[11] Hall was a professor of Sociology at the Open University who appeared regularly on television programs broadcast on the BBC, and had been embroiled in a public debate with Rushdie about *Handsworth Songs*, a self-consciously unconventional collage of news reports, eyewitness footage, interviews, and abstract imagery.[12]

In an article entitled "Threatening Pleasures" in the British film journal *Sight and Sound*, Bhabha, Gilroy, and Hall discussed whether *Young Soul Rebels* subverted stereotypes that reduced Black cultural groups to a few simple, essential, and "natural" characteristics (such as irrationality, rhythm, animism, oneness with nature, and sensuality).[13] Bhabha expressed his disappointment with what he considered the film's rather sentimental ending (in which the gay and straight couples go home, clean their records, and dance together). Gilroy did not disagree with Bhabha's point, but he invited further discussion about the final frame in a film that struggled to convey a pluralized and open version of the Black subject as well as "anti-racist, polysexual, democratic aspirations" to a mainstream audience. If filmmakers were to avoid the pitfalls of essentialism as exemplified by American film and British sitcoms, they would not fix the idealized and "mystified black community offered by the barber's shop." Nor would they cast all of their utopian aspirations into the basket of the "'mixed race' family." They would need to think more creatively about translating the language and communicative moments in the underground rave, the pirate radio station, and the alternative media. The last word in the article was given to Hall, who accepted the ending of the film as a "sort of 'coda'—almost a moment out of time," and particularly liked "the way Billibud, the white boy, dances; a kind of tentativeness at first, as if he's learning to dance, learning to match his steps and rhythms to theirs. It has the tentativeness of emergence for me, a kind of utopian emergence."

Portrait of Paul Gilroy in 1991.
Photo: Paul Tozer

Small Acts: Thoughts on the Politics of Black Cultures

Paul Gilroy's *Small Acts* was published by Serpent's Tail, an independent publishing house in London that had previously published Val Wilmer's *As Serious as Your Life*.[14] Its cover image was an extract from Sonia Boyce's painting *Talking Presence* that represented St. Paul's Cathedral, a double-decker bus, and other iconic landmarks of London from oblique angles. On its back cover, Stuart Hall endorsed a collection of essays, interviews, and conversations by a former student that touched on a broad range of Black cultural production on both sides of the Atlantic. Such images and endorsements were supplemented with chapters that departed from the more stately lines of English culture familiar to locals and tourists by reflecting on *The Other Story* (the first art exhibition of British African, Caribbean, and Asian modernism, which Boyce created co-operatively with three other female artists) and citing Hall's observations about the plurality of forms that racism has developed within and between societies.[15] In conjunction with its reflections on the ethics and aesthetics of vernacular intellectuals such as Boyce and Hall, *Small Acts* revealed how Black music magazines, activist-oriented journals, record stores, dance halls, and concerts, among other venues, were part of a Black public sphere. That is to say, they were important sites in which individuals could come together to freely and openly discuss, identify, and symbolize societal problems and, through that interaction, generate a range of collectively authored material and symbolic resources that could influence political action in local, transnational, or comparative diasporic contexts.[16]

Although some readers have found it difficult to discern Gilroy's engagement with visual culture, religion, and the life of the spirit in the Black diaspora,[17] *Small Acts* contrasted the bold work of Black British artists and the communitarian elements of Rastafarianism with "England's moribund cultural order."[18] Aside from its reflections on the first art exhibition of British African, Caribbean, and Asian modernism and interviews with artists and filmmakers such as David Bailey and Isaac Julien, *Small Acts* reflected on the visual pleasures of record sleeves that made their mark on the dreams of young soul rebels when they attached them to their bedroom walls. It also alluded to the role that the Rastafari concept of livity played in the political imaginations of Black Britons who sought to disassociate law from oppressive or discriminatory governments, "politrick-sters," and police.[19] Gilroy did not believe that such discrimination in the "overdeveloped world" was confined to overt acts of aggressively racist policing, violence, or political speeches. *Small Acts* thus drew attention to the exclusionary acts of aesthetes who separated truth, justice, and beauty from each other, and noted how John Ruskin's evaluation of J.M.W. Turner's famous painting of *Slavers Throwing Overboard the Dead and Dying: Typhoon Coming On* relegated the information that the ship was carrying enslaved people to its footnotes.[20]

Small Acts also communicated Gilroy's interest in developing Black popular modernism that avoided the pitfalls of "therapeutic essentialism" and "anti-essentialism."[21] On the one hand, he painted a rather derisory picture of "a posse, sorry, a party of African American tourists who were doing one of those tours led by Doc Ben [Yousef Ben-Jochannan]" in search of their ancestral roots and nostalgia for a scale of life associated with rural living, as he sought to construct a healthier basis for the writing of cultural history and the calculation of political choices for Black people in postcolonial cities.[22] On the other, Gilroy proposed a form of anti-anti-essentialism that was distinct to what he identified as the premature anti-essentialism of cultural workers who were more concerned with the pursuit of funding from an international film circuit than the building of a base or context for their art within Black British communities.[23]

Although Gilroy could be a paranoid reader who suspected that artists who claimed to work "inside and against" multination-als would quickly forget the "against" part when their cheques were signed,[24] he did not disrupt the language and style of interna-tional conferences and art exhibits that propose a London-centric approach to England and a New York–centric view of the United States. In a chapter based on a presentation to a conference to com-memorate the decade 1900–1910, for example, he proposes that

Black Britons (rather than Londoners) do not have to approach questions of race and raciology via events in New York, although "New York should, of course, remain prominently marked on the map that we make as part of comprehending them."[25] In another chapter based on a presentation to a conference on Black Popular Cultures, he concedes that he does not "pretend to understand everything that [the New York rapper] Tim Dog's performance means in *the United States*, but in *London* it has very particular meanings and effects."[26] Such use of New York and London as entry points to talk about the United States and Britain (or at least England) provides two revealing examples of why his work would be associated with a cosmopolitan "New York–London nexus" and a "metropolitan academic climate" in the mid-1990s that popularized concepts of "fusion, hybridity and syncretism as explanatory tools for the analysis of cultural formation."[27]

The Black Atlantic: Modernity and Double Consciousness

Building More Stately Mansions, a 1944 painting by the African American artist Aaron Douglas, was a fitting choice to grace the front cover of *The Black Atlantic*. Its concentric bands of muted color, which suggest waves of history and knowledge that link the Black builders of pyramids, temples, and churches to the Black constructors of skyscrapers in the twentieth century, magisterially illustrate Gilroy's approach to the expressive cultures of an African diaspora that were ceaselessly in motion and, in the words of Amiri Baraka, a "changing same."[28]

There are numerous overlaps between *Small Acts* and *The Black Atlantic*. Both texts would praise Toni Morrison for her imaginative and moving excursions into the "relationship between terror and memory, sublimity and the impossible desire to forget the unforgettable,"[29] use Spike Lee to illustrate the pitfalls of cultural protectionists who associate mixing and hybridity with regression,[30] and portray Afrocentricity as something born amid the pain of American cities facing a crack epidemic rather than a rich and productive basis for the writing of cultural history.[31] However,

The Black Atlantic spends substantially more time demonstrating its engagement with postmodern and postcolonial theory in the Western academy than *Small Acts* did. The author of *Small Acts* had translated the "ecstatic bodily pleasures" of listening and dancing for audiences who rejected a "moribund English culture" and "morbid celebrations of England and Englishness";[32] the author of *The Black Atlantic* constructed a text that foregrounded slave suicide, fatalism, pain, and death drive as the dominant features of Black modernity.[33] In a text published by an independent publishing house in London, Gilroy struggled to create and sustain a Black British identity that included postcolonial migrants from Africa, Asia, and the Caribbean; in a book published by Harvard University Press and Verso, he sought to reconstruct the lives and circumstances of "slave-descended" intellectuals from Europe, Africa, the Caribbean, and, above all, America who lovingly borrowed, respectfully stole, or brazenly hijacked the art of others to make it fit their political and emotional needs. Revealingly, *The Black Atlantic* includes a memorable passage in which Gilroy recounts the poverty and hopelessness he encountered on his quest to find a record store in the Black city of New Haven (while he was a visiting professor at Yale University in the early 1990s), rather than any analysis of politically infused acts of pleasure on British dance floors.[34]

On some occasions in the text, Gilroy uses the life and work of African American intellectuals to argue that the presentation of a public persona was a founding motif within the expressive culture of the *African diaspora*.[35] On other occasions, it is specified that the articulation of personal history within imaginative writing is an important cultural and aesthetic motif in *African American letters*.[36] Whether generalizing about an African diaspora (via the autobiographies of African American intellectuals) or African American letters (via the creative artistry of writers he claims as ideal ancestors or prototypes for today's Black would-be Europeans[37]), the subjects of Gilroy's attention carefully organize their thoughts in "self-consciously polyphonic forms" that combine sociological writing "with personal and public history, fiction, autobiography, ethnography, and poetry."[38] He not only noted that Du Bois's *Souls of*

Black Folk tended to begin most chapters with one epigraph drawn from the canon of European literature and another extracted from one of the Black American "sorrow songs"[39]—but he developed a text that opened each chapter with at least one observation from a white thinker who has entered into the canon of Europe-centered material on the history and legacy of the Enlightenment, and one from a Black vernacular intellectual who provides material and symbolic resources to transform Euro-American social theory, philosophy, and cultural criticism.[40] To disrupt the Euro-American academic establishment and "myopically Eurocentric theories," Gilroy also noted how Frederick Douglass and Friedrich Nietzsche pondered post-sacral modern values at roughly the same time and, as described in chapter two, demonstrated the connections between the everyday lifeworld of urban Black Americans such as Richard Wright and the existential anxieties of European savants such as Søren Kierkegaard.[41]

When writing about a Black British Arts movement in the 1980s, Gilroy suggested that the emphasis placed on the success of a Black Audio Film Collective within the international film festival circuit masked a failure to cultivate a "base or context for the type of films they want to make within the black communities in this country."[42] So, when he outlined his desire to map a Black Atlantic network of cultures spanning Africa, North and South America, the Caribbean, and Europe in international conferences held in New York, Gilroy remarked that his "intellectual journey across the Atlantic" was not a flight from Black cultural politics in the United Kingdom. It was, instead, a means to generate new resources for Black Britons "to comprehend doubleness and cultural intermixture."[43] Many scholarly reviews were unconvinced by this framing of *The Black Atlantic* and wondered whether it was acclaimed *because* it resonated and reflected an anti-materialist, cultural turn in North American and European academic institutions.[44]

The Black Atlantic has been adjudged to be too academic or dependent on a cultural turn, as well as not academic enough for literary critics and historians who tend to demonstrate the breadth of their reading with extensive endnotes or footnotes rather than trust their readers to identify their allusions and influences. On the one hand, critics felt that *The Black Atlantic* was weighed down by "forbidding abstraction,"[45] and its "affirmation of black debts to European philosophy" could only be considered a counter-model of social emancipation from a "very specific and academic perspective."[46] On the other hand, professional literary critics and historians claimed that it did not demonstrate any substantive engagement with Marxist literature on world-systems theory[47] or Cedric Robinson's *Black Marxism*.[48] Such comments may reveal more about the fetishization of footnotes among historians, and the belief that it is vitally important to bestow recognition on Black radical thinkers by explicitly naming and citing them, than about a text that was enhanced by conversations with Robinson and developed substantive case studies of Du Bois and Wright that were clearly in dialogue with Robinson's analysis of Du Bois, Wright, and other Black radicals who seemed destined to articulate the idea of struggle rather than create it.[49]

With that said, it remains striking that *The Black Atlantic* (unlike *Small Acts*) did not acknowledge its debt to the art historian Robert Farris Thompson, who had coined the term the "black Atlantic" in his 1983 book *Flash of the Spirit: African and Afro-American Art and Philosophy*.[50] In his pursuit of a "proper job" in academia,[51] Gilroy adopted the language of cultural theorists who wish to assert the originality and significance of their projects with the phrase "what I am calling" and repeatedly talked about "what I am heuristically calling the black Atlantic world," "I call the black Atlantic," "I want to call the black Atlantic," and "I have labelled the black Atlantic."[52] Readers of *The Black Atlantic* may also be unaware that Edward Said's *Orientalism* served as its model and inspiration.[53] Said does not appear in the book's index and only features in three of its footnotes. One has to turn to a review of Said's *Culture and Imperialism* Gilroy wrote for the *New Statesman* in 1993 to find Gilroy expressing admiration for Said's "resolutely principled" work and its exploration of "representations of western supremacy that have been gored by cultural historians and literary critics to whom empire was a non-event or sideshow."[54]

While Said provided Gilroy with a wealth of symbols and concrete evidence to push the politically radical and openly interventionist aspirations of British Cultural Studies into closer dialogue with Postcolonial Studies, *The Black Atlantic*'s challenge to any simplified periodizations of modern and premodern periods demonstrated more substantive engagement with feminist theory. Said was willing to respond to questions about his gender politics by invoking his upbringing in the male world of boarding schools and expressing his feeling that "in the relationships between the ruler and the ruled in the imperial or colonial or racial sense, race takes precedence over both class and gender."[55] Gilroy's examination of modernity and double consciousness in *The Black Atlantic* repeatedly encouraged more critical reflection about a "plural reading public fractured along the experiential fault lines of gender, race, and class."[56] It also translated Stuart Hall's well-known aphorism about race being the modality in which class is lived (to invite further reflection about an analogous formation: how gender is the modality in which race is lived[57]), and was transformed and boosted by the special and uniquely creative work of African American women such as June Jordan, bell hooks, and Toni Morrison.

Rather than examine what the book says about race and gender, critical commentary has tended to lament the relative absence of case studies about the life and work of Black women. In response to questions about the preponderance of case studies about African American men in *The Black Atlantic*, and how they were used to represent a Black diaspora in a way that studies that focused on African American female authors or African writers were not, Gilroy has acknowledged that the life, work, and political culture of Ida B. Wells-Barnett was appropriate to the heuristic project of mapping a Black Atlantic (one thinks, for example, of her lectures and talks in the United Kingdom against the barbarity of lynching in America). He has also noted that, if he were to begin the project in the twenty-first century, he would have included a case study on the life and work of Anna Julia Cooper, a distinguished scholar and educator who attended the first Pan-African Conference in 1900 and received her PhD from the University of Paris–Sorbonne in 1925.[58]

★

The next chapter moves between 1984 and 1996 to chronicle Armond White's contributions to Black Atlantic exchange as the arts editor for the *City Sun*, a Brooklyn-based Black newspaper with the tagline "speaking truth to power." His cultural criticism has some obvious affinities with Paul Gilroy's thoughts on Black cultural politics. It similarly esteemed Toni Morrison's work, used Spike Lee's films to illustrate the contradictions of a Black bourgeoisie, and appeared in a paper that advertised academic workshops featuring Edward Said.[59] There were, however, some important distinctions between the two critics as they navigated a Black public sphere, shared their evaluative judgments about diaspora identities and aesthetics, and considered the commodification of Blackness.

As we have seen, Gilroy would find little value in Lee's advertisements for Nike and a Black bourgeoisie that "has gradually become parasitic on the rich culture of the black poor" with an essentially commercial and conservative view of Black culture.[60] He would express a secularized faith that talented artists would express an anti-capitalist stance that would colonize "greedy and hostile cultural industries" or, at the very least, suffuse it with their utopian content.[61] In contrast, White was open to the possibility that commercial advertisements offered filmmakers such as Lee the opportunity to sharpen their visual imagination.[62] He considered advertisements and music videos to be art forms that offered filmmakers the opportunity to transform perceptions of minority groups and reach a much broader audience than artists who are feted with grants and awards for their installations in museums and art galleries.

Although White admired the punk ethics of independent filmmakers who challenged racist hierarchy and capitalist indoctrination by producing fair and sensible portraits of racialized minorities and working-class cultures, his cultural criticism also engaged with feminist intellectuals inside and outside of academia in a manner that evoked Edward Said's rather sweeping comments about race taking precedence over class and gender in colonial contexts more than Paul Gilroy's substantive dialogues with intellectuals such as bell hooks about Third World liberation. White sought to translate the work of postcolonial critics who talked about imperialist white supremacist capitalism, and reserved his greatest praise for male artists who communicated "democratic, ethnically diverse, politically courageous art" to a popular audience with wit and imagination.[63] As we shall see, he was an aesthete who admired soulful artists who clarified the confounding contradictions of capitalism rather than an advocate for political transformation that would abolish the contradictions and hierarchies of racial capitalism.

In underdeveloped countries that acquire independence there is almost always a small number of upstanding intellectuals, without set political ideals, who instinctively distrust the race for jobs and handouts that is symptomatic of the aftermath of independence. The personal situation of these men (breadwinners for an extended family) or their life story (hardship and strict moral upbringing) explains their clear distrust for the smart alecks and profiteers. These men need to be used intelligently in the decisive struggle to steer the nation in a healthier direction.

Frantz Fanon (1961)

It looks like everything is in place for American film culture's most exciting display of new talent and upstart sensibilities since the seventies renaissance—only this time by African-American film-makers. . . . Everything is set—everything except a new school of critics who can demonstrate a feeling for non-Hollywood styles and nonwhite artists. Above all, critics who can lead public thinking and discussion about these movies toward a meaningful understanding of art and politics . . . not a moonlighting Ivy League prof with the right bloodlines, a rock-'n'-roll refugee with a credible hairdo, or even an ax-grinding freelancer but someone who (this may sound radical) *who knows film.*

Armond White (1991)

5.
ENLARGING *THE AMERICAN CINEMA*

Armond White vs. the Straight Middle-Class White World (and the Black Bourgeoisie)

In 2010, the British journal *Sight and Sound* invited critics to list the five most inspirational books ever written about film. Armond White described his first pick, Pauline Kael's *Kiss Kiss Bang Bang*, as an original, "personal, inspiring history of cinema." He hailed his second selection, Andrew Sarris's *American Cinema*, as "a one-man tour de force that cements the case for the auteur theory."[1] After listing Richard Dyer's *Heavenly Bodies* in third place ("academic thought . . . that still relates to pop, pleasure and real life") and Kael's *Reeling* as his fourth choice ("the only example of a great film era (the 1970s) meeting a worthy, attentive journalist"), he rounded out his list with *The Resistance*, his own book about popular culture that "shook the world." Although he did not provide a pithy description for the book he authored, one suspects that White would not be disappointed with a tagline that considered his writings on film, music, and culture between 1984 and 1994 to be a worthy successor to Kael and Sarris, his "film critic mom and pop."[2]

In marrying the strengths of Kael and Sarris, White writes against the grain of cinephiles who rigidly defend the honor of Team Kael or Team Sarris and claim that the two most prominent American film critics of the 1970s could never have found each other attractive. He does not mention, for example, that Sarris described Kael as a rather parochial "Berkeley babe" with a flair for self-promotion,[3] or that Sarris and was cited as an ally in Renata Adler's notorious essay condemning Kael's "hysterical" and "worthless" writing.[4] Rather than emphasize the family squabbles between Kael—a critic who claimed that she rarely, if ever, rewatched a movie and consistently refused to compile end-of-year lists—and Sarris—a critic and academic who was willing to re-evaluate former positions after careful, repeated viewings of films and to develop evaluative lists and concise summaries of directorial and non-directorial figures that he designated as the authors of films—White sought to synthesize their work to rise above the fray of petty journalists and timid scholars. He was proud to point out that his "film critic mom" had supported his entry into the New York Film Critics Circle and his "film critic pop" stood up for him during a meeting of the circle "that turned nasty."[5]

Whereas chapter three outlined White's creative engagement with Kael's work as a movie-struck kid from Detroit in the 1970s, this chapter transmutes White's cultural criticism in the 1980s and '90s into an updated version of Sarris's famous compendium of auteurs. In doing so, I synthesize thousands of White's reviews of film, music, and expressive culture for the *LA Weekly*, the *Village Voice, Emerge, Film Comment* and, above all, the *City Sun* (a Brooklyn-based Black newspaper where White worked as arts editor for many years). This rich archive of resistance aesthetics has been overlooked by film critics (one reason, perhaps, why White felt compelled to offer an advertisement for himself in *Sight and Sound*'s collection of inspirational film books). It is also absent from histories of American culture and politics during the Reagan, Bush, and Clinton administrations, and underappreciated in scholarly works in or about those decades that pertain to Black Studies (in, for example, theoretical and historical accounts of the birth of a New Black Aesthetic, the cultural and political expression of a hip hop or post–civil rights generation, the decline or diversification of the Black public sphere, the end of the innocent notion of the essential Black subject, and the thesis that class was becoming more of a deciding factor in the life chances of Black Americans than race[6]).

In scrutinizing the tone and texture of Armond White's reviews of film, music, theater, and other art forms between 1984 (when he joined the *City Sun*) and 1996 (when the *City Sun* ceased publication), this chapter reveals some reasons why he is often ignored and derided by film critics and Black academics who believe that he transgresses the boundaries of acceptable discourse and disrupts the integrity and significance of their professions. On the one hand, I document his belief that American film critics were more concerned with protecting their jobs than provoking readers into fresh thinking. On the other, I provide context for his contention that Black public intellectuals were more concerned with securing high-profile roles in Ivy League universities and prominent positions in media institutions than disrupting the privilege and dominance of "the straight middle-class white world."[7]

The *City Sun* and *The American Cinema*

When Detroit elected its first African American mayor in 1973, White did not presume that politics could be confined to the formal political realm and managed by experts. Quite the contrary, he responded to the shifting of the racial architecture in his hometown by asking the readers of the *South End* to do some fresh thinking about the sources of political legitimacy in the pulpit, protest march, nightclub, dance floor, and festival stage as well as the polling booth. When his arrival at the *City Sun* coincided with Jesse Jackson's 1984 presidential campaign, White also considered it the responsibility of principled critics to uncover the political truths within popular culture.

The publisher and editor-in-chief of the *City Sun* was a former businessman and civil rights activist named Andrew Cooper. After his successful lawsuit against racial gerrymandering led to the creation of New York's 12th Congressional District and the subsequent election of Shirley Chisholm, the first Black woman to be elected to the US Congress, Cooper had turned to journalism. In 1977, he started the Trans-Urban News Service to train journalists from racial or ethnic groups that were underrepresented and disadvantaged in the profession, and produce reporting relevant to marginalized communities. In his role conducting this news service, Cooper was well situated to identify the significant disparity between the racial make-up of the readership and editorial staff of mainstream media outlets in New York.[8] He also perceived a substantial decline in the circulation and quality of the *Amsterdam News*, the nation's oldest Black newspaper, which had achieved a circulation of around 80,000 in the 1960s. By 1983, its circulation had fallen to approximately 41,000, and its publisher, Wilbert Tatum, proposed a 20 percent pay cut to ease operating costs. Cooper also complained about the paper's misspelled headlines, uninspiring design layouts, and obsequious approach to political elites.[9] In 1983, for example, Tatum demanded that his editor run, verbatim, an article by the white New York City mayor Ed Koch. Shortly after his editor complied with this order, but also wrote a piece criticizing Koch's insensitivity to racial minorities, he was fired.[10]

Sensing that there was a need and an opening for a new Black newspaper that would challenge Mayor Koch and any politicians who failed to advance the interests of the communities they purportedly served,[11] Cooper hired consultants to compile statistics, analyze census data, and construct a profile of the kind of reader who might support a new Black newspaper. In 1984, he co-founded the *City Sun* with Utrice Leid, a Trinidadian American journalist and activist who served as the paper's managing editor until 1992. They shepherded a publication that carried original stories and a diverse array of Black writers such as Thomas Sowell, a prominent conservative commentator, and Benjamin Hooks, the executive director of the National Association for the Advancement of Colored People. The *City Sun* was also one of the few New York papers to carry continuing, in-depth African news in the 1980s, and publicized events such as the Biko Lives Festival from the Free South Africa / Free the South Bronx Network that celebrated the life and legacy of Steve

Biko, an anti-Apartheid activist-intellectual and theorist of Black Consciousness.[12]

White joined the *City Sun* after he put his MFA in Film History, Theory, and Criticism from Columbia University on hold in 1983,[13] but he did not leave behind the lessons he had learned from Andrew Sarris and other "life-changing teachers" at that institution. White considered Sarris's *American Cinema*—which organized auteurs into categories such as "pantheon directors" who transcended their technical problems "with a personal vision of the world," expressive and esoteric directors with "difficult styles or unfashionable genres or both," and "talented but uneven directors with the mortal sin of pretentiousness"—to be one of the few seminal books about film.[14] As arts editor for the *City Sun,* he would develop a list of Black movie history after 1967 (a new era of Black people "taking part in the creation of their own myths"[15]) and express what Sarris believed was missing from the book he wrote in 1968 (i.e., convey a deep appreciation for dissonant, against-the-grain temperaments).[16]

In keeping with White's appreciation of punk and hip hop artists who mounted an aggressive challenge to mainstream culture in the 1980s and '90s, and of pop artists who transmitted the pleasures of American multiracial democracy or modern consciousness without being preachy or didactic, this chapter translates White's reviews of art and culture into a revised and updated version of *The American Cinema* that includes mavericks and malcontents in music and film.[17] To do so, I adapt the categories and epigrammatic evaluations that Sarris used to make a powerful case for the theory of cinema authorship in the 1960s to reveal the philosophical commitments, political implications, and intellectual coherence of the work White generated for debate, discussion, and examination in a Black public sphere during the 1980s and '90s. Rather than follow the conventions of an academic essay or the weekly reviews of film, music, and Black expressive culture in which White responded quickly and journalistically to social and political events, I have organized White's cultural criticism into five categories—Serious Pop Artists; Sense and Sensibility; Oddities, One-Shots, and Newcomers; R-E-S-P-E-C-T; and Let the Mourning Begin—and selected filmmakers and musicians that may be used to illustrate these categories as well as the challenges and opportunities facing a rebel generation that debated the ethics of "selling out" and "spreading out" into mainstream American culture. I have listed the years of birth of these artists and critics to demonstrate how White was consistently engaging with individuals who, like him, were born in the 1950s, as well as older cohorts that he associated with the struggle to dismantle racial stereotypes and younger cohorts that he associated with the careerism, commodification, classism, and caution of a post–civil rights generation.

Serious Pop Artists

These American directors and musicians were esteemed by White because they imposed their vision on the world without sacrificing difficulty, falling prey to obscurity, or selling cheap thrills, unedifying entertainment, and exploitative material.

Steven Spielberg (b. 1946)

Selected Films: Jaws (1975), *Close Encounters of the Third Kind* (1977), *Indiana Jones and the Temple of Doom* (1984), *The Color Purple* (1985), *Indiana Jones and the Last Crusade* (1989), *Hook* (1991), *Schindler's List* (1993)

As a young critic at the *South End* in the 1970s, Armond White worried that Steven Spielberg might squander his undeniable talent to pursue a commercial hit. In contrast to reviewers who considered Spielberg's *Jaws* to be a masterful piece of suspenseful drama, White believed that its "Hollywood flash" failed to honor the efficiency, honesty, and unpretentiousness of B-movie thrillers.[18] As a more experienced critic in the 1980s and '90s, White would continue to praise filmmakers who embraced B-movies as a genre that offered them the opportunity to convey their maverick, rebellious spirit. Yet he would also reject the presumptuousness of critics who assumed that Spielberg was, at best, a talented entertainer. In White's reviews,

Spielberg was cast as a serious artist working within a Hollywood system, that is, someone who "spread out" to impose his personal vision on the world rather than someone who "sold out" to achieve commercial success at any cost.

In 1973, White had praised Martin Ritt, the Jewish director of *Sounder*, a film adaptation of a prize-winning children's book about Black sharecroppers during the Great Depression fighting to obtain a decent education for their children, for his profound connection with downtrodden people. Thirteen years later, he similarly described Spielberg as a Jewish director who combined "childlike artistry" with "psychological complexity" in *The Color Purple*, his adaptation of Alice Walker's Pulitzer Prize–winning epistolary novel about African American women's struggles for empowerment in the early twentieth century.[19] Such refusal to accept the presumption that films needed to choose (adult) complexity or (childlike) wonder informed White's critique of mainstream films that were "insultingly childish" *and* art-house films that succumbed to the curse of strained seriousness and pretentiousness. Furthermore, it reflected White's abiding interest in analyzing Black Consciousness within the context of Western art. He would connect his reading of *The Color Purple* to his interest in advancing a multiracial or "mulatto-minded" *American* American culture that included the African diasporic choreopoems of Ntozake Shange and the silent films of D.W. Griffith that framed Black people as problems rather than people facing problems.[20] White celebrated the commercial and critical success of *The Color Purple* because he hoped that it would lay to rest the old lie that "politically conscious, aesthetically advanced, multicultural, pop cinema" with Black protagonists would struggle to find a popular audience.[21] He did not scold audiences who contributed to the commercial success of *The Color Purple* as he had rebuked the audiences of *Star Wars* and other films he deemed regressive and nostalgic. Nor did he chastise other film critics who contributed to its critical success as he would do following the acclaim received by films such as *Mississippi Burning* and *Cry Freedom*, which featured self-flattering white movie heroes but were unable to portray political or psychological nuances in Black characters.[22]

Spielberg could do little wrong in White's eyes in the 1980s and '90s. While White would denounce other directors for their token-ism, he would praise Spielberg's ability to enlarge "the mythology of Peter Pan [in *Hook*] to include non-white children by showing Peter passing sovereignty on to a Black boy."[23] Although White had consid-ered the slow, suspenseful pacing of *Jaws* to be a sappy concession to the anxieties of small-town USA (and acknowledged the racist tropes in *Raiders of the Lost Ark*), he asserted that the slow, suspenseful pacing of *Indiana Jones and the Last Crusade* was an opportunity for the audience to think more deeply about "racist-colonialist vanity."[24] His cultural criticism repeatedly used Spielberg's example to shame other minority filmmakers who sacrificed "the meaning of their lives, the ingenuity of their talent, before the ideal of our country's dominant ideology: the Heterosexual White Boy."[25]

Although White believed that artists from minority ethnic groups were able to express greater humanity and universality when they embraced their ethnicity (and exposed the spurious humanism and universality of mainstream entertainment that revolves around a straight, white, middle-class world), this does not mean that he was willing to accept the "commonplace but mistaken political notion that a filmmaker should make movies only about his own ethnic group."[26] White would assert that Spielberg mattered as a Jewish filmmaker who took on the task of entertaining the world with popular art and "essential, kinetic . . . cinema," and bristle at "literal-minded" reviewers who only respected Spielberg as an art-ist, or considered him award-worthy, when he directed a film like *Schindler's List* that could be included within "the not-always-artful but often sanctified tradition of Holocaust movies."[27] Recalling and recycling his earlier work as a movie-struck kid in Detroit—who had expressed concern that Spielberg may succumb, rather than transcend, the conventions of B-movies and commercial flash—White sought to make his mark on the dreams of his readers in New York as a middle-aged critic who expressed concern that Spielberg may succumb, rather than transcend, the conventions and strained seriousness of epic period dramas that appealed to the liberal senti-mentality of Oscar voters.

Michael Jackson (1958–2009)
Selected Music Video: "Black or White" (1991)

The American Society of Composers, Authors and Publishers honored Armond White with a Deems Taylor Award in 1992 for his outstanding coverage of music in print and media the previous year. His award-winning article on Michael Jackson's music video "Black or White" brought together his love of cinema and music by claiming the video as the "outstanding film of 1991," and identified Jackson, not the listed director John Landis, as the film's auteur.

Revealingly, White connected the ideological transitions and tours across the Global South in Jackson's video to the cross-cutting between Georgia and Africa in the letters sequence of Spielberg's *The Color Purple* as well as the design of the mothership in *Close Encounters of the Third Kind* (which Spielberg had based on a refinery he'd observed at night in India).[28] That is to say, White used such a comparative approach to argue that Jackson was a proponent of "morally complex art" and "authentic pop art."[29] He did not mention that the music video's use of computer technology, which morphed individuals from different racial groups, might also be compared to the type of pseudo-anthropological approach to racial transgression in Benetton advertisements in the early 1990s that emptied any critical, radical, or challenging content from multiculturalism.[30]

Prince (1958–2016)
Selected Films and Albums: Purple Rain (1984), *Under the Cherry Moon* (1986), *Lovesexy* (1988), "Batdance" (1989), *The Black Album* (1994)

Thesis: in 1984, White proclaimed Prince to be an artist who authentically conveyed American multiculturalism to the world. *Antithesis:* in 1986, he diagnosed the Purple One as a calculating entertainer who suffered from the "self-hatred of a man longing to escape himself and his heritage" and who would do anything to achieve mainstream success.[31] *Synthesis:* in 1989, White accepted Prince as a brazen figure who "*almost* redeems the [more] obvious commercial calculation" of movie franchises.[32]

In his dialectical approach to Prince's art and artistry, White provides us with one of the few critical accounts of the Purple One to address the issues of race and racism directly.[33] In his examination of *Purple Rain* in 1984 ("the most financially successful movie without a white principal player"), he sought to clarify the political and spiritual meaning of a Black artist who crossed over to white audiences without compromising their personal vision or ethnic identity. In securing financing outside the Hollywood film industry, and refusing to qualify or excuse its character or story, *Purple Rain* revealed to White how Black creative artists could produce authentic, original, and independent contributions to American culture.[34] He interpreted the film as a "trashy . . . crude . . . and tawdry" form of American entertainment that was shallow in a good way (i.e., able to expose the pitfalls of strained seriousness in "message movies") rather than shallow in a bad way (i.e., exploiting demeaning stereotypes about Black masculinity, displaying technical wretchedness, and contributing to "widespread social desolation"[35]).

Prince's directorial debut in *Under the Cherry Moon* received the worst picture, worst director, and worst actor awards from the seventh annual Golden Raspberry Awards. White was similarly unimpressed by the film but examined its cultural politics in greater depth than critics who merely resented a pop star sliming into film culture with a vanity project. Noting that the only woman in *Under the Cherry Moon* who was deemed undesirable was dark-skinned, White expressed concern about the film's propagation of Eurocentric beauty standards. He also proposed that the film's bland cocktail of "commercial calculation, self-absorption and Uncle Tomism" meant that it inflicted upon the audience "the least interesting Black character to be portrayed on film in the post–civil rights era."[36] Rather than impose Prince's will on the world, it demonstrated the perils of artists attempting to flee their ethnic and national roots.

In 1988, White expressed thanks that Prince was able to use music videos to disrupt dramatic storytelling conventions about sex and race in America that could then be embraced by a global audience.[37] He found the impudent, alternative world of the medium well suited to the "fierce idiosyncrasy," "schizogenius," and "rebel authenticity" of an artist who was interested in exploring sin and salvation, Saturday night and Sunday morning, and other startling and surprising contradictions without "the *usual* marketing conceits."[38] Prince's music video for *Batman* was, for example, a welcome contrast to the "Trump-like edifices" that took it for granted you could "force-feed the public a baroque fantasy about a white millionaire vigilante 'taking back the streets,'" demonize the homeless, and presume that young men of color accused of sexual assault against a white woman were guilty, so long as you had enough arrogance and money.[39]

More generally, White was interested in claiming music videos and commercials as opportunities for shrewd auteurs to "define the popular image and public profile of a social group that is little understood or usually negatively shown" and reach audiences who might never tour art galleries to view video installation artists who are hailed as prestigious national treasures by academic and cultural institutions.[40]

Honorable mentions

White also celebrated other directorial and non-directorial auteurs who challenged a Hollywood system that a) tolerated stereotypical or non-threatening *individuals* from outside a straight, white, middle-class world while b) remaining hostile to authentic representations of ethnic *groups* in America that do not conform to a WASP ideal. White's reviews would, for example, discuss the following:

- "The brave artopolitical leaps of **Robert De Niro**."[41]
- The "transcendent" art of **Bernardo Bertolucci**.[42]
- The intransigent maverick **Robert Altman**, who conveyed layers of chaos in American democracy with sensitivity.[43]
- The struggles of **Martin Scorsese** and **Francis Ford Coppola** to "balance independence with compromise to the Hollywood system."[44]

- **Brian De Palma's** "modern consciousness."[45] White defined this amorphous concept by referring to De Palma's refusal to offer the audience a single person to identify with. In other words, he celebrated De Palma as a pop artist because he produced original, personal work within the commercial realm that represented American diversity and steered clear of exaggerated individualism.

Sense and Sensibility

White admired these directors and musicians from North America and Europe for their ability to delve beneath the surface of memory to address race and sex issues in modern living, and to expose the artistry, pain, beauty, vulnerability, and psychological angst of oppressed people.

Alex Cox (b. 1954)

Selected Films: Repo Man (1984), *Straight to Hell* (1987), *Walker* (1987)

In the summer of 1977, White confessed that he had started to find it more "satisfying listening to radio and records than going to most current movies."[46] Such dissatisfaction with the general state of movies did not mean that he was unable to appreciate the childlike splendor and emotional maturity of *Close Encounters of the Third Kind* that winter. Nor was it evidence that he always got satisfaction from tuning in to the radio—he had, after all, associated the sounds of Mick Jagger and David Bowie and other "androgynous rock stars" from the United Kingdom with "insipid flashiness" and "perversion."[47] It was, instead, a sign that he was concerned about the end of a golden era of independent American cinema that artfully balanced commercial and artistic interests, and open to listening to and learning from Detroit radio stations that were a testing ground for new music from around the world.[48]

In the mid-1980s, when he believed that the counterculture had been extinguished, White could not help feeling nostalgic about the vibrant, active intelligence of punk artists of the late 1970s and early '80s. While he dismissed the "bad nostalgia" of Americans who pined for the supposedly good old days of safe, segregated, suburban communities, he insisted that his fond memories of punk were justified because "little current music is as questioning, daring, visionary or exciting."[49] He particularly esteemed the English director Alex Cox and his attempts to channel the revolutionary zeal of punk into mainstream film. White welcomed the democratic, anti-authoritarian "subculture consciousness" of artists like Cox into his vision of a brave, rebellious American spirit ("Unlike most foreign directors . . . Alex Cox understands the [American] culture very well"[50]).

White found the rotten reviews of Cox's *Straight to Hell* evidence that most people who write about movies were wedded to the norms of "middle-class stability and aesthetics that the movie rejects."[51] Many movie critics and executives deemed Cox's film about William Walker, an American mercenary who usurped the presidency of Nicaragua in 1856, to be too political and violent because of its willingness to draw direct parallels between Walker's colonial adventures in the nineteenth century and American intervention in the area in the 1980s. According to White, the difficulties Cox faced in making the film proved that Hollywood executives had little empathy with liberation struggles in the Third World (as if further proof were needed). White also used the critical opprobrium heaped on the film by his colleagues as a reminder that he was surrounded by film critics who preferred to watch films set in the Global South that delivered flattering portraits of white protagonists rather than examine the psychology of non-white supporting characters.

Morrissey (b. 1959)
Selected Albums: Viva Hate (1988), *Kill Uncle* (1991), *Southpaw Grammar* (1995)

In his autobiographical portrait of an artist who was young, clumsy, and shy, Morrissey recalls the moment he spotted the American writer and social reformer James Baldwin sitting alone in the lobby of a grand Barcelona hotel in 1986:

> History books overlook James Baldwin because he presented an unvarnished view of the American essence—as blunt and rousing as print would allow. His public speeches were intoxicating, his motivational palette of words so full of fireworks that you smile as you listen—not because of humour, but because he was so good at voicing the general truth, with which most struggled. His liking for male flesh gave the world a perfect excuse to brush him aside as a social danger, and he was erased away as someone who used his Blackness as an excuse for everything. In fact, his purity scared them off, and his honesty ignited irrational fear in an America where men were draped with medals for killing other men yet imprisoned for loving one another. Pitifully, on this Barcelona day, I do not have the steel to approach James Baldwin, because I know very well that I will jabber rubbish, and that his large, soulful eyes will lower at someone ruefully new to the game. Shortly thereafter, he is dead.[52]

Following Baldwin's death in 1987, White sympathized with Morrissey's criminally vulgar shyness and claimed him as an artist who shared Baldwin's ability to convey the struggles of unco-opted, *non-mainstream* minorities to produce fair, sensible pictures of race, class, and gender in the United States and Europe.[53] He appreciated the challenge of listening to Morrissey's "sly wit,"[54] which roused people into radical action without falling prey to the pitfalls of sophomoric calls to rage against the machine.[55] He identified with an "extroverted introvert" who understood how to embrace and transcend dichotomies by fusing rock and punk, responding to an unjust society with sadness and optimism, and being cynical about media institutions without being cynical about life.[56]

Public Enemy (an American hip hop group co-founded by Chuck D, b. 1960, and Flavor Flav, b. 1959)

Selected Albums: It Takes a Nation of Millions to Hold Us Back (1988), Fear of a Black Planet (1990), Apocalypse 91 . . . The Enemy Strikes Black (1991), Muse Sick-n-Hour Mess Age (1994)

After associating hip hop with juvenile posturing in the early 1980s, White began to appreciate the political possibilities of the genre when he listened to Whodini's *Funky Beat* in 1986. However, it was the release of Public Enemy's *It Takes a Nation of Millions to Hold Us Back* in 1988 that convinced him that hip hop could be a force to confront racial hierarchy and capitalist indoctrination in the "solipsistic, regressive 1980s."[57] He welcomed the group's collectively authored protest against white supremacy and media gatekeepers who perpetuated the idea that Black Americans wanted nothing more than to enter the national consciousness as bland, non-confrontational individuals.[58]

Such appreciation for Public Enemy was nuanced rather than hagiographic. Just as he called on the introspective Morrissey to advance his art and escape "beleaguered isolation" by listening more carefully to the call and response of Public Enemy,[59] White invited the American rappers to develop their artistic practice by learning from the British artist's ability to reject masculinist priorities and identify with the dispossessed without celebrating criminality.[60] White was particularly concerned that Public Enemy's overly defensive and didactic declarations of masculine hardness would prevent them "being the visionary warrior-philosophers they imagine"[61] and would throw away the baby of the civil rights movement with the bathwater of its middle-class leaders, processes, and agendas.[62] He consistently encouraged artists to deepen and extend the work of Public Enemy with collaborative ventures that facilitated conversations across an American public fractured along the experiential fault lines of gender, race, and class. White appreciated, for example, the Lionel Martin–directed music video for "Night of the Living Baseheads" and the opening montage to Spike Lee's *Do the Right Thing*, which expressed the power of Public Enemy's "Fight the Power" via the boxing and dancing of Rosie Perez, an Afro Nuyorican artist.

Isaac Jullen (b. 1960)
Selected Films: Looking for Langston (1989), *Young Soul Rebels* (1991)

As the arts editor for a newspaper that covered events across the African diaspora and the Global South,[63] White had a platform to confront Hollywood's colonization of taste and Americans who were uninterested in "World cinema or music."[64] Nonetheless, this challenge to the parochialism of white America did not result in diasporic criticism that decentered the United States. Among the thousands of reviews White published as arts editor of the *City Sun*, less than fifty addressed films or music from the United Kingdom, and less than twenty ranged even further to examine films from Australia, Belgium, France, Iran, Burkina Faso, and Korea. White found it difficult to feel like a citizen of the world when he was drawn to American filmmakers and felt "chauvinist pride" during international film festivals.[65] He presumed that American artists who migrated to homes outside of the United States also became "distanced from the world,"[66] and described the pop artist Terence Trent D'Arby leaving America for the United Kingdom "only to rediscover [the United States] in his heart and most profoundly in his very Black voice."[67] As I have argued elsewhere, White's work may be situated within a tradition of African American intellectuals, such as James Baldwin, who questioned the parochialism of whites in the United States while maintaining that "Negroes do not, strictly speaking, exist in other countries."[68] Although Baldwin lived and worked in Europe for many years, he steadfastly wrote for an imaginary reader located in Harlem.[69]

Some of the distinctions between global African Americans and more expansive, diasporic approaches are exemplified in White's reviews of Isaac Julien, the Black British director of films such as *Looking for Langston*, which sought to claim Langston Hughes and James Baldwin as Black, American, gay, historical icons "from across the ocean and across art forms."[70] Although White was sympathetic to Julien's revolutionary challenge to the totems and taboos of African American culture,[71] he lamented that the British filmmaker lacked "the common touch" and populist candor of hip hop. According to White, Black British artists such as Julien, Martina Attille, Maureen Blackwood, Nadine Marsh-Edwards, and Robert Crusz (the co-founders of the Sankofa Film and Video Collective) and the Black Audio Film Collective provided a different approach to "the black independents in the United States. The difference is virtually the same that divides other European filmmakers from their American counterparts—an art versus entertainment approach to film. . . . This is really radical filmmaking, which may mean that these collectives are a folk art movement educated beyond the sophistication of the average audience."[72] White also championed Julien's attempts to reach a more mainstream audience in *Young Soul Rebels* (which, as discussed in chapter four, was informed by Paul Gilroy's examination of the cultural politics of "race" and nation in *There Ain't no Black in the Union Jack*, and sought to balance artistic and commercial interests while making bold claims for "the movements that emerged amid punk and the anti-fascist movements" in the late 1970s[73]).

One brief note in White's review of *Looking for Langston* about Julien's "curious propensity towards using slightly foreign, light-skinned types" may be connected to his reviews on commercial films and music videos that deployed "half-breeds" to "appeal to our most liberal senses" and "dissipate the energy of black rage."[74] Such brief, yet notable, asides about racial intermediaries and racialized ways of seeing may also clarify one connective tissue between more parochial forms of African American Studies, Global African American Studies, and diasporic approaches to race and identity that aspire to decenter or deprovincialize the United States. That is to say, White's blend of anachronistic, offensive, and impressionistic language about mixed-race individuals may be connected to an African American intellectual tradition that includes xenophobes such as Harold Cruse (who alluded to mixed-race individuals being a group favored by white liberals in the United States[75]), as well as global African Americans such as Malcolm X (who believed in a Black culture that embraced 1,001 shades of Blackness while remaining wary about what he termed "mongrel-complexioned children" and the political commitments of Blacks who had white husbands or wives).[76] They also evoke the work of diasporic intellectuals such as Fanon, who expressed concern about the sickness of neocolonialism that projected images of young, sexually available "half-breed" boys and girls for Western tourists, while diagnosing the sickness of American racism and race thinking.[77] Such suspicions of racial mixing and mixture are understandable given histories of colonialism and slavery that emphasize how "mulattoes" distanced themselves from Blackness in pursuit of material or psychological benefits. Yet, as the Afro-Jewish philosopher Lewis Gordon reminds us, this does not necessarily mean that they are ethical.[78] They may, for example, be misappropriated by audiences who find it unusual to come across radicals that they associate with "light-skinnedness" and conservatives that they phenoperceive as "dark-skinned."[79]

Honorable mentions

White's reviews repeatedly praised auteurs who exposed the sickness of Europe's "provincialism and political oppression"[80] and serious artists who challenged Americans to produce a healthier popular culture that reflects the country's variety rather than some conformist fantasy. For example, White praised:

- **Linton Kwesi Johnson** as a "zealous English artist."[81]
- **Hanif Kureishi** as a dramatist of "the dreams and human errors of the Third World, punks, gays," who provided a "rich perspective on the world that maybe only minority artists can restore to the movies."[82]
- **Sonya Madan** as someone who was raised under British colonialism but managed to mature into a revolutionary artist who contests ongoing coloniality and miseducation like "C.L.R. James, *early* Salman Rushdie, Terry Eagleton, Isaac Julien, and Hanif Kureishi."[83]

- **Mike Leigh** as a filmmaker who enhanced the world's sense of art by making cinema about people with bad coifs, facial blemishes, awkward gaits, and bad grooming. White believed that African American filmmakers could benefit from Leigh's unsparing, yet humane, method of seeing through characters' delusions about themselves and their unawareness of social structures. This was, however, supplemented by the *American American* critic asserting that the British filmmaker's "implicit judgment of stereotyped behavior" meant that he fell short of the full, awesome flux of life and "spiritual discovery" in independent American filmmakers such as Robert Altman.[84]
- The **Geto Boys** as a hip hop group that incisively critiqued the modern world's prevailing savagery "just like Mike Leigh's great, unsettling 1993 movie *Naked*."[85]
- **De La Soul** as an imaginative and innovative hip hop group replete with moral intelligence that reminded audiences that hip hop surely—and sorely—needed "some spirituality."[86]
- **Fishbone** as non-sellouts and creative anarchists who defied all musical labels.[87]
- **Samuel Fuller** as a filmmaker who uses the B-movie format as an opportunity to stay ahead of cultural gatekeepers in the media and academia.[88] In contrast to spuriously independent filmmakers who catered to the clichés and values of Hollywood, White considered Fuller to be a true radical who challenged staid, polite forms of American racism and hypocrisy with depth and imagination. White's admiring reviews of Fuller's films remind us that the critic who grew up perceiving B-movies as "cheap, decrepit and omens of abject failure" in Detroit had become a New York–based critic who respected the eccentricity of "artists and working people not 'good' enough or 'normal' enough to be successful at the A-movie level or with mass popularity."[89]
- **André Téchiné** as a director of films about family bonds, homosexuality, and exile that gave the past "the vivacity of contemporary experience" and avoided what White considered the pitfalls of nostalgia.[90]

- Terence Davies as the director of a film that reminded White that nostalgic "sentiment isn't [always] a shameful word." Davies's *The Long Day Closes*—which tells the story of a gay British boy called Bud, his loving family, his austere religious community, and his cinephilia—resonated with White's memories of a childhood in which he searched for a way to unlock the hidden secrets of pop culture and gay identity within a large family and a religious community in Detroit. In homage to Davies's film, White would call his regular column for *Out* magazine, a gay lifestyle magazine, "Our Bud at the movies."[91]

Oddities, One-Shots, and Newcomers

This pairing of "oddities, one-shots, and newcomers" is an opportunity to consider why academics considered White's political judgments "limited on the question of feminism."[92] For while White associated the feminist and Afrocentric vision of female auteurs with their strained seriousness (rather than his failure to connect with the meaning of their work), he championed male auteurs who reflected his abiding interest in a serious examination of existentialism and masculinity in American cities.

Julie Dash (b. 1952)
Selected Film: Daughters of the Dust (1991)

In the first feature film by an African American woman distributed theatrically in the United States, Julie Dash explored the African folkways of three generations of Gullah women on Saint Helena Island off the coast of South Carolina and Georgia. *Daughters of the Dust* was nominated for a Grand Jury Prize and received the Excellence in Cinematography award from the Sundance Film Festival in 1991. In his dissenting opinion to critics who hailed the film as "an unprecedented achievement in terms of world cinema and African achievement," White considered it "slow, precious crap" that was bereft of the "frivolity, dance, humor" and kinetic energy that he deemed indispensable to popular art.[93]

While White celebrated filmmakers such as Terence Davies for explorations and examinations of nostalgia that resonated with minorities and subcultures in urban cultures, he could not support or identify with Dash's nostalgia for a rural, matriarchal, Afrocentric past. Just as he rejected the nostalgia of films that narrowly catered to European and Euro-American sensibilities, he was wary of reading the film solely within an African tradition and what he deemed "dishonest," "ideological," and "weak" forms of Afrocentric nostalgia.[94] While arguing that *Daughters of the Dust* "only resonated with a cultural elite" and was a "dreadful Black bourgeois fantasy of refined cinema,"[95] it is worth noting that White found it "more adventurous and less sentimental" than Jane Campion's *The Piano*. As much as White recoiled from the fantasies of a Black middle-class, he was even more offended by what he characterized as the white feminism of *The Piano*, its limited engagement with race and class privilege, and the critical acclaim bestowed upon it by his predominantly white peers and the Academy Awards.[96]

Wendell B. Harris Jr. (b. 1954)
Selected Film: Chameleon Street (1989)

When he sat on the jury at the 1990 Sundance Film Festival, White took great pleasure in awarding the Grand Jury Prize for US Dramatic Film to Wendell Harris's *Chameleon Street*. Its wry analysis of a smart, calculated Black male protagonist from Detroit who displayed "wily and mighty personal conviction" aligned with White's preference for art that examined nationalism and racism as circumstances "under which people act individually" rather than as forces that drive and circumscribe characters.[97] Few other films spoke as directly to White's hopes and dreams as *Chameleon Street* did in its ability to assault the standards held by most people, who obediently accept their assigned social roles while sensitively examining the vulnerabilities and tensions of disenfranchised people. White would insist that this film—created by an artist whose family had founded Prismatic Images, a multi-award-winning film/video/audio production facility in Flint, Michigan, in 1979—deserved to be ranked alongside Ralph Ellison's *Invisible Man* and Martin Scorsese's *Taxi Driver* as a classic example of American existentialism.

R-E-S-P-E-C-T

White considered these actors and directors to be representative of an upstanding civil rights generation. He maintained that their personal and artistic ambitions were aligned with political campaigns to achieve transformative change and a more perfect union of American states.

Sidney Poitier (1927–2022)
Selected Films: Lilies in the Field (1963), *Shoot to Kill* (1988)

In his reflections on the racial politics of American cinema, James Baldwin recognized Sidney Poitier's ability to smuggle moments of intelligence and wit into films that may have been produced to appeal to the "virtuous sentimentality," "cowardly obtuseness," "guilty eroticism," and "excessive and spurious emotion" of white liberals.[98] White similarly appreciated Poitier's challenge to the "sentimental indulgence," "venal sentimentality," "treacly emotions," and "weak nostalgia" of American films.[99] He believed that Poitier's image "refused invisibility and disregard" and that his achievements as a dignified Black trailblazer and Academy Award winner forced millions of viewers to take the civil rights movement seriously.[100]

In the 1980s and '90s, White consistently questioned the ability of Black actors to assert their dignity and independence in a manner that honored Poitier's pioneering role as a civil rights standard-bearer who defied preconceptions and prejudices about Black people and characters.[101] This is not to say that White expected actors to develop a safe, technically sophisticated pastiche of Poitier's work or image.[102] Quite the contrary, he wanted them to build upon Poitier's legacy and move with the times to expose the "liberal caution" and "old naïve notion of cultural-political utopia that idealizes achievement of success and equality that sparked the endeavors of Blacks who were desperate to access the middle class."[103] In reviews of Denzel Washington's performances, for example, White would contrast Poitier's ability to embody a "spiritual revolution" with Washington's symbolization of an "era of stalemate" during the 1995 US government shutdown.[104] Just as White tuned in to punk music and Motown records when movies in the late 1970s seemed to lack the "imaginative force" that they had once had, he looked to rap artists to speak to the pop audience in the 1990s with more urgency and effectiveness than Washington and other Black filmmakers and movie stars.[105]

Honorable mentions

- White considered **Bill Gunn** to be "the most fearless Black artist of his lifetime" and a director who was willing to upset a "sense of Black pride that is usually set in codes of Black heterosexual machismo."[106]
- White reappraised **Melvin Van Peebles** in the 1980s and '90s. While writing at the *South End*, White had considered Van Peebles a shoddy initiator and representative of Blaxploitation films. At the *City Sun*, White hailed him as an independent thinker who assaulted the "white bourgeois filmgoing experience" and praised his "down and dirty miscegenation" in the 1990s as a welcome challenge to contemporary Black filmmakers who were ineffective in confronting sexism, classism, or racism in a hip hop exploitation era.[107]
- Although White did not consider **Charles Burnett** an "ideal pop artist," he respected his seriousness and facilitated a letter-writing campaign to protect Burnett's *Glass Shield* when the Miramax production company, co-founded by Harvey Weinstein, threatened it with cuts or shelving in 1995.[108]

Let the Mourning Begin

In these reviews, White railed against the hype accorded to hacks who copied the work of the imaginative artists who went before them and the barely concealed careerism of his contemporaries as well as younger artists from a post–civil rights generation. He lamented the extinction of a counterculture that supported original, challenging, and independent filmmaking in America as well as the demise of a radical, lively, and independent Black press.

Henry Louis Gates Jr. (b. 1950)

Selected articles for the New York Times: "2 Live Crew, Decoded" (1990), "Black Demagogues and Pseudo-Scholars" (1992)

The notion of a public sphere was familiar to many academics following the publication of *The Structural Transformation of the Public Sphere* in 1989, an English translation of Jürgen Habermas's historical and sociological study of literary journals, salons, and newspapers that emerged in Western Europe in the late eighteenth and early nineteenth centuries. Habermas proposed that individuals could freely and openly come together to discuss and identify societal problems in these networks and, through rational-critical discussion, form a public that could influence political action in local and national contexts. While outlining the history of a bourgeois public sphere that disrupted feudal forms of authority, Habermas also considered its decline and how a refeudalized public sphere emerged that merely had the appearance of openness via public relations, opinion polls, and the manufacture of consent. This refeudalized public sphere was connected, in no small part, to technological developments and a culture industry in the twentieth century that produced networks for individuals to follow and pledge allegiance to icons.

Rather than retain Habermas's focus on a literary public sphere, scholars and activists considered how a Black public sphere included oral and aural practices in radio stations, churches, barbershops, and other places and networks that countered the exclusionary violence of much public space in the United States.[109] White consistently engaged with the work generated by academic conferences and workshops about Black cinema and a Black public sphere while working for the *City Sun* (which advertised workshops and panels about the culture wars featuring prominent intellectuals such as Edward Said, Cornel West, and Sylvia Wynter[110]). However, he was not interpreted as an upstanding intellectual who attempted to put the knowledge gleaned from Western universities at the disposal of a broad audience. Nor was he included in the lists of Black public intellectuals that proliferated in the mid-1990s.

Excluded from the system of awards and patronage accorded to Black public intellectuals, White defined himself as a critic who could not be bought and cast doubt on the principles of "mediocre" and middle-class Black "race hustlers" and "eggheads" who slimed their way into the ranks of mainstream opinion as freelancers and op-ed columnists.[111] While also targeting the likes of Michael Eric Dyson and bell hooks,[112] White's ire was most frequently trained on Henry Louis Gates Jr. White accused Gates of capitalizing on white America's guilt and loathing toward Black culture to achieve grants, genius awards, and publishing opportunities with the *New York Times*.[113] He labeled the Harvard professor a cautious and compromised responder to the terms of public discourse set down by the white liberal media—the "national conversations about race" that rely on platitudes about what unites us or divides us rather than critical analyses of cultures that may be read within, across, outside, or against the nation-state. Moving beyond the boundaries of polite academic discourse, White portrayed Gates as a parasite who was more interested in securing his status as an intermediary between Blacks and whites in America than in cultivating imaginative and inventive Black cultural expression.

It is possible to interpret such animosity as stemming from the "narcissism of minor differences" between two male critics of a similar age who shared similar perspectives, as well as White's frustration that Gates sublimated his ideas for well-heeled readers of American dailies, weeklies, or quarterlies. On the one hand, White would adapt Gates's much-discussed op-ed for the *New York Times* in 1990, in which he defended 2 Live Crew from an overly "literal-minded" reading that failed to appreciate that the hip hop crew were "acting out" the "stereotypes of the over-sexed Black female and male,"[114] by challenging literal-minded critics who complained about the sexism of the Geto Boys. In 1996, White contended that any sexism in their new album resulted from the Geto Boys' desire to get their point across to a popular audience mired in American patriarchy and was so outlandish that any conscious listeners would discern its absurdity.[115] On the other hand, White claimed that Gates's 1998 article about the mix of hip hop and politics in the film *Bulworth* conspicuously repeated points he had made in the *City Sun* in 1992 (and were republished in a collection of his writings about film, music, and culture between 1984 and 1994[116]).

Spike Lee (b. 1957)

Selected Films: Do the Right Thing (1989), *Jungle Fever* (1991), *Malcolm X* (1992), *Clockers* (1995)

Having discovered that individuals are unlikely to confess any personal feelings or actions that may be considered racist, pollsters often ask their subjects whether their *neighbors* are racist. Similarly, journalists are usually more comfortable suggesting that their *readers* might assume that African Americans uncritically support artists from their racial group. The introduction to White's reviews in the *American Movie Critics* anthology by Phillip Lopate, an American film critic, essayist, fiction writer, poet, and teacher, offers a revealing example of this rhetorical move when it sets up the possibility that some readers may think that White would be sympathetic to the films of Spike Lee because they are both African American. To prevent imaginary readers from holding such beliefs, Lopate notes that White wrote a negative review of *Malcolm X* as well as a positive review of *Do the Right Thing*.[117] Rather than limit one's focus to the issue of whether White was predisposed to be charitable to Black artists, and simplistically ask whether he responded to a film with

a thumbs-up or thumbs-down, it may be more productive to consider how White expressed his standards of journalistic integrity and
critical analysis in his "positive review" of *Do the Right Thing* as well
as his "negative reviews" of *Malcolm X*, *Jungle Fever*, *Clockers*, and
other Spike Lee joints.

White's review of *Do the Right Thing* in *LA Weekly* was sugges-
tively titled "Rebirth of a Nation" to position Lee as an auteur who
went behind the veil to join Griffith, Altman, Scorsese, and other
filmmakers who brought new elements to the American cinema.
According to White, *Do the Right Thing* filled the gap left by white
filmmakers who fled for the safe, ersatz sophistication of European
movies. The film, set in a multiracial working-class Bedford-
Stuyvesant neighborhood of Brooklyn, also laid down a gauntlet to
purportedly Black cultural productions made for and/or by white,
liberal, middle-class Americans. Although he remained wary of Lee's
tendency to be schematic and sentimental, White maintained that
Do the Right Thing was worthy of celebration because it conveyed
the impudent integrity of hip hop and Black radio without condescending to a Black working class in an "*overly* didactic or preachy"
manner.[118]

Whereas White perceived *Do the Right Thing* as a film that could
seriously convey the realities and fantasies of women and men who
were working-class, urban, and American, his reviews of the subsequent films that Lee made tended to emphasize the confusion of
a filmmaker who symbolized the contradictions and arrogance of
a Black middle class. He would reprimand Lee's *Jungle Fever* for its
failure to perceive that college is a dead-end for many working-class
kids and young Blacks and its failure to show how New Yorkers were
capable of communicating across racial lines.[119]

White's review of *Malcolm X* similarly focused on Lee's inability
to produce a challenging, difficult film when he received considerable
financing from Hollywood studios and mainstream Black entertainers.[120] Much like Amiri Baraka's indictment of Lee as a middle-class
Negro who wanted to alleviate his class guilt, White accused Lee of
being a shameful figure who commodified Malcolm X and failed to
acknowledge his connections to Frederick Douglass, Marcus Garvey,

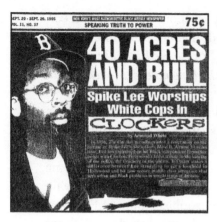

Front page of the *City Sun*, September 20–26, 1995.

and other Black historical figures who galvanized opposition to slavery and colonialism. Believing it within his rights as a critic to discern potentially selfish motivations of filmmakers,[121] White associated Lee's practice with that of careerist Blacks who wanted to be accepted by Hollywood by asserting their racial distinctiveness rather than demonstrating artistic talent and originality.

In contrast to his review of *Do the Right Thing*, which compared Lee's talent and creativity to that of Altman and Scorsese, White's review of *Malcolm X* contended that Lee lacked the skill, grace, and imagination of auteurs such as Orson Welles and Brian De Palma to make history come alive. In short, White supplemented the *City Sun's* attacks on Black politicians that they deemed venal and self-serving by depicting Lee as a non-threatening emblem and commercial token who imitated contemporary hip hop artists so that he could put on a "show as a maverick for white liberals."[122] White compared Lee to Gates and other Black public intellectuals as a parasite who exploited Black political issues and white "guilt feelings" for their career advancement.[123] He also contended that Lee was a slavish entertainer who made films that "worshipped white cops" rather than a principled artist capable of exposing the realities of state brutality and institutional racism in a non-facile and undogmatic manner.[124]

Eddie Murphy (b. 1961)

Selected Films: Beverly Hills Cop (1984), *Beverly Hills Cop II* (1987), *Coming to America* (1988), *Boomerang* (1992), *Vampire in Brooklyn* (1995), *The Nutty Professor* (1996)

In one of his final acts as the arts editor for the *City Sun*, White deliberately paired his reviews of stand-up performances from Paul Mooney and Chris Rock. In one review, he portrayed Mooney as an experienced comedian born in 1941 who had written for Richard Pryor but had not secured widespread commercial success or popular acclaim. In the other review, he described Rock as an up-and-coming stand-up born in 1965 whose *Bring the Pain* special for HBO had made him one of the most commercially and critically acclaimed stand-ups in America.[125] More pointedly, he admired Mooney's insightful way of sorting through the pain of Black experience to gain a better understanding of life, and depicted Rock as a selfish opportunist who appealed to audiences taught to laugh rather than think.

Such barbed comments were characteristic of reviews in which White sought to contrast the artistic and political struggles of a civil rights generation with the apolitical and amoral careerism of a post–civil rights generation. These broad generalizations about an older generation that deserves to be respected, and a younger generation that is lost and confused, sit uncomfortably with White's professed commitment to producing criticism that is nuanced, sensitive, and expressive of an openhearted engagement with difference. His reviews of Eddie Murphy are particularly revealing examples of the tensions inherent in White's opinionated reviews of Black comics whom he associated with the selfishness of Rock and a post–civil rights generation rather than the ability of Mooney and a civil rights generation to clarify political hypocrisy and misunderstanding.

In the 1980s and '90s, White repeatedly targeted Eddie Murphy as "a kid with no heart, no mind" who was willing to recycle stereotypes of servile, shufflin' Blacks to advance his career.[126] He described Murphy's deeply insensitive jokes about Blacks, gays, and other minorities in America as a "cocaine-induced, sitcom-inspired" update to Stepin Fetchit (the first Black actor to become a millionaire in the 1930s, who was widely condemned by African Americans for his portrayal of harmful, negative stereotypes). He mourned Murphy's failure to become the "vibrant, handsome young representation of post–civil rights era black youth . . . [and] act out the era's cynical knowingness about politics, offering a common ground where no one shies away from the facts of racial difference."[127] Such wasted potential was a reminder that it was foolhardy to praise Black achievers or women who break the glass ceiling when mainstream approval invariably "destroys ethnic character and self-esteem."[128]

In a review of *Coming to America*—Murphy's romantic comedy about an African prince who journeys to New York in search of a bride he can genuinely love and respect—White drew attention to scenes like a tacky female beauty pageant in which the contestants parade under a Black Awareness Rally banner. While such scenes may help boost Murphy's earnings, they dismiss the struggles of a civil rights movement by considering "the very idea of Black politics or the political expression of Black pride . . . absurd." Anticipating academic discussions about speaking and shrieking commodities from a post–civil rights era who entered the American mainstream with performances that attacked the Black poor, rejected public displays of introspection, and expressed unambiguous misogyny and homophobia,[129] White diagnosed Murphy as a casualty of a period of arrested social advancement for Black people in the 1970s. To go further, White depicted Murphy as an avatar of the ignorance and craven commercialism of a "TV generation" that uncritically supported American capitalism and recycled the racial stereotypes that had confined and defined Black people in the early twentieth century.[130]

White's review of *Coming to America* provoked Murphy into purchasing a third of the *City Sun*'s advertising space for its next issue to publish an open letter that responded to what he considered an unprecedented and vicious attack.[131] Defending his right to produce "simple" films that do not push politics, history, and "dark-skinned, light-skinned paranoia" down the throats of their audiences, Murphy pointed to the box-office success of *Coming to America* as evidence that he was more in tune with the desires of the Black community than White was.[132] The stakes of the debate were clear to White, whose rebuttal emphasized the importance of Black independent journalism that called out "scoundrel-entertainers" who "understand the tastes, morals, and values of the Black community enough to make it enjoy its own humiliation" and "refuse to address the history of slavery or the varied realities of racism and poverty, to insult women and gay people."[133] He also implored Murphy to read "Du Bois, Garvey, Fanon, and Frederick Douglass" rather than disingenuously claim that he is compromising with Hollywood executives "for the benefit of the entire race."[134]

White would repeat his concerns about the direction of Murphy's Hollywood career in the 1990s. He noted, for example, the typical values of monogamy and light-skinned females that were evident in *Boomerang*. However, he was alive to the possibility of Murphy maturing and would acknowledge that there was a subtly ethnic approach in *The Nutty Professor*, Murphy's "closest to likable movie."[135] Much like he had reappraised Melvin Van Peebles and Blaxploitation films because he believed that they were more original and challenging than the films that were produced during a "hip hop exploitation era" in the 1980s and '90s, White would reappraise Murphy and the artists he deemed dishonorable when he perceived American culture to be under attack from an even more significant threat from "Internet hordes" and a "Millennial generation" in the twenty-first century.

Dishonorable mentions

- **Alan Parker** was one of many white (and foreign) directors that White identified with the sickness of racism and white condescension that perpetuated inauthentic and racist portrayals of American history and culture. Decades before many of his colleagues in the New York Film Critics Circle, White exposed the condescension of white savior movies such as Parker's *Mississippi Burning* in the 1980s. To go further, he refused to accept the premise of Parker that an American audience was not radical or sophisticated enough to identify with the plight of Blacks without sympathetic white surrogates. He also called out film critics for their complicity in rendering an all-American identity synonymous with whiteness, particular articles in the mainstream media that claimed that Gene Hackman, the co-lead of *Mississippi Burning*, had "America's face."[136] White perceived that such a tendency to associate all-American values with whiteness reflected a film culture that canonized Robert Redford for his "blue-eyed blondness" and worshipped "white beauty standards."[137] He also made the case that such possessive investment in whiteness reflected a broader political culture that expressed contempt for non-white, non-affluent people and derided manifestations of Black rage as evidence of Black irrationality rather than a necessary ingredient in social transformation.[138]

- **Roger Ebert** was the first film critic to receive a star on the Hollywood Walk of Fame and the most prominent face of film criticism on American television. Rather than celebrate Ebert as a pioneering film critic, White portrayed him as the man who destroyed the profession and debased an American public sphere by "judging a film's content by the demographics of the audience . . . and then playing to the Nielsen [ratings]."[139]

- White's bête noire was **Quentin Tarantino.** Rather than add further critical acclaim to a filmmaker praised as the savior of American independent film, White described Tarantino as an overhyped auteur who took the aesthetics and conventions of a French new wave without their ethics and convictions; a "white negro" who made Blaxploitation films with predominantly white casts; a director corrupted by the stereotypes he consumed on TV and video as a child; a nihilist incapable of expressing spiritual beauty or humanistic values through dynamic movement and action; and an opportunist who exploited race-mixing rather than transcending racial politics like the pop artists he featured on his soundtracks.[140]

- Disgusted by **Albert and Allen Hughes**'s *Dead Presidents*, White suggested that the shocking, hateful Black males in the film were possibly a result of the brothers' identity and Oedipal conflicts as children of a Black American father and a white Armenian mother from Detroit.[141]

- According to White, **John Singleton** reflected the misguided view that "toughness and stoicism" were the essence of African American masculinity[142] and constructed films that were "too forthright, too artless, and too confused to consciously employ political symbolism."[143] Rather than follow academics and journalists who listed films such as Singleton's *Boyz n the Hood* under the New Black Realism label, White would file such commercially successful films under the label "hip hop exploitation movies."

- **Snoop Dogg, Dr. Dre, Nelson George, Keenen Ivory Wayans,** and **Samuel L. Jackson**—White did not suffer this foolish five gladly. As arts editor for the *City Sun*, White had considerable leeway to use language that would have been difficult to smuggle past editors at other papers. He denounced these musicians, writers, and actors as "venal reprobates" who allowed "listeners from the non-core audience to disregard hip-hop's substance of personal expression, social commentary, cultural transformation," "untalented opportunists," "showbiz prostitutes," "shameless Hollywood panderers," "moral idiots," and "Hollywood whores."[144]

The strident, militant tone of the *City Sun* did not deter advertisers such as the Afrocentric clothing line Primitive (which was modeled by Laurence Fishbourne before he starred in commercially successful films such as *Boyz n the Hood* and *The Matrix*) or white individuals who used its classified advertising to search for Black sexual partners who wanted "cream" to add to their coffee. It may also have helped the paper to develop articles and positions that were repeated and engaged by other New York media outlets, even if they were not cited or acknowledged. It was not, however, particularly attractive to larger companies that the owners of the *City Sun* hoped would support a lively and independent Black newspaper, and the paper would not achieve the weekly circulation of 65,000 that it promised in its business plan. One of the reasons Utrice Leid gave for her departure from the paper in 1992 was its inflation of the circulation figures to secure better advertising rates.[145] When city marshals evicted staff from its offices on October 21, 1996, the City Sun company owed over $380,000 in back taxes as well as money to its printers.

After the *City Sun* folded, White formed City Sun Employees Inc. to organize fundraisers to provide some material support for former colleagues.[146] He collaborated with former contributors to the *City Sun* as part of the writing collective of *First of the Month*, an occasional print journal and "website of the radical imagination." In their mission statement, the writing collective outlined their ongoing commitment to an accessible, non-patronizing approach. They wrote with and for people who believed in the power of a "60s word *soul*," "a more democratic politics of culture," and the importance of platforms in which they might "come together and, in ways that enhance all parties, *disagree*."[147]

The next chapter considers how the generous agonism with which Armond White prodded the tastes and boundaries of a liberal public sphere as a film critic for the *New York Press*, an alternative weekly that he joined in 1997, may be read in parallel with Paul Gilroy's abiding interest in sustaining "a kind of fragile community composed of people who disagree with one another, constituted by the fruitful mode of disagreement that grows with discipline and mutual respect."[148] More specifically, we will place White's ongoing opposition to Quentin Tarantino and other "faithless bloodhounds" and "secular progressives" in America who directed films that he found bereft of any "edifying, Christian love" in dialogue with Gilroy's distinct yet related project to sustain a sense of a humanist community while navigating neoliberal academic institutions in the United States and the United Kingdom.

It may well be that in middle-age, people get so befuddled and desperate and obsessive about their loss of youth and vision (both in eyesight and outlook) that they start thinking stupidly and selfishly. Through the influence of popular culture, they can only think of their spiritual dilemma in banal soap opera terms.

Armond White (1974)

In *Another Year*, [Mike] Leigh demands that viewers look past the superficiality and guile that, in youth, is not fully answered for. Doing so permits Leigh to make a landmark cinematic discovery: middle age as the moment of self-consciousness.

Chagrin, obligation, judgment, desperation, the hard facts of middle age, make the movie fascinating even as it defies thrill-hungry, narcissistic film culture.

Armond White (2006)

6.
MIDDLE-AGED, GIFTED, AND BLACK
Structures of Feeling in the Black Atlantic

What works of popular culture spoke to American prize-giving institutions as they prepared to meet the social and political challenges of the twenty-first century? On January 23, 2000, *The Sopranos* picked up the most awards at the 57th Golden Globes. It remains one of the most popular and acclaimed shows from a "golden era of television" that featured white male anti-heroes who, like President Bill Clinton, were called upon to address the personal and political costs of lying to their families. *American Beauty*, a drama about a sexually frustrated suburban father, garnered five Academy Awards at the Oscars held on March 26, 2000. Destiny's Child won a Grammy in 2001 for "Say My Name," a song about the discovery of an affair that also spoke to the demands of minority groups for recognition and respect.

High Fidelity, a movie about a middle-aged record store owner in Chicago who tracks down his ex-girlfriends to discover what went wrong in his relationships, was largely overlooked by America's prize-giving establishments.[1] It did, however, make its mark on headline writers at the *Village Voice*, who selected "Hybrid Fidelity" as a suitable title for a review of Paul Gilroy's *Against Race*. Although the review did not mention that Gilroy was a contemporary of Nick Hornby, whose book about a fogeyish record store owner in London provided the foundation for *High Fidelity's* screenplay, it did draw attention to Gilroy's determination to defend hybridity as a source of excitement and strength while propounding some fogeyish perspectives about the deskilling of popular music.[2]

References to the anxieties and neuroses of male baby boomers born in America or Britain may obscure as much as they reveal. While Hornby's novel would engage with a generation of music lovers who celebrated Bruce Springsteen as a white rock-music avatar of the American working class, *Against Race* was written with and for a multiracial cohort that had more enthusiasm for the Trenchtown rock of Bob Marley. Although Hornby did not ignore the impact of punk on suburban consumers, *Against Race* delved more deeply into the politically infused pleasure of music that emerged when punks and soul rebels rocked against racism in underground venues and outdoor concerts. Hornby's middlebrow fiction would not demand that its readers rethink the terms that they heard on the evening news about a special relationship between the United States and the United Kingdom; Gilroy's book, modeled on Hannah Arendt's *The Origins of Totalitarianism*, would confront bourgeois barbarism in the overdeveloped world. *High Fidelity* was transplanted from London to Chicago to make it more accessible to American filmgoers; beyond changing the title of the book published as *Between Camps* in the UK, *Against Race* made fewer concessions to readers who wanted to know more about the specific material, legislative, economic, and artistic movements in the United States that influenced the shape and contours of African American culture.[3]

Rather than connect Gilroy to Hornby and a boomer identity that is preoccupied with the thoughts and feelings of white, middle-class men, this chapter connects his attempts to deprovincialize American Studies to the aspirations of a multiracial cohort of transatlantic rebels. More specifically, it moves between 1997 and 2011 to compare Gilroy's work to Armond White's reflections on America and the world for the *New York Press* (a free alternative weekly that styled itself as a quasi-anarchic alternative to the *Village Voice*). In 1997, White was one of three critics in a lively, radical film section in the *New York Press*, and Gilroy was a professor of Sociology and Cultural Studies at Goldsmiths College in London who was traveling to New York to deliver conference presentations, attend live music venues, dig into the crates in record stores, and pick up the latest issues of alternative weeklies from sidewalk newspaper boxes. By 2011, White was the only film critic for a paper that was on its last legs and Gilroy had returned to England to become the inaugural Anthony Giddens Professor of Social Theory at the London School of Economics after sojourning in the US as a professor of Sociology and African American Studies at Yale.

The first section, *Armond Dangerous* and *Against Race*, moves between 1997 and 2001 to connect Gilroy's structures of feeling to White's early reviews for a film section in the *New York Press* in which he was one of three thought-provoking critics granted space to review films from around the world. The second, Mourning and Melancholia, attends to White's search for humane art that could help Americans see through their bewilderment in the aftermath of 9/11 as well as Gilroy's concerns about British elites who followed US scripts and statecraft about war in Iraq and policies intended to address "race relations."[4] The third section, Moral Criticism and Moral Economies, documents White's work as a self-styled defender of the dignity and significance of film criticism in dialogue with Gilroy's attempts to feed some images back into the conversations about Black British identity and history between 2006 and 2011.

Armond Dangerous and Against Race

Founded in 1988 by Russ Smith, a libertarian Republican who believed that the state had no business criminalizing sex work, gambling, and drugs, the *New York Press* was a free print publication that included a diverse range of political commentary as well as crime and human interest stories that ventured into the underground worlds of satanism and cockfighting. It strove to foster a rivalry with the *Village Voice*, the first alternative newspaper in the United States, and many journalists at the *Press* interpreted the *Voice*'s decision to became a free publication in 1996, after decades of carrying a cover price, as a sign that they had forced their rival to buckle.[5] In 1997, the editors of the *Press* announced that Armond White would be joining a film section that provided Godfrey Cheshire (a fellow member and former chair of the New York Film Critics Circle who had recommended him for the job) and Matt Zoller Seitz (a former media columnist for the *Dallas Observer* who had an encyclopedic knowledge of American pop culture) the opportunity to practice long-form journalism. Over the next three years, Cheshire and Seitz would partake in full and frank debates with their new colleague and, on occasion, the *Press* would feature multiple reviews of the same film.

While White's colleagues were willing to politely point out what they felt he was missing or projecting onto the screen, readers would write letters to the paper expressing their frustration with White's "nauseatingly elitist" language and failure to understand that most people go to the movies in search of light entertainment with their dates or families.[6] Others would set up an *Armond Dangerous* blog to parse and critique his film reviews, making White one of the few film critics to be the subject of such sustained exegetical attention and commentary.

Like a heelish member of the Detroit Pistons, White also antagonized fellow members of the New York Film Critics Circle. While a critic at the *City Sun*, White accused Georgia Brown, a film critic at the *Village Voice*, of liberal condescension and racism when she expressed her discomfort with films in which "handsome, brooding, dark-faced" heroes were "done in by inexorable social forces."[7] At the *New York Press*, White similarly wrote against the grain of Brown's colleagues and friends when they positively reviewed the films directed by her son Noah Baumbach. Equating flattering reviews of Baumbach's sophomore film *Mr. Jealousy* to "shameless" nursery gifts, White contended that *some viewers* of the self-absorbed, almost entirely white world portrayed by Baumbach may be more inclined to suggest "retroactive abortion."[8] J. Hoberman, a long-standing film critic at the *Voice* and one of White's colleagues in the New York Film Critics Circle, would later interpret this as evidence that *White* had called for Baumbach's abortion, as would film publicists who did not offer White an invitation to attend a critics' screening of Baumbach's 2010 film *Greenberg.*[9]

White sublimated his spats with film critics and publicists into reviews that questioned their tendency to dismiss humane filmmakers he esteemed—such as Altman and Spielberg—as unstructured, unsentimental, or manipulative. White's fervent advocacy for the "democratic, ethnically diverse, politically courageous art" of such pop artists led him to expunge any doubts he had once had about their earlier work.[10] On the twentieth anniversary of the theatrical release of Robert Altman's *3 Women*, for example, he hailed its "bold vision of eccentricity" as a means to critique the limitations of American film and television in the late 1990s. He did not repeat the claims he had made as a movie-obsessed kid from Detroit that the film was "artsy-fartsy B.S."[11] Similarly, White's distaste for Hollywood blockbusters in the 1990s meant that he departed from the positions taken by a brash young critic for the Detroit media who had denounced the crudeness and Hollywood flash of Spielberg's *Jaws* in 1975. He had evolved into a middle-aged critic who praised *Jaws* as a "revitalization of forgotten silent-film aesthetics, along with a new, good-humored sensibility."[12]

White often compared Spielberg's pop art in the early twenty-first century to the aesthetics of D.W. Griffith's silent films in the early twentieth century. Without ignoring the racism of Griffith's films, he celebrated the artistry of a filmmaker who had made a mark on the dreams of his fellow Americans. To go further, he would join colleagues in protesting the decision of the Directors Guild of America to drop Griffith's name from its Lifetime Achievement Award in 2000. According to White, such a symbolic, performative gesture was a "depressing example of 'political correctness' as an erasure, and rewriting, of American film history."[13]

In White's reviews, the term "political correctness" is often associated with the regression of movie art—the casting of uncharismatic figures because they align with the diversity strategies

Portrait of Armond White in 2000.
Photo: Chris Whitney

imposed by "leftist cynics," "social justice warriors," and other phantom menaces to American existentialists.¹⁴ Although he had first heard the term "political correctness" in the 1970s and didn't consider it a new phenomenon, White perceived it to be more prevalent and more dangerous in the late 1990s and early 2000s. He was increasingly finding it difficult to sustain a sense of humanist community and identified with the French-Swiss filmmaker Jean-Luc Godard, who had turned to auto-critiques because "there was no longer a community he could address by making new films" and talked to himself "as all serious critics must."¹⁵ His reviews at the *Press* before 9/11 would, however, find some crumbs of hope in American auteurs who enlarged and revised the emotional and aesthetic triumphs of Altman, Spielberg, and Griffith. He was particularly impressed by white auteurs such as Brad Bird, Wes Anderson, Walt Whitman, and David Gordon Green, claiming that they honored and updated a tradition of pop artists and American mavericks by subjecting white privilege to X-ray-exact critical scrutiny or treating the experiences of minorities, subcultures, and eccentrics with humanity.¹⁶

While White was beginning a new chapter in his career at the *New York Press*, Gilroy was processing what it meant to drop the "young" from "young soul rebel." At a conference about music, myth, and popular culture at the Dia Center for the Arts in New York in 1997, Gilroy confessed that his demographic, geographical, and generational affiliation had, relatively recently, started to feel like a curse.¹⁷ Three years later, in the book published by Harvard University Press as *Against Race*, he disclosed that he bore a "generational affliction"

as he critiqued commodified Black cultures in the United States and the United Kingdom that he associated with pseudo-performances and video-based simulations, Americocentric Millennial nationalism, and authoritarian populism.[18] The distinctive energy of the text is informed by an author meditating on what it feels like to have live concerts and music, which were at the very center of his identity as a young soul rebel, mediated by television, "sports and computing."[19] He was not just a member of a community of interpreters who communicated his life-changing experiences with the music of male performers such as Bob Marley in the 1960s and '70s—he was also a professor of Sociology and African American Studies at Yale University who drew on the interviews and cultural productions of male performers such as Ice Cube, Snoop Dogg, and R. Kelly at the dusk of the twentieth century to argue that a culture industry had colonized and commodified the rebel spirit of Black popular culture and turned it into a distracting accompaniment for the postmodern self-discipline of working out.[20]

One of the most intriguing passages in *Against Race* finds Gilroy casting a sociological eye over corporate multiculturalism that privileged the ideal, superhuman Black athlete, model, or icon.[21] Echoing Frantz Fanon's writings about the eroticization of the Black athlete and the creation of sporting heroes to reinforce passive consumption to political hierarchies, Gilroy argued that "an exemplary black physicality, mute and heroic, has been conscripted into service to build a militarized and nationalized version of planetary popular culture in which the world of sports counts for more than the supple, subtle public relationships improvised around the gestalt of song and dance."[22] The first part of this sentence connects the problem of mute and heroic Black physicality, which is unfettered with doubt, vulnerability, and humanity, to the problem of militarized and nationalized propaganda. It leaves the reader wondering if Gilroy might tolerate the muteness and heroism if it were enlisted in pursuit of non-violent, diasporic identities that might make "today's black political imaginary" more democratic and cosmopolitan.[23] The second part of the sentence reveals a writer unwilling to countenance any nostalgic representations of a period in the 1970s and '80s when "the gestalt of song and dance" involved white, male, working-class fans standing in soccer stands delivering monkey chants to Black players, terrorizing Black fans, and bringing together a distinctive blend of homoeroticism, homophilia, and homophobia. Gilroy remained a utopian writer who imagined a future in which the gestalt of song and dance or doubt, vulnerability, and humanity had not been extinguished by comfortable, all-seater stadia or corporate cultures that turn the sublime skills of professional athletes into superhuman feats of neoliberal conviction.

Although *Against Race* was over four hundred pages in length, it retained an elliptical style that extends few olive branches to readers desirous of more practical, comprehensive, or conventional guides to political resistance.[24] More than any of Gilroy's previous books, it addressed the ethics of Black Atlantic artists and critics moving into overground spaces. As the soul rebel witnessed multinational corporations appropriating Bob Marley's image after death, he meditated on what Marley's life and work might mean for readers in the over-developed world who wished to consider the ethically charged role of interpreters. He celebrated Marley's ability to perceive hybridity and mixture as sources of excitement and strength rather than as symptoms of weakness and pathology. He also argued that Marley's spiritual connection to Africa, which did not involve making his physical home in the continent, expressed a "more difficult cosmo-politan commitment."[25] As much as such a celebration of difficulty went against the grain of quick-fix and oversimplified corporate multiculturalism, and challenged audiences to pursue "creative recycling rather than immoral disposability,"[26] it was also used as evidence that Gilroy's work was written with and for "First World" readers and had little value for activists and intellectuals who make Africa their physical home while expressing difficult commitments to national liberation, anti-colonialism, and cosmopolitanism.[27]

Mourning and Melancholia

After Godfrey Cheshire's dismissal in December 2000, Armond White and Matt Zoller Seitz shared the film reviewing duties at the *New York Press*. In 2001, both critics would write reviews that demonstrated the impact of Cheshire, a creative and diligent champion of a New Wave of Iranian cinema, and convey their esteem for Pauline Kael after she died in Great Barrington, Massachusetts, on September 3, 2001. Then, after citizens of Saudi Arabia, the United Arab Emirates, Lebanon, and Egypt hijacked planes to attack New York and Washington, both critics would seek to communicate their trauma and anger to their readers.

In the wake of 9/11, White's reviews would mention, in passing, the hurt that caused him to reject all directors from Iran, Egypt, or Middle Eastern countries who had previously renewed his humanity and appreciation of others.[28] Conjoined with such inchoate Orientalism and Islamophobia was a concern that American films were increasingly incapable of harnessing their potential to speak intelligently to everyday people with spiritual insight, philosophical speculation, and historical understanding. White's incisive review of Vin Diesel's performance in *xXx*, for example, debunked Diesel's claim that he wanted to make films for "all the invisible kids, the ones who don't fit into one ethnic category" and then find themselves "lost in some limbo."[29] It proposed that such marketing talk threatened to distract us from the deleterious impact of action-adventure films and video games in which juvenile American males trashed European history and Western civilization. The review called on imaginative critics to pierce beyond the surface of the press releases they received from movie studios and publicists to generate deeper questions about Diesel's mainstream ascension and the manner in which slavery remained a consciously and unconsciously felt problem in American life.

White thus took the opportunity to remind his readers at the *Press* that Diesel's image in popular culture could be compared to a gay, mixed-race porn actor who used the historically loaded name of Dred Scott, an enslaved African American who had unsuccessfully sued for his freedom in a landmark legal case in 1857. In a context in which American politicians sought to justify a war in Iraq, White targeted the lies of filmmakers who peddled tired, colonial tropes of white soldiers battling anonymous Black hordes. This meant exposing the limitations of Ridley Scott, who, after a career in British advertising, directed *Black Hawk Down*, a film about the US military's 1993 raid in Mogadishu, and Lorne Michaels, the Canadian producer of the television sketch show *Saturday Night Live*, who permitted the mayor of New York City, Rudy Giuliani, to pose in front of a wall of police and fire officers and then claim that the all-white, all-male cast represented the sacrifice and indomitable spirit of all New Yorkers.

Seeking to restore and recuperate film criticism (or, more polemically, "Make Film Criticism Great Again"), White would regularly repeat Pauline Kael's contention that film critics needed to be a bulwark between the audience and advertising. He would deliver panegyrics about the time he'd spent as a graduate student at Columbia University studying with Andrew Sarris and other inspirational teachers. He would fondly recall healthy disagreements and discussions with classmates in the 1980s who, while being shut out from high-profile media outlets in New York, remain "better thinkers about film than anybody who's writing criticism currently."[30] Aside from looking back to times and spaces in America in which he felt more alive, White searched more intently outside of the United States. His reviews for the *Press* between 2001 and 2006 would praise "achingly soulful" artists from Europe, South America, and Asia— such as Roy Andersson, Morrissey, Terence Davies, Mike Leigh, André Téchiné, Isaac Julien, Stephen Chow, Julián Hernández, and John Boorman—who made films and music that he associated with belief "in the power of community and doing the humane thing."[31]

The words "depressing," "indignation," "parochial," "tepid," and "disturbing" in the opening paragraph of Paul Gilroy's *Postcolonial Melancholia* reveal much about the shape and contours of a book written in the wake of 9/11 and a "belligerent, sanctified and resolutely Churchillian Britain [that] was aligned politically with the worst and most backward features of the latest U.S. imperial adventures."[32] *Postcolonial Melancholia* began its life as the Wellek Lectures in critical theory at the University of California, Irvine in 2002, and was revised while Gilroy endured "long New England winters [in Connecticut and New Haven]" as a professor at Yale as well as "many brief, painful, and exhilarating journeys back to the [English] homeland" he was never sure that he had.[33]

Although it has been critiqued for its "mindfully vicious" use of Condoleezza Rice and Colin Powell as examples that prove African Americans could be conscripted to justify the war in Iraq,[34] the primary targets of the book are British politicians, political scientists, and sociologists who assume that they need to follow or catch up to the scripts and statecraft about race devised by American authorities. It repeatedly expresses hope for the transfiguration of politics away from the inconsistencies and shallowness of the New Labour project and "Phony King Tony [Blair] and his crony courtiers."[35] Since the prime minister and leader of New Labour who led Britain into war in Iraq is only three years older than Gilroy, *Postcolonial Melancholia* strategically assigned him to a different *"political and cultural* generation"—one that speaks the same language of Little Englanders who are proud of a British Empire and suspicious of immigrants from outside Western Europe or "white dominions" such as Australia, Canada, New Zealand.[36]

Postcolonial Melancholia is dedicated to Gilroy's children and the memory of Rachel Corrie and Thomas Hundall, young members of the international solidarity movement active in the Gaza Strip who were killed by the Israeli military. Corrie and Hundall are described as determined figures who placed themselves between the "vulnerable victims of the occupation and the military firepower of the Israeli army" and are distinguished from their English forbears who believed that they were entitled to use military force to establish and extend a British Empire.[37] They are deployed in Gilroy's text as exemplars of non-national solidarity that he finds more difficult, principled, and open than the limited codes of human-rights talk, medical emergency, and environmental catastrophe that proliferate among academics and journalists.[38] Gilroy does not approach the study of racism and racialization as a technical problem to be managed and administered with experts, evidence-based solutions, algorithms, and other tidy models of governance.[39] In a pointed rejoinder to critics who claim that his utopian work is "tainted, ignoble, and unpolitical," Gilroy contends that what often passes as serious, competent, formal politics incubates *para*political technologies and ongoing colonial violence.[40] In the tradition of authors such as C.L.R. James and David Graeber, he associates "policy" with the negation of politics and the idea of people managing their own affairs.[41]

In addition to advancing a vision of worldly political activism by planetary humanists who left their homes in Europe to expose injustice in the Middle East, *Postcolonial Melancholia* calls attention to the power of unkempt, unruly, and unplanned multicultures.[42] The book contrasts the "chaotic pleasures of convivial postcolonial urban world" with the unconvincing or banal narratives used by nations and corporations that wished to demonstrate their commitment to equity, inclusion, and diversity.[43] It expresses its utopian hopes in solidarity with the political intelligence and moral values of "ordinary multiculturalism" and "mundane encounters with difference" rather than corporate or commodified multiculturalism designed for the 1 percent. It suggests that convivial multicultures in Britain's urban areas articulate a healthier future for the nation than the tawdriness of "cheap patriotism."[44] It also contests the narrow horizons of conservative writers whose praise of the so-called natural landscape excludes "all urban and metropolitan space from the forms of moral and aesthetic rearmament that are necessary if the country is to be reinvigorated and restored."[45]

Whereas Gilroy's discussions of feral multicultures and "real multiculturalism" in the 1990s had drawn attention to the insinuating rhythms of the streets, his work in the twenty-first century about the richness and complexity of Europe's convivial multicultures—spaces in which "one set of habits flows into others and all of them are altered by that encounter"[46]—engaged with the Streets, a music project developed by the English rapper Mike Skinner that playfully grappled with the impact of American film and culture. In contrast to Gilroy's engagements with live music and underground raves in twentieth-century Britain, *Postcolonial Melancholia* looked to the politics and ethics that were consumed by "screenies." It interpreted the carnivalesque comedy of Sacha Baron Cohen on late-night television shows, for example, as a witty and intelligent exposé of the generational gaps between members of a British establishment who grew up viewing world maps in which huge swaths of territory were colored pink to signify British dominions, on the one hand, and tech-savvy youngsters who grew up viewing music videos that blended British, Caribbean, and American cultures, on the other.

Gilroy was, in short, seeking to recycle "some *images*" back into the sorts of conversations that people have about history.[47] Rather than merely use the term "recycling" to critique African American musicians who translated the work of more daring and principled artists in the past for well-heeled audiences in expensive seats,[48] he used it to refer to ideas that he deemed necessary to repeat to generate a healthier political future.[49] In calling for a new, planetary humanism, Gilroy delivered two calls for action. First, historians of Europe's repressed, denied, and disavowed Blackness "must become willing to say the same things over and over again in the hope that a climate will eventually develop in which we will be able to find a hearing." Second, "we must be prepared to step back audaciously into the past."[50]

Gilroy's review of Michael Haneke's *Caché* is one notable demonstration of his awareness that repetition is often necessary to generate a political response. His commentary on the film, which received the European Film Award for Best Film and the Best Director Prize at the Cannes Film Festival in 2005, was significantly different to that of European critics and scholars who praised Haneke's ability to examine guilt critically. It also developed a dissenting position to European thinkers who consider guilt to be a "responsible emotion" in contradistinction to the more "destructive" and narcissistic emotion of shame.[51] According to Gilroy, *Caché* did not do enough to unsettle Europeans who had become resigned to the discomfort, complexity, ambiguity, and *shame* of empire. He suggested that the film projected the dangers of shame onto a migrant character who commits suicide rather than offer its European audiences any "clear sense of how to act justly or ethically."[52] Gilroy called for creative artists and critics to transform "paralyzing guilt" about the imperial past into "a *more productive* shame that would be more conducive to the building of a multicultural nationality that is no longer phobic about the prospect of exposure to either strangers or otherness."[53] Although his review did not cite Armond White's earlier review of the film, it shared White's frustration with a film that displayed little interest in portraying characters from France's Algerian community with any "psychological gravity and complexity."[54]

Moral Criticism and Moral Economies

In December 2002, a small investment group called Avalon Equity Partners, which controlled the largest gay newspaper group in the United States, purchased the *New York Press*. Soon after acquiring the *Press*, Avalon moved the staff of its other media publications into the *Press*'s offices and, as the paper found many of its advertisers gravitating to online sources, undertook the first of what would be several rounds of firings and pay cuts. The new owners of the *Press* did not hire anyone to replace Matt Zoller Seitz when he left the paper after the death of his wife.

As the sole film critic for a paper that was determined to cut costs and no longer granted its writers room for long-form journalism, Armond White was unable to use one thousand words or more to unpack his assertions about America, race, and the movies. Responding to such constraints, he inaugurated a "better than list" in 2006 that ingeniously transformed the mere ranking of films into an end-of-year or mid-year reckoning. These lists would incisively address what he perceived as the vices of much-hyped films and the virtues of films that were often overlooked or underrated, and continue after Manhattan Media, a company that publishes a variety of community and political newspapers and lifestyle magazines (such as *New York Family*), purchased the *Press* in 2007.

White's better-than reviews were catnip for readers and writers who associated film reviewing with the practice of thumbs-up or thumbs-down that Roger Ebert had popularized as a co-presenter of *Siskel & Ebert at the Movies*. After being sent a table that purported to list movies that White considered either good or bad, Ebert concluded that White was a "troll."[55] The first film critic to be awarded a star on the Hollywood Walk of Fame did not consider the possibility that White might find a movie good and bad (by, for example, praising the cinematography, soundtrack, or acting in a motion picture that he found morally objectionable or poorly written). Nor did Ebert do any journalistic legwork to check a table that erroneously claimed *Terminator Salvation* was a "good movie according to Armond" (even though White's review of the film had described it as "junk" and "over-valued schlock"[56]) and placed *Tropic Thunder* in the "bad movies according to Armond" (even though White had praised the film's "keen insight" and scrutiny of media icons and symbols).[57]

Although White believed that critics were entitled to question the motivations of artists and their peers, he was also quick to respond to any aspersions against his professional integrity. In 2010, he asserted that Ebert was a dishonest "shill" who was given the platform of a television show without having the foundation or training of a serious film critic. He resented the fact that Ebert "became an example of what a film critic does for far too many people" and fatally damaged the reputation of film criticism as a dignified, significant, and independent art form.[58] When the *New York Press* was discontinued on September 1, 2011, White would become editor at *City Arts* (a review of New York's culture and a division of Manhattan Media); he would not join his former colleagues Cheshire and Seitz and contribute to RogerEbert.com.

After leaving his post at Yale and returning to the UK in 2005 to become the Anthony Giddens Professor of Social Theory at the London School of Economics, Paul Gilroy championed the special gifts of a transitional generation poised between "citizen-immigrants of the 1950s," such as Stuart Hall, and the more assertively British-born groups that followed them.[59] His photographic history *Black Britain* (which features a foreword written by Hall) is both an attempt to restore Black Britain's patchy political memory and a guide to the particular sensibility of a writer who identifies with a rebel generation that came of age in the late 1960s and early '70s.[60] Gilroy sought to position his political and cultural generation as lucky rather than lost—the beneficiaries of "an unusually eloquent, militant and musically rich culture" that helped them to fold traces of past suffering into political and cultural resistance so that they could interpret and transcend their space and time formation and "imagine a better future for blacks, Africa, and the wider world."[61]

Although *Black Britain* drew on a collection of Getty images from popular publications in the UK, Gilroy contended that the photographs he selected should not be written off as "tainted by their commercial origins."[62] He argued that it may be more productive for the writing of cultural history and the calculation of political choices to approach them as an archive that grants us access to Black British communities and multiracial environments that are often hidden and overlooked. His faith in the ability of cultural critics to imaginatively use found objects with origins in the commercial realm was combined with moral criticism that ardently defended vernacular intellectuals who appropriated the bureaucratic language of the UN Declaration of Human Rights to colonize the "inhospitable infrastructure of greedy and hostile cultural industries."[63] It was also conjoined with his war of position against professionals who appropriated lively and creative work for the empty dreams of corporate multiculturalism and consumer culture.[64] Gilroy remained a writer who appreciated sanctified healing spaces and a "banality of good" that he connected to everyday, normal, and ordinary encounters with racialized difference, and a critic of the banality of cheap, therapeutic forms of diversity and tokenism.[65] *Black Britain* also paired photographs of multiracial protesters in London opposing the American-led invasion of Iraq with passages that called on historians and journalists to describe how young people were actively resisting "a generic, US-based blackness" and the broken edifice of a British nation that seduce "the vulnerable and ignorant" into a military-industrial complex.[66]

In *Darker than Blue*, a slim volume of three essays published in 2010 based on his W.E.B. Du Bois Lectures at Harvard University four years earlier, Gilroy lamented the fading role of redemptive, soulful humanism in Black popular culture in Britain and the United States.[67] Although he did not wish to capitulate to nostalgia, he could not avoid the sense of loss that emerges when he contrasts his memories of a "glorious parade of Black Atlantic performers that flowed through London's musical scenes between 1969" (when he first started going out to enjoy live music) "and the more recent point, when deskilling aesthetic stagnation, and what can politely be called 'recycling' all intervened to make live performances less alive and less pleasurable."[68] Gilroy called on the members of his rebel generation to reintroduce a critique of consumer capitalism "into the vacuum that black political thought has become" and to communicate the green politics of Black idioms that may be hard to detect in popular music that celebrates conspicuous consumption of gas-guzzling cars and blood diamonds.[69] Just as he sought to develop a photographic history of Black Britain that would not merely become a handsome presence on coffee tables in the overdeveloped countries, Gilroy hoped that "something gritty and important" remained in his memories of underground musical cultures even when the "project-managing pimps of corporate multiculturalism" sought to commodify them.[70]

Although American readers have asked what his work meant for "national conversations" between Black and white in the United States (or what it means for Gilroy to translate or direct his analysis of African American cultures to a European audience), it may be more productive to read the text as one in which he resolutely calls for dialogue across generations and between academics and artists in postcolonial cities in Europe and elsewhere. Although the author of *Darker than Blue* did not claim to be an artist who brings newness into the world, he was determined to distance his position from "timid" and "selfish" scholasticism, corporate forms of multiculturalism for the 1 percent, *and* sclerotic forms of nationalism.[71] In the final chapter of *Darker than Blue*, Gilroy acknowledged that the shiny, multicultural glamour of the Obama administration had great power, resonance, and appeal around the world. Yet he also suggested that its ongoing participation in the "war on terror" would lead many to view Obama as a "smiling human cipher" for a foreign policy that propagated decadence, bullying, and injustice.[72] As much as he recognized why many African Americans wished to "close ranks" and operationalize their long-delayed membership in the national community, Gilroy could not help feeling that it may also be a sign of African American disengagement from an African and Black diaspora (or reflective of a belief that, if there is to be transnational exchange, American voices should be the dominant ones that instruct others how to build capacity for diversity and inclusion).[73]

In the coda to this tale of two critics, we will further examine Gilroy's attempts to disrupt the hegemony of "spectacular viral narratives of cruelty, triumph and uplift sourced from African American culture and experience" in the wake of Obama's election as the forty-fourth president of the United States.[74] I suggest that Gilroy's reading of Steve McQueen's *12 Years a Slave* as a refusal to engage with slavery and suffering in ways that conform with African American narratives[75]—*and* White's reading of McQueen's film as a distressingly familiar example of the "Obama effect" on American films, which confused brutality, violence, and misery with a humane reckoning of African American history, creativity, and resistance—may be read as elegies for a rebel generation that will never be satisfied by politicians who contend that the United States of America is the greatest nation on earth or speak about national identities and creative artists in oversimplified, banal terms.[76]

The half-caste appears in a prodigal literature. It presents him, to be frank, mostly as an undersized, scheming and entirely degenerate bastard. His father is a blackguard, his mother a whore. His sister and daughter . . . follow the maternal vocation.

But more than this, he is a potential menace to Western Civilisation, to everything that is White and Sacred and majusculed.

Cedric Dover (1937)

Contrary to the stereotype, simply having "mixed" parentage seems not to have been a handicap . . . but rather to have conferred some interpretive advantages and stimulated . . . [Bob Marley] towards useful insights into the character and the limits of both identity and groupness. . . . Once again, hybridity, mixture and contaminating combination can be seen as sources of excitement and strength, rather than symptoms of weakness and pathology.

Paul Gilroy (2010)

CODA
Guess Who's Coming to the Awards Dinner

Following the assassination of Martin Luther King Jr. on April 4, 1968, few people expected the Oscars to speak to the revolutionary mood in Black America. Nonetheless, the decision to award the Oscar for best original screenplay to *Guess Who's Coming to Dinner* was a particularly sobering example of how the Academy of Motion Picture Arts and Sciences could appear anemically liberal and tone-deaf to many Americans during the most sustained period of social unrest in the country since the Civil War. The film's early scenes have Joanna "Joey" Drayton returning from her Hawaiian vacation with some exciting news to share with her parents. She has met Dr. Prentice, an accomplished physician, medical professor, assistant director for tropical medicine at the World Health Organization, and Nobel Prize candidate. She intends to marry him. Oh, and he seems to be under the impression "that the fact that he's a Negro and I'm not creates a serious problem."

The visit of Dr. Prentice is thus used as an invitation to ask Mr. Drayton, a newspaper publisher, and Mrs. Drayton, the owner of an art gallery, the blunt question that was often posed to white liberals who opposed racial discrimination and laws prohibiting interracial marriage: *Would you let your daughter marry one?* It also grants them the opportunity to reveal their possessive investment in the question that remained, over fifty years after W.E.B. Du Bois identified it in *The Souls of Black Folk,* central to white liberal interactions with university-educated Blacks: *How does it feel to be a problem?*

One of Mr. Drayton's conversations / interrogations / Platonic dialogues with Dr. Prentice is worth quoting at length given the election of Barack Obama, a child of a white woman and a Black man who met while they were studying at the University of Hawai'i in the 1960s, as president of the United States in 2008.

Mr. Drayton: Have you given any thought to the problems your children are going to have?
Dr. Prentice: Yes, and they'll have some. And we'll have the children. Otherwise I don't know what you'd call it but you couldn't call it a marriage.
Mr. Drayton: Is that the way Joey feels?
Dr. Prentice: She feels that every single one of our children will be the president of the United States and they'll all have colorful administrations. . . .
Mr. Drayton: How do you feel about the problem?
Dr. Prentice: Frankly, I think your daughter is a bit optimistic. I'd settle for secretary of state.

Dr. Prentice responds to the questions posed by Mr. Drayton by acknowledging the prurient interest in interracial relationships and insisting on the supposedly inextricable, biological link between marriage and procreation. As Jared Sexton (a professor of African American Studies and Film and Media Studies at the University of California, Irvine and, with Saidiya Hartman, David Marriott, and Frank Wilderson, often cited as a prominent contributor to the theory of Afro-pessimism) suggests in *Amalgamation Schemes,* the so-called interracial relationship has to await the legitimization of multiracial people before it can enter the American public sphere as a "renovated family affair."[1] The price of such inclusion into the elite cadres of American political and social life seems to be a cruel inversion of Frantz Fanon's famous prayer: "O my body, make of me always a man who questions!"

The Oscar-winning screenplay did not construct a coherent and rational Black doctor who asks pertinent and probing questions to destroy the sickness of racism. Although Dr. Prentice may be wondering what problems Mr. Drayton foresees for his "coffee-colored grandchildren," he doesn't ask his potential father-in-law to specify what problems are uppermost in his mind. (Is he concerned about the problem of racial profiling, the problem of state violence, and/or the problem of so-called identity confusion?) Prentice is framed as a man of science who is willing to consider the possibility that children who are considered a problem in twentieth-century America may grow up to supervise its foreign service and immigration policy in the twenty-first century. He is not a radical figure who seeks to expose the constellation of wicked problems that anemic liberalism cannot solve.

Armond White and Paul Gilroy grew up supplementing the generic questions in scripts celebrated by American prize-giving institutions in the late 1960s and '70s with material and symbolic questions generated by radical intellectuals located inside and outside of academia. In the 1980s and '90s, they pursued careers as independent critics, provocateurs, and mavericks who refused to accept the opinions of small groups of cultural gatekeepers about what constitutes excellence. In the twenty-first century, when *Guess Who's Coming to Dinner* has been played for laughs in *Guess Who* (a 2005 comedy film about an African American family meeting their daughter's white boyfriend for the first time), and recycled by *Get Out* (a 2017 comedy-horror that invited audiences to scratch the surface of a white liberal couple who voted for Obama and encouraged their daughter to bring home her Black romantic and sexual partners), they have entered into what may be called different "structures of relation." White has been cast as the "Kanye West of film criticism" after being expelled from the New York Film Critics Circle.[2] After returning from "exile" in the United States, and feeling shut out from African American political and social thought, Gilroy has been described as perhaps "the most influential intellectual writing in Britain."[3]

After viewing *12 Years a Slave* in 2013, White wondered whether the Black British director Steve McQueen had consciously set out to construct a film that appealed to white liberals, secular audiences, and prize-giving institutions that had been conditioned to accept Black freakishness or superpathology by a spate of films made in the wake of Barack Obama's 2008 election as president (including *Precious, The Help, Beasts of the Southern Wild,* and *Captain Phillips*).[4] Gilroy was not unaware of the hollowness and superficiality of American institutions that incorporate non-white individuals into their privileged cadres when he wrote an article about *12 Years a Slave* for the *Observer*. Yet rather than align McQueen with prominent African Americans, such as Barack Obama (whom he described as a "smiling human cipher" for campaigns to seduce young people into the shiny glamour of progressive neoliberalism), Gilroy portrayed him as a deadly serious artist who demonstrates how human beings fought "off the sub-humanity imposed upon them by their status as commercial objects."[5] In other words, he chose to situate McQueen, a friend and former student of Caribbean descent, in the tradition of Bob Marley and diasporic intellectuals who quietly colonized "greedy and hostile cultural industries" with their rebel spirit (even if their revolutionary commitments are often repressed, marginalized, or domesticated by official and corporate cultural industries after their deaths).[6]

In this coda, I consider how we might delve beneath the surface of the two critics' disagreements about *12 Years a Slave*. Is it what White might call a family quarrel between Black Britons and their African American cousins? Is it what Gilroy, who remains sensitive to the limitations of family metaphors and the suppression of historical memory in the American public sphere, might describe as a transatlantic dialogue in which Black British artists refuse to let American voices drown out all of the others? Or is it a reminder that their seriously soulful criticism respects thoughtful disagreements about creative artistry in contrast to the ruthless reduction of cultural criticism to a set of binary choices between pantomime heroes or villains, likes or opprobrium, celebration or cancellation?

The Obama Effect

In 2004, Barack Obama delivered a keynote address to the Democratic National Convention that challenged political pundits who sliced and diced Americans into red states and blue states as well as "a black America and a white America and Latino America and Asian America."[7] Such rhetoric aligned with White's unease with the type of "cultural fragmentation that sorts moviegoers by age, political proclivities, race, and gender [that] cannot be mended by taste or education."[8] However, White was suspicious of a politician he equated with unprincipled actors of color who traded in their "personal vitality" for a "smoothness" that might pass muster with mainstream America.[9] He was a paranoid reader of a political candidate who not only reminded white liberals of Sidney Poitier, the American-Bahamian actor who'd portrayed Dr. Prentice, but also seemed to be a golden child of Prentice and Joey Drayton destined to have a colorful administration as president of the United States.[10]

In 2008, White reflected on Obama's superheroic feat in becoming the first Black presidential candidate of a major party by comparing his political persona to that of the actor Will Smith, who was starring in *Hancock* as a Black superhero who improves his public image with the help of a white suburban family. He assigned both Obama (born in 1961) and Smith (born in 1968) to a post–civil rights generation that had exploited the gains achieved by a civil rights generation composed of African American "civilians, politicians, artists and consumers: from Marvin Gaye to Julian Bond, Toni Morrison to Angela Davis, Kareem Abdul-Jabbar to August Wilson."[11] White portrayed the politician and the actor as unprincipled opportunists who only embraced a racial identity when it could be distanced from "radical, upstart black nationalism, liberation theology and prophetic Christianity" and connected to a bland and non-threatening beige identity.[12] He wanted to clarify that they were avatars of a post–civil rights generation he associated with profiteers and careerists. White did not want them to be confused with *his* political and cultural generation, which he connected to a civil rights movement, a 1970s protest ethic, and the do-it-yourself intransigence and independence of punk. In short, White's reviews were informed by a desire for Black politicians to outwit, circumvent, or challenge a liberal media. They responded to a context in which media outlets repeated the romantic racism of celebrity journalists such as Barbara Walters (who made a point of emphasizing Obama's "white blood"[13]), and politicians such as Joe Biden (who declared that he found Obama appealing because he was "articulate and bright and clean and nice-looking"[14]), as much as the content of Obama's political speeches.

In a brief article published in an online film website during Obama's historic presidential campaign, the Australian critic Adrian Martin contended that White was an intriguing example of someone who appeared progressive because he was a "black, gay, supporter of edgy pop culture," but also performed the role of a "post 9/11" conservative by taking "his adversaries to task for their lack of religious education, or their 'kneejerk liberalism.'"[15] Such commentary offers what Obama might call a teachable moment about some of the Manichean thinking that bedevils many of White's interlocutors. In one camp, they place progressives who are tolerant to sexual and racial minorities; in another, conservatives who cling to their religion and guns. Such binary thinking often marginalizes or represses radical critiques of liberals and conservatives. That is to say, White's position does not seem particularly intriguing or strange to a radical participant of Pride Parades and Caribbean carnivals who knows that corporate interests could appropriate Black, gay, and "edgy" identities.[16] It might not seem odd to readers who know that religious instruction and liberation theology have been employed in the service of anti-colonial liberation. It may even seem entirely reasonable when scholars, such as the Yale historian Robin Winks, have been considered progressive guides to Black history even when they portrayed Black radicals as purveyors of "superficial analysis" that stirred up "thoughtless, needless and frustrated destruction."[17]

The Kanye West of Film Criticism vs.
Britain's Most Influential Intellectual?

When he served as chairman of the New York Film Critics Circle in 2010, White implored his peers to "uphold the dignity and significance of film criticism" rather than descend to the standards of online commentators who were intimidated by independent thinkers.[18] He argued that film critics had a duty to uphold the tradition of forebears such as Pauline Kael, Andrew Sarris, and Frank S. Nugent, the first chair of the Critics Circle, who were models of personal conviction and cinematic literacy, and defy the pernicious influence of Roger Ebert, online hordes, and review aggregator sites such as Rotten Tomatoes that responded to "movies like thrill-hungry teenagers, colluding with commercialism."[19]

When the New York Film Critics Circle honored Steve McQueen with one of the hundreds of awards that *12 Years a Slave* received from prize-giving bodies in 2013 and 2014, White loudly proclaimed his belief that his colleagues had colluded with Hollywood hype and liberal cant. Terms such as "garbageman" and "doorman" were heard from White's table when McQueen accepted his award and, after blogs and news outlets began carrying stories about the alleged heckling of McQueen, an emergency meeting of the Critics Circle was convened. On January 13, 2014, White was expelled from the circle for a failure to uphold the "*integrity* and significance of film criticism."[20] Intriguingly, the New York Film Critics Circle strategically modified White's earlier call for independent thinking to defend the *dignity* and significance of film criticism. Their public pronouncement suggests that White had damaged their idea of a film critics' circle in which reasonable professionals might achieve consensus about film and the boundaries of acceptable discourse to approach the kind of authority bestowed on a scientific community. Put slightly differently, they treated White like a deplorable member of the public who refused to follow the science.

Mark Kermode, one of Britain's best-known writers and broadcasters on cinema, similarly found it difficult to believe that White had praised *Norbit*, a 2007 comedy starring Eddie Murphy that a majority of critics had derided as a cruel, crass, stereotypical film (it received a 9 percent rating on Rotten Tomatoes). Judging White to be more of a performance artist rather than a critic who could be taken seriously, he did not feel under any obligation to acknowledge White's trenchant criticism of Roger Ebert. In fact, Kermode argued that Ebert was a thoughtful, intelligent writer who was "*universally revered*" by his peers in the twenty-first century.[21]

Three months after the *Observer* announced that it had hired Kermode as its new film critic, the left-liberal Sunday newspaper published an article by Paul Gilroy abut the controversy surrounding *12 Years a Slave*. In it, Gilroy disagreed with White's characterization of the film as "torture porn" without dismissing him as an unserious critic. In fact, he contended that White was a serious critic who revealed the deep distrust of Hollywood and the deep hostility to Black British directors and actors telling stories that are considered African American, within African American social and political thought. According to Gilroy, such hermeneutics of suspicion reflected a widespread and "enduring sense that the bleak history of racial slavery is the exclusive property of African Americans."

In the first time that he cited the work of his American contemporary, Gilroy omitted to mention White's extensive body of work. He did not, for example, note White's reviews of British films such as *Amazing Grace* and *Belle*, which make it abundantly clear that he does not believe that racial slavery is the exclusive property of African Americans.[22] Gilroy seemed to be on relatively firmer ground when he sought to use White to illustrate wider currents in African American political and social thought that counseled African Americans to move away from the dubious psychological identification with slavery even while the legacies of slavery and Jim Crow segregation are still at large.[23] White's reviews have, after all, criticized proponents of a "New Jim Crow" thesis as "race hustlers" peddling the idea that "contemporary racial issues can be approached in the same way as racism of the past" as if "black Americans by and large have not experienced progress."[24] However, this does not necessarily mean that White has counseled African

Americans to move away from a dubious psychological identification with slavery per se. Much like Laura Chrisman's review of *The
Black Atlantic* took issue with Gilroy's moribund vision of Black
modernity that foregrounded slave suicide, fatalism, pain, and death
drive as its dominant features, White encouraged African Americans
to be critical of representations of slavery in films like *12 Years a Slave*
that focused on abjection, suffering, shame, and death and have little to say about iconoclastic, ironic, and scatological aesthetics, let
alone collective resistance.[25]

Black Atlantic Exchange in the Digital Age

In 2014, Armond White began writing for the *National Review*
website (the digital arm of a conservative magazine that had, in the
1950s, opposed civil rights and claimed that Blacks were culturally
inferior to whites). White's reviews on this platform have repeated
neoconservative soundbites by pathologizing "brazen" activists
in the Occupy movement,[26] the "petulance of the Black Lives
Matter crusade,"[27] politically correct "snowflakes,"[28] Marxist critics
who "dominate the academy,"[29] and other supposed enemies of
Western civilization. Although he does not particularly care about
the Oscars—as his maître à penser Pauline Kael remarked, serious
film critics don't talk about them—White has come to accept that
they are a convenient way to get people's attention.[30] He has written
about hashtags such as #OscarsSoWhite, which call attention to the
lack of diversity in nominations for the Academy Awards. He has
also responded to complaints that *Selma* (a historical drama about
the 1965 voting rights marches from Selma to Montgomery directed
by the African American filmmaker Ava DuVernay) was snubbed
by Academy voters after the cast and crew protested the death of
Eric Garner and racist police brutality. White argues that the calls
to diversify the Oscars are driven by self-serving artists and publicists, such as DuVernay, who believe that Black people are entitled
to awards "not because they are good but because they are black."[31]

Although film critics have tried to make sense of White's
recent work by diagnosing him as a "gay African-American

fundamentalist-Christian aesthete" consumed by rage,[32] it may be more accurate to identify resentment—a particularly virulent expression of politicized anger—as the primary force animating his late style. The barely concealed subtext of White's ire with contemporary manifestations of totalitarianism—which he has associated with a younger generation that has been "miseducated" by "Marxist Professors" and "itself misappropriated racial virtue and become fascist"—is a concern that the authentic resistance against white supremacy he has chronicled over the past fifty years will be scrubbed from the historical archive like Stalinists scrubbed Trotsky's image from the lineups of Soviet revolutionaries.[33]

White fears that few people are left who understand what it means to align their intellectual projects with "principled" Black politicians and preachers who called on Black individuals to move from "ethnicity to ethicalness to excellence" in the 1970s.[34] He is concerned that the radical challenge posed to the solipsistic, regressive forms of white supremacy by hip hop groups such as Public Enemy and the Geto Boys in the 1980s and '90s has been parasitically seized by a ruling class. Although White was willing to tolerate *Roots* as an understandably oversimplified distillation of American slavery and its afterlife for a television audience in the 1980s,[35] he could not countenance Ava DuVernay's *13th* as an understandably oversimplified distillation of the intersection of race, justice, and mass incarceration for a Netflix audience in 2016. To go further, he resented DuVernay's decision to give screen time to an "aristocratic group of black achievers" rather than hip hop artists who exposed the "corruption affecting the Clinton-era black urban mindset" and the "range of America's human tragedy" with wit and imagination in the 1990s.[36]

Resentment is one of the many emotions that give White the power to slap and embrace the readers of his film reviews for *National Review*. He resents the attention granted to the music video for Childish Gambino's "This Is America" as evidence of Millennial "groupthink and its attendant anxiety," which plunders the minstrel motifs of Jim Crow segregation to make oneself feel "woke."[37] He resents the power of Marvel Studios, a subsidiary of Walt Disney

Studios, to bully organizations and schools into buying tickets for people to "see themselves represented on screen." He resents the unimaginative, infantile, and banal representations of Africa in *Black Panther* so much that he feels nostalgic for the "straight-up, feel-good" piece of "black anthropology" of *Coming to America* (when reviewing it thirty years earlier, he had considered *Coming to America* incapable of revealing "the natural communal, spiritual beauty" of Africa).[38] He even resents *Lincoln* (2012), directed by Steven Spielberg, and Spielberg's video for the 2013 White House Correspondents (which preceded Spielberg being awarded the Presidential Medal of Freedom by Obama in 2015), as "devious" celebrations of President Barack Obama.[39]

No longer able to celebrate Spielberg as an *American* American producer and director of triumphant and transcendent pop art, White searched for other figures who might produce art that combined childlike wonder and adult sophistication. One of the American creative artists he championed as an heir to Spielberg's mantle was Kanye West. He described the rapper as a cultural producer who combines childlike innocence with "a sense of communal morality, a stress on self-discipline, that many hip-hop artists have forsaken."[40] Following West's visit to the studio of the tabloid news website TMZ on May 2, 2018, and his contention that the existence of slavery for hundreds of years "sounds like a choice . . . it's like we're mentally imprisoned," White suggested that the "Millennium's greatest hip hop artist" had transcended the "liberal, Democratic Party politics" that have been laid out for African Americans "for at least the past 50 years."[41] Writing against the grain of journalists who believed that the college dropout needed to be schooled by historians to prevent the tragic dissemination of untruths about "the happy slave,"[42] he contended that West intuited the radicalism and conservatism of soul musicians who transcended political division in the 1960s.

In contradistinction to opinion writers who believed that West was farcically echoing the contemporary alt-right,[43] White claimed that West was upholding the tenets of punk artists who laid down a gauntlet to a straight, middle-class world in the 1970s. Turning the tables on journalists lauded and amplified by American cultural gatekeepers, who argued that West craved attention and "white freedom" in advance of his album release,[44] White framed him as a victim of liberal bullies and self-serving Democratic politicians who, when they call for a national conversation about race, really mean "listen to me."[45] In short, White praised West's understanding and recycling of American history in contrast to overhyped artists and entertainers who exploited it to achieve attention and awards.

Paul Gilroy's late style has made few distinctions between the corporate multicultural glamour associated with Disney Studios (including the regal bearings of Beyoncé, *Black Panther*, and the Obamas) and Kanye West's ironic appetite for branded seriousness. Obama, Beyoncé, Jay-Z, 50 Cent, and Kanye all appear as a roll call of African American icons that have been used to transform the soulful artistry that inspired Gilroy as a young Black teenager into something less pleasurable and stimulating. He does not approach them as serious artists who have wrested a Black radical tradition away from a conformism that threatens to overpower it, or as sly figures who smuggle moments of dissidence into commodified cultures. Gilroy has connected the gaggle of American celebrities to a broader surrender to global business enterprise and the "project-managing pimps of corporate multiculturalism."[46]

In many of our platforms, such differing interpretations of McQueen and West might spark the fan of outrage and set the stage for online battles. One thinks, for example, of the attempts of Michael Eric Dyson to roast Gilroy by awarding him a "Ringo Starr award" and claiming that he trashes "most American intellectuals" and "black folk . . . in public lectures."[47] Alternatively, one may consider the long stream-of-consciousness footnote in Fred Moten's *Black and Blur* that doubled as a poetic game of *Jeopardy*. If the answer is "the Great Tribunal of Rational Men, The National-Cosmopolitan Star Chamber," Moten phrased his response in the form of the question, "to whom is Gilroy speaking . . . who the fuck does he think he's talking to?"[48] Yet such interventions seem to tell us as much about Dyson's role within an American punditocracy, and Moten's position within the Great Tribunal of Black Critical Thought or the

University of Minnesota Press / Duke University Press star chamber, as about Gilroy's role within academic and media establishments in contemporary Europe that are, rhetorically at least, committed to equity, diversity, and inclusion.

In moving between analog and print archives and digital cultures, I have collected evidence in *Thinking While Black* for scholars who wish to situate Paul Gilroy within what may be termed a Black postmodernist intellectual "tradition" (elucidating, for example, Gilroy's desire to unmoor tradition from merely closed or simple tradition, and assert the complex, dynamic potency of Black Atlantic and diasporic cultures that are determinedly "non-traditional" traditions[49]). I have also assembled material that may permit researchers to locate Armond White within a Black conservative intellectual tradition that includes some high-profile libertarian figures who rhetorically target a range of imagined fifth columnists (political correctness, cultural Marxism, and so on).[50] Above all, however, I have been struck by the determination of these idiosyncratic writers, and the rebel generation to which they belong, to complicate the progressive or conservative camps that academics, journalists, and politicians repeatedly frame as dichotomous alternatives. Gilroy's progressive campaigns against neoliberalism and privatization, for example, have been accompanied with notes about the quiet virtues of rambling and an "appreciation of nature";[51] discomfort with calls for safe spaces on university campuses that he associates with cheap, therapeutic approaches to race thinking rather than richer, healthier challenges to racism;[52] and Adornian comments about the dangers of listening to bad music and watching bad music videos, which share some discordant affinities with conservative pundits on FOX News.[53] Similarly, White's broadsides against "secular progressives" for a conservative platform in the twenty-first century remains remarkably similar to the anti-liberal rhetoric he developed for the radical and countercultural *South End* in the 1970s and the resistance aesthetics of his dissonant, against-the-grain criticism in the 1980s and '90s.

In White's ability to antagonize cinephiles and academics— as well as his overgeneralized attacks on political correctness, puritanical mores, and "cancel culture"—and Gilroy's willingness to test the boundaries of polite academic discourse, we have access to two related yet distinct approaches to the writing of cultural histories and the calculation of political choices. Rather than spend an inordinate amount of time and space quibbling about their tone, I have considered it more productive to scratch beneath the surface of the inevitable omissions and exaggerations in their attempts to illuminate the ongoing search for ideal communicative moments between artists and their audiences. In attending to White's fulsome praise of Kanye West and vigorous prosecution of Steve McQueen, for example, this book has reconstructed the political commitments and spiritual beliefs of a critic who believes that secular elites threaten to flood a 1970s protest ethic with nihilism and cynicism. Delving beyond Gilroy's critical support for McQueen and healthy skepticism about West's public persona, it has recorded the efforts of a thinker to map the politics and poetics of Black Atlantic cultures that overflow from the containers that organized religion, the modern state, and consumer capitalism provide for them.

There is a danger that studies of artists and thinkers support the uncritical celebration of heroic figures whose authority we should respect. Such celebration may result in the ahistorical claiming of radicals as guides for contemporary activists struggling against a changing same of anti-Black racism and xenophobia. It can lead to a summary dismissal of any evidence that taints messianic heroes, icons, and prophets of Black liberation. In turning to the stories of two unabashed humanists, I have sought to draw attention to agents and avatars of a rebel generation who associate disagreement, dissent, and iconoclasm about the ethics of circumventing liberal media and spreading out into mainstream spaces with solidarity, love, and collegiality rather than with barriers to them. Instead of focusing on what White, Gilroy, and their political and cultural generation can do to help contemporary activists and pundits celebrate or condemn the distribution of energy and interest around systemic racism, Afro-pessimism, and the Black Lives Matter movement, I have asked what successive generations can do to think with and through the work of soul rebels. Each generation may discover, fulfill, or betray its mission in relative opacity, but in carefully constituting and consulting an archive of seriously soulful intellectuals who have combined steadfast advocacy of lively and radical approaches to racism with a willingness to nimbly adopt new subjects and positions, we have access to precious, productive, and playful resources to translate the politically infused acts of pleasure of a rebel generation with a little less opacity and strained seriousness.

NOTES

Preface

1   To give one notable example, Mark Anthony Neal describes Harold Cruse, an African American writer whose work included vehemently anti-Caribbean rhetoric, as a father figure to a post–civil rights generation born after the March on Washington for jobs and freedom in 1963 in *Soul Babies: Black Popular Culture and the Post-Soul Aesthetic* (London: Routledge, 2002). Some implications of such a US-centric approach are evident in Neal's analysis of R. Kelly, which liberally borrows from Paul Gilroy's insights in *Against Race* but only chooses to cite a Chicago-born informant—rather than acknowledge Gilroy's planetary humanism—in its endnotes (pp. 17, 197n43). Revealingly, Neal's *Looking for Leroy* also reveals the pitfalls of national consciousness as it seeks to map the diverse and cosmopolitan roles chosen by African American musicians, directors, and actors without a concomitant interest in the creative artistry of non-American members of the African diaspora. When discussing, for example, the career of the African American actor Avery Brooks it does not focus on the American and extra-American characters he played. In contrast, it does not mention the non-American work of the Black British actor Idris Elba, and only mentions the fictional African American character Elba portrayed on HBO's *The Wire*. Mark Anthony Neal, *Looking for Leroy: Illegible Black Masculinities* (New York: New York University

Press, 2013). On Cruse's xenophobia, see Winston James, *Holding Aloft the Banner of Ethiopia* (New York: Verso, 1998), 262–91.

2   Linton Kwesi Johnson, "Riots, Rhymes and Reason," April 18, 2012, lintonkwesijohnson.com. Also see David Austin, *Dread Poetry and Freedom: Linton Kwesi Johnson and the Unfinished Revolution* (Toronto: Between the Lines, 2018).

3   Armond White, cited in Marc Jacobson, "No Kiss Kiss, All Bang Bang," *New York Magazine*, February 13, 2009.

4   Paul Gilroy, *Black Britain: A Photographic History* (London: SAQI, 2007), 248; Paul Gilroy, *The Black Atlantic: Modernity and Double Consciousness* (Cambridge, MA: Harvard University Press, 1993), 40.

5   Paul Gilroy, "Introduction: Race Is the Prism," in *Selected Writings on Race and Difference: Stuart Hall*, ed. Paul Gilroy and Ruth Wilson Gilmore (Durham, NC: Duke University Press, 2021), 16.

6   Phil Scraton, *Hillsborough—The Truth* (London: Random House, 2016).

7   "The Conservatives are polling *visible minorities* on same-sex marriage . . . the Tories see the same-sex message as a wedge they can drive between the Liberals and *immigrant Canadians* . . . appealing to the socially conservative attitudes of new arrivals" in *"the ethnic press."* John Ibbitson, "Same-Sex Will Smite Harper," *Globe and Mail*, February 18, 2005. Emphasis added. Also see Will Kymlicka, *Finding Our Way: Rethinking Ethnocultural Relations in Canada* (Toronto: Oxford University Press, 1998), 87; Daniel McNeil, *Sex and Race in the Black Atlantic: Mulatto Devils and Multiracial Messiahs* (London: Routledge, 2010), 69.

8   David Cronenberg, *Free Thinking*, BBC Radio 4, October 8, 2014. Also see Stephen Harper, Closing Remarks, G20 Summit, Pittsburgh, September 25, 2009.

9   Stuart Hall, "Race and Moral Panics in Post-war Britain," in *Five Views of Multi-Racial Britain* (London: Commission for Racial Equality, 1978).

10 Carol Tator and Frances Henry, *Racial Profiling in Canada: Challenging the Myth of "a Few Bad Apples"* (Toronto: University of Toronto Press, 2006), 141. Frances Henry was appointed to the Royal Society of Canada in 1989 and received an award for excellence in race relations from the Ministry for Multiculturalism and Citizenship in 1991. In biographical statements, she describes herself as one of Canada's leading experts in the study of racism and anti-racism and a pioneer of research in this field. Carol Tator was president and acting executive director of the Urban Alliance on Race Relations for many years and assisted all three levels of government, universities and colleges, all of the former boards of education in Metro Toronto, humanservice organizations, and various other public-sector agencies as a private race relations consultant. Frances Henry and Carol Tator, "Contributions and Challenges of Addressing Discursive Racism in the Canadian Media," *Canadian Journal of Communication* 34 (2009): 711–13.

11 Frances Henry and Carol Tator, *The Colour of Democracy: Racism in Canadian Society* (Toronto: Nelson, 2009), 235. Also see Daniel McNeil, "Even Canadians Find It a Bit Boring: A Report on the Banality of Multiculturalism," *Canadian Journal of Communication* 46, no. 3 (2021): 403–29; Daniel McNeil and Chris Russill, "'Multicultural Snake Oil' and Black Cultural Criticism: A Conversation with Daniel McNeil," *Canadian Journal of Communication* 46, no. 3 (2021): 663–87.

12 Frances Henry, "Black Power in Montreal," *Literary Review of Canada* 21, no. 6 (2013).

13 Mark Fisher, "Precarity and Paternalism," *K-Punk*, February 11, 2010.

14 Peter Hudson and Aaron Kamugisha, "On Black Canadian Thought," *The C.L.R. James Journal*, 20, no. 1/2 (2014): 3–20; Katherine McKittrick, *Dear Science and Other Stories* (Durham, NC: Duke University Press, 2021).

15 Armond White, "Fellini's 'Borey Lyndon,'" *South End*, April 5, 1977; Paul Gilroy, "Artist and Empire: The Long Nineteenth Century," Tate Britain and the School of Arts at Birkbeck University of London, November 25, 2015.

16 Ben Miller and Christian Jacobs, "Call for Papers: Doing the Global Intellectual History of Social Movements," Freie Universität Berlin / Humboldt-Universität Berlin, August 19–21, 2021.

17 Paul Gilroy, "Threatening Pleasures," *Sight and Sound* 1, no. 4 (1991).

18 Editorial, *South End*, September 21, 1967. There were approximately 2,500–3,500 Black students at Wayne State University during the 1960s. This meant that Wayne had a higher Black enrollment than all of the schools of the Big Ten and Ivy League combined. It also meant that, in a city that was rapidly on its way to a Black majority, less than 10 percent of the student population at Wayne was Black. James A. Geschwender, "The League of Revolutionary Black Workers: Problems Confronting Black Marxist-Leninist Organizations," *Journal of Ethnic Studies* 2, no. 3 (1974).

19 Editorial, *South End*, September 28, 1972.

20 Lewis Gordon, "Black Intellectual Tradition," in *Encyclopedia of American Studies*, ed. Simon J. Bronner (Baltimore: Johns Hopkins University Press, 2018); Laura Chrisman, "Journeying to Death: Gilroy's Black Atlantic," *Race & Class* 39, no. 2 (1997).

21 Armond White, *The Resistance: Ten Years of Pop Culture That Shook the World* (New York: Overlook Press, 1995), 310.

22 Frantz Fanon, *The Wretched of the Earth*, trans. Richard Philcox (New York: Grove Press, 2004), 99, 121.

23 Paul Gilroy, "12 Years a Slave: In Our 'Post-racial' Age the Legacy of Slavery Lives On," *Observer*, November 10, 2013.

24 Paul Gilroy, *Darker than Blue: On the Moral Economies of Black Atlantic Culture* (Cambridge, MA: Harvard University Press, 2010), 122; Armond White, "Discourteous Discourse," *New York Press*, September 28, 2010.

1. Theories in Motion

1   Owen Glieberman, "Why Armond White Got Kicked Out of the Critics Circle," *Entertainment Weekly*, January 13, 2014.

2   Vikki Bell, "Historical Memory, Global Movements and Violence: Paul Gilroy and Arjun Appadurai in Conversation," *Theory, Culture and Society* 16, no. 2 (1999): 23; Paul Gilroy, "A Dialogue on the Human," in *Retrieving the Human: Reading Paul Gilroy*, ed. Rebecka Rutledge Fisher and Jay Garcia (Albany, NY: SUNY Press, 2014), 216.

3   Tommie Shelby and Paul Gilroy, "Cosmopolitanism, Blackness, and Utopia," *Transition* 98 (2008): 123.

4   Gilroy, "A Dialogue on the Human," 210.

5   Jonathan Flatley, *Affective Mapping: Melancholia and the Politics of Modernism* (Cambridge, MA: Harvard University Press, 2008), 25, 26. Also see Raymond Williams, *The Long Revolution* (London: Chatto & Windus, 1961), 64.

6   Gilroy frequently uses the phrase "it bears repetition" in his work. See, for example, Gilroy, *The Black Atlantic*, 105, 155, 218, 223; "Exer(or)cising Power: Black Bodies in the Black Public Sphere," in *Dance in the City*, ed. Helen Thomas (London: Palgrave Macmillan, 1997), 24, 32; *Against Race: Imagining Political Culture Beyond the Color Line* (Cambridge, MA: Harvard University Press, 2000), 59, 165, 196, 237; "After the Great White Error ... the Great Black Mirage," in *Race, Nature, and the Politics of Difference*, ed. Donald S. Moore, Jake Kosek, and Anand Pandian (Durham, NC: Duke University Press, 2003), 90; *Darker than Blue*, 30, 33, 71, 77, 82, 137; "Shameful History: The Social Life of Races and the Postcolonial Archive," *Moving Worlds: A Journal of Transcultural Writing* 11, no. 2 (2011): 25, 30; "'My Britain Is Fuck All': Zombie Multiculturalism and the Race Politics of Citizenship," *Identities* 19, no. 4 (2012): 384; "Multiculture and the Negative Dialectics of Conviviality," in *Retrieving the Human,* ed. Fisher and Garcia, 100; *Selected Writings on Race and Difference*, 9, 14.

7   Paul Gilroy, "To Be Real: The Dissident Forms of Black Expressive Culture," in *Let's Get It On: The Politics of Black Performance*, ed. Catherine Egwu (Seattle: Bay Press, 1995), 21; *Against Race*, 81.

8   Armond White, "REAL Black Movies Needed," *South End*, November 20, 1972.

9   Daniel McNeil, "The Last Honest Film Critic in America: Armond White and the Children of James Baldwin," in *Film Criticism in the Digital Age*, ed. Mattias Frey and Cecilia Sayad (New Brunswick, NJ: Rutgers University Press, 2015), 61–78; "Ethnicity, Ethicalness, Excellence: Armond White's All-American Humanism," *African American Arts: Activism, Aesthetics, and*

Futurity, ed. Sharrell D. Luckett (New Brunswick, NJ: Rutgers University Press, 2020), 69–88.

10   Pauline Kael, back-of-the-dust-jacket endorsement for White, *The Resistance*; Jeffrey Ferguson, *The Sage of Sugar Hill* (New Haven, CT: Yale University Press, 2008); Ralph Ellison, *Shadow and Act* (New York: Vintage, 2011); Albert Murray, *The Omni-Americans: New Perspectives on Black Experience and American Culture* (New York: EP Dutton, 1970); Malcolm X, *The End of White World Supremacy: Four Speeches* (New York: Simon and Schuster, 2020); Harold Cruse, *The Crisis of the Negro Intellectual: A Historical Analysis of the Failure of Black Leadership* (New York: New York Review of Books, 2005); James Baldwin, *Collected Essays* (Library of America, 1998).

11   Stanley Crouch, "Aunt Medea," *New Republic*, October 19, 1987; Armond White, "Can't Trust It," *City Arts*, October 16, 2013.

12   Adolph Reed Jr., "What Are the Drums Saying, Booker?," *Village Voice*, April 11, 1995; White, *The Resistance*, 310.

13   Cornel West, "Pity the Sad Legacy of Barack Obama," *Guardian*, January 9, 2017; Adolph Reed Jr., "Obama No," *Progressive*, April 28, 2008; Armond White, "Pursuit of Crappyness," *New York Press*, July 9, 2008.

14   Eric Lott, "Public Image Limited," *Transition* 68 (1995): 65.

15   Armond White, "To the Best, Their Due," *City Sun*, December 17, 1986; "A Lesson in Ethnic Ethics," *City Sun*, April 9, 1986; "Echobelly Shows Britpop the First This Time," *City Sun*, March 20, 1996.

16   Gilroy, *The Black Atlantic*, 33. See also Paul Gilroy, "Nationalism, History and Ethnic Absolutism," *History Workshop Journal* 30, no. 1 (1990): 114–20; "Diaspora," *Paragraph* 17, no. 3 (1994): 207–12; "Diaspora and the Detours of Identity," in *Identity and Difference*, ed. Kath Woodward (London: SAGE, 1997), 301–46.

17   Lott, "Public Image Limited," 61.

18   After claiming that White is "as unparochial as anyone writing," Eric Lott confuses Manchester and London and mixes up BBC and Channel 4, which is roughly comparable to a buccaneering British critic confusing Boston and New York and mixing up PBS and ABC. Eric Lott, *The Disappearing Liberal Intellectual* (New York: Basic Books, 2006), 108, 111–12, 128.

19   Thomas Delapa, "Review of *Film Criticism in the Digital Age*," *Journal of Film and Video* 69, no. 2 (2017): 54–56.

20   Armond White, "Basque to the Future," *Film Comment* 24, no. 1 (January 1988).

21   "Casting the Holy Ghost: Reading Film and Identity with Armond White and Daniel McNeil," *Vitamin D Podcast*, August 22, 2016.

22   Armond White, "Yes, and It Counts: Public Enemy's Mad Rhymes for Mad Times," *City Sun*, February 15, 1994.

23   Richard H. King, "Traditions, Genealogies, and Influences: Gilroy's Intellectual Roots and Routes," in *Retrieving the Human*, ed. Fisher and Garcia.

24   Paul Williams, *Paul Gilroy* (London: Routledge, 2013).

25   Paul Gilroy, Tony Sandset, Sindre Bangstad, and Gard Ringen Høibjerg, "A Diagnosis of Contemporary Forms of Racism, Race and Nationalism: A Conversation with Professor Paul Gilroy," *Cultural Studies* 33, no. 2 (2019): 173–97.

26   Paul Gilroy, "Travelling Theorist," *New Statesman & Society*, February 12, 1993.

27   David Widgery, *Beating Time: Riot 'n' Race 'n' Rock 'n' Roll* (London: Chatto & Windus, 1986).

28   Gilroy, "A Dialogue on the Human," 208.

29   Eric Lott, "Review of *The Black Atlantic: Modernity and the Double Consciousness*," *Nation*, May 2, 1994. Also see, for example, Jim Cullen, "Review of *Darker than Blue: On the Moral Economies of Black Atlantic Cultures*," History News Network, January 24, 2010.

30   Gilroy, *The Black Atlantic*, 17; C.L.R. James, *Notes on Dialectics* (London: Allison and Busby, 1980).

31   Gilroy, *The Black Atlantic*, 122; "Diaspora," 211–22.

32   Paul Gilroy, *Small Acts: Thoughts on the Politics of Black Cultures* (London: Serpent's Tail, 1993), 113–14n3.

33   Armond White, "Political View of a Mafia King," *South End*, February 7, 1975; "Zwick on His Feet: Fighting Black," *Film Comment*, January 1990; "Underground Man," *Film Comment*, May 1991.

34   Gilroy, *Small Acts*, 14; "Introduction: Race Is the Prism," 5.

35   Chrisman, "Journeying to Death"; Adrian Martin, "Illuminating the Shadows: Film Criticism in Focus," panel discussion, Mary and Leigh Block Museum of Art, Northwestern University, May 4, 2012; Vince Mancini, "2010: The Year in Armond White Quotes," *Filmdrunk*, December 29, 2010; "Film Criticism or Op-Ed Piece: Armond White and the Smugness of Torture Victims," *Filmbrain*, June 29, 2006.

36   Armond White, "Regression of Movie Art Award Winner," *South End*, July 21, 1977; "Lucas Lacks the Force," *South End*, June 8, 1977; "Weekend Film," *South End*, July 18, 1977.

37   Paul Gilroy, "Record Reviews," *City Limits*, September 10, 1982; June 17, 1983.

38   Richard Iton, *In Search of the Black Fantastic: Politics & Popular Culture in the Post–Civil Rights Era* (Oxford: Oxford University Press, 2008); Michael Denning, *Culture in the Age of Three Worlds* (London: Verso, 2004); Emily J. Lordi, *The Meaning of Soul: Black Music and Resilience since the 1960s* (Durham, NC: Duke University Press, 2020).

39   Gilroy, *Small Acts*, 207. Also see Gilroy, *The Black Atlantic*, 200.

40 White, *The Resistance.*

41 Steve Biko, *I Write What I Like: Selected Writings* (Chicago: University of Chicago Press, 2002).

42 Huey Copeland, *Bound to Appear: Art, Slavery, and the Site of Blackness in Multicultural America* (Chicago: University of Chicago Press, 2013); Eddie Chambers, *Black Artists in British Art: A History since the 1950s* (London: I.B. Tauris, 2014).

43 Armond White, *The Resistance,* 310; "Whose Black Cinema Is it Anyway?," *City Sun,* April 27, 1994. Also see Armond White, "History Gets Lost in The Matrix," *First of the Month,* June 2013.

44 Adam Begley, "Black Studies' New Star: Henry Louis Gates Jr.," *New York Times,* April 1, 1990; Cornel West, *Race Matters* (Boston, Beacon Press, 2001), xii; bell hooks, *Class Matters: Where We Stand* (New York: Routledge, 2012).

45 Gilroy, "Diaspora," 212; "A Dialogue on the Human," 208.

46 White, *The Resistance,* 310.

47 John Semley, "Armond White Is the Kanye West of Film Criticism," *Now Magazine,* January 7, 2014.

48 Gilroy, "A Dialogue on the Human," 210.

49 Jackson Lears, "One Hundred Seconds," *Raritan* 40, no. 1 (2020): ii–v.

50 Barack Obama, *Dreams from My Father: A Story of Race and Inheritance* (New York: Time, 1995), xv.

51 Paul Gilroy, "Analogues of Mourning, Mourning the Analog," in *Stars Don't Stand Still in the Sky,* ed. Karen Kelly and Evelyn McDonnell (New York: New York University Press, 1999), 263.

52 Armond White, *New Position: The Prince Chronicles* (New York: Resistance Works, WDC, 2016), 109.

2. Black and British

1 Paul Gilroy in *Twilight City* (dir. Reece Auguiste, 1989).

2 Daryl Cumber, "Beryl Gilroy: A Bio-Literary Overview," *MaComère* 1, no. 1 (1998): 1–3; Peter D. Fraser, "Obituary: Beryl Gilroy," *Guardian,* April 18, 2001.

3 Gilroy, *Black Britain,* 81.

4 Gilroy, Sandset, Bangstad, and Høibjerg, "A Diagnosis of Contemporary Forms of Racism, Race and Nationalism."

5 Gilroy, *The Black Atlantic,* 200.

6 Gilroy, *Small Acts,* 207; Richard Green and Monique Guillory, "Question of a 'Soulful Style': An Interview with Paul Gilroy," in *Soul: Black Power, Politics, and Pleasure,* ed. Richard Green and Monique Guillory (New York: New York University Press, 1998), 252; Gilroy, *Darker than Blue,* 122.

7 Gilroy, *The Black Atlantic,* 86.

8   Gilroy, *Black Britain*, 197.

9   Paul Gilroy, "Steppin' out of Babylon—Race, Class and Autonomy," in *The Empire Strikes Back: Race and Racism in 70s Britain*, ed. Centre for Contemporary Cultural Studies (CCCS) (London: Hutchinson & Co, 1982), 278.

10 Cyril Osborne, Speech to the House of Commons, January 17, 1961, Parliamentary Debates, Commons, Vol. 634, 1960–61, col. 1933. In the pages of the *Spectator*, Osborne also declared his opposition to the creation of a "chocolate-coloured Afro-Asian mixed society." C. Osborne, *Spectator*, December 4, 1964.

11 Conservative Central Office News Service Press Release, September 29, 1967, Bodleian Library, Oxford, CPA, PPB 16.

12 Patrick Cosgrave, *The Lives of Enoch Powell* (London: Bodley Head, 1989), 228.

13 Andrew Roth, *Enoch Powell: Tory Tribune* (London, Macdonald & Co. 1970), 341.

14 Jenny Bourne, "The Beatification of Enoch Powell," *Race and Class* 49, no. 4 (2008): 85–86.

15 Simon Heffer, *Like the Roman: The Life of Enoch Powell* (London: Faber and Faber, 1998), 448. On the impact and legacy of Powell's speech see, for example, Andrew Crines, Tim Heppell, and Michael Hill, "Enoch Powell's 'Rivers of Blood' Speech: A Rhetorical Political Analysis," *British Politics* 11 (2016): 72–94; Sarfraz Manzoor, "Black Britain's Darkest Hour," *Observer*, February 24, 2008; Conor Friedersdorf, "Learning from 1968's Leading Anti-immigration Alarmist," *Atlantic*, April 23, 2018; Camilla Schofield, *Enoch Powell and the Making of Postcolonial Britain* (Cambridge: Cambridge University Press, 2013).

16 Powell's concern about "importing" Black Power was also expressed in letters and conversations. Writing in the *Daily Telegraph* on December 23, 1967, he complained about the BBC's decision to broadcast an interview with Stokely Carmichael. In his notes on a meeting with Enoch Powell on November 6, 1969, Michael Strachan recorded Powell's belief that a Black Power movement would soon emerge in the UK.

17 "An Evil Speech," *Times*, April 22, 1968.

18 Stuart Hall, "The Great Moving Right Show," *Marxism Today* 23, no. 1 (1979): 14–20.

19 Paul Gilroy, *There Ain't No Black in the Union Jack* (London: Unwin Hyman, 1987) 206–7.

20 Gilroy, *Small Acts*, 158.

21 Gilroy, *The Black Atlantic*, 40.

22 Gilroy, *Small Acts*, 207; "Paul Gilroy on Two Electrifying Performances by the Voices of East Harlem," in *Epiphanies: Life-Changing Encounters with Music*, ed. Tony Herrington (London: Strange Attractor, 2015), 69–71.

23   Gilroy, *Darker than Blue*, 147.

24   Green and Guillory, "Question of a 'Soulful Style,'" 252.

25   Gilroy, *Darker than Blue*, 127.

26   Paul Gilroy, "Convention on Modern Liberty," Institute for Education, February 28, 2009.

27   Gilroy, *Small Acts*, 12.

28   Max Farrar, "Paul Gilroy—In Conversation," *darkmatter*, May 7, 2007.

29   Gilroy, *There Ain't No Black in the Union Jack*, 151.

30   Gerry Dawson (David Widgery), "The Politics of Pornography," *Socialist Worker*, September 24, 1971.

31   David Renton, "The Life and Politics of David Widgery," *Left History: An Interdisciplinary Journal of Historical Inquiry and Debate* 8, no. 1 (2002).

32   At least thirty-one Black people were killed in racist murders in England between 1976 and 1981. Widgery, *Beating Time*, 17, 40.

33   Renton, "The Life and Politics of David Widgery"; Paul Foot, "David Widgery," *New Left Review* 196 (1992).

34   Widgery, *Beating Time*, 61.

35   Widgery, *Beating Time*, 62.

36   Margaret Thatcher, *World in Action*, ITV, January 30, 1978. Thatcher's stance was widely interpreted as a sign of the Conservative Party appealing to voters who may have considered supporting the National Front, especially when the National Front's vote plummeted in the 1978 local elections.

37   *Resistance through Rituals: Youth Subcultures in Post-War Britain* was first published in 1975 as Working Papers in Cultural Studies 7/8.

38   Farrar, "Paul Gilroy—In Conversation."

39   CCCS Mugging Group, "Some Notes on the Relationship between the Societal Control Culture and the News Media, and the Construction of a Law and Order Campaign," in *Resistance through Rituals: Youth Subcultures in Post-War Britain*, ed. Stuart Hall and Tony Jefferson (London: Hutchinson, 1976); Stuart Hall, Chas Critcher, Tony Jefferson, John Clarke, and Brian Roberts, *Policing the Crisis: Mugging, the State and Law and Order* (London: Macmillan, 1978).

40   Dick Hebdige, "Reggae, Rastas and Rudies," in *Resistance through Rituals*, ed. Hall and Jefferson.

41   Iain Chambers, "A Strategy for Living," in *Resistance through Rituals*, ed. Hall and Jefferson.

42   John Clarke, "The Skinheads and the Magical Recovery of Community," in *Resistance through Rituals*, ed. Hall and Jefferson.

43   Angela McRobbie and Jenny Garber, "Girls and Subcultures," in *Resistance through Rituals*, ed. Hall and Jefferson.

44   Graham Murdock and Robin McCron, "Consciousness of Class and Consciousness of Generation," in *Resistance through Rituals*, ed. Hall and Jefferson.

45 Paul Corrigan and Simon Frith, "The Politics of Youth Culture," in *Resistance through Rituals*, ed. Hall and Jefferson.

46 Dermot Kavanagh, *Different Class: The Story of Laurie Cunningham* (London: Unbound, 2017).

47 Steven Seidman, *Posters, Propaganda, and Persuasion in Election Campaigns around the World and through History* (London: Peter Lang, 2008), 153.

48 Gilroy, *There Ain't No Black in the Union Jack*, 65.

49 Paul Gilroy, "Leafleteer's Prose," *Race Today Review* 1984, 37.

50 Paul Gilroy, "Preface," in *The Empire Strikes Back*, ed. CCCS, 7.

51 Paul Gilroy, "C4—Bridgehead or Bantustan," *Screen* 24, no. 4–5 (1983): 131.

52 Gilroy, "C4—Bridgehead or Bantustan," 132.

53 Robert Miles, "Les jeunes d'origine immigrée en Grande-Bretagne," *Les Temps Modernes* 540–41 (1991): 133–65; Tariq Modood, "Political Blackness and British Asians," *Sociology* 28, no. 4 (1994): 859–76.

54 Geoffrey K. Fry, *The Politics of the Thatcher Revolution: An Interpretation of British Politics, 1979–1990* (London: Springer, 2008), 169.

55 Owen Hatherley, "The Government of London," *New Left Review* 122 (2020): 81–114.

56 John Gyford, *The Politics of Local Socialism* (London: Taylor & Francis, 1985), 19.

57 Gilroy was a research officer for the GLC between January 1982 and August 1985. *Emergency* ran from 1982 to 1984.

58 Max Farrar, "Love and Dread in Modern Times," *Emergency* 1, no. 2 (1983/84): 1–8.

59 Gilroy, *Small Acts*, 104. Emphasis original. Also see Gilroy, *The Black Atlantic*, 159.

60 Val Wilmer, *As Serious as Your Life: Black Music and the Free Jazz Revolution, 1957–77* (London: Serpent's Tail, 1977).

61 "A Portrait of Val Wilmer," BBC Radio 3, September 4, 2019.

62 Hilda Kean, "The Transformation of Political and Cultural Space," in *London from Punk to Blair*, ed. Joe Kerr and Andrew Gibson (London: Reaktion Books, 2012).

63 Paul Gilroy, "Singles," *City Limits*, June 17, 1983.

64 Paul Gilroy, "Review of Claus Ogerman / Michael Brecker 'Cityscape,'" *City Limits*, September 10, 1982.

65 Paul Gilroy, "Afrika Bambaataa Live Show," *City Limits*, November 19, 1982.

66 Paul Gilroy, "Review of Linval Thompson, 'Baby Father,'" *City Limits*, March 11, 1983; "Recent 45s," *City Limits*, July 22, 1983.

67 Paul Gilroy, "Review of Michael Smith, 'Mi Cyan Believe It,'" *City Limits*, November 19, 1982.

68 Paul Gilroy, "Review of Sly Dunbar, 'Sly-go-ville,'" *City Limits*, August 20, 1982.

69 Paul Gilroy, "Review of Barbara Mason, 'Another Man,'" *City Limits*, January 20, 1984.

70 Paul Gilroy, "Review of Grandmaster Flash and the Furious Five, 'The Message,'" *City Limits*, October 22, 1982.

71 Hannah Arendt, *The Human Condition* (Chicago: University of Chicago Press, 1958).

72 Gilroy, *There Ain't No Black in the Union Jack*, 219.

73 Gilroy, *There Ain't No Black in the Union Jack*, 285.

74 Paul Gilroy, "Mixing It: How Is British National Identity Defined and How Do Race and Nation Intersect," *Sight and Sound* 3, no. 9 (1993): 24–25.

75 Gilroy, *There Ain't No Black in the Union Jack*, 105, 215, 269.

76 Paul Gilroy, "There's a Riot Going On," *Emergency* 1, no. 2 (1983/84): 56–60.

77 Linton Kwesi Johnson, "Five Nights of Bleeding," *Selected Poems* (London: Penguin, 2006).

78 Gilroy, *There Ain't No Black in the Union Jack*, 221.

79 Gilroy, *Black Britain*, 219.

80 Gilroy, "C4—Bridgehead or Bantustan?," 136.

81 Gilroy, "There's a Riot Going On."

82 "'Community' Relations: A Non-Starter," *Race Today*, April 1973.

83 Gilroy, *There Ain't No Black in the Union Jack*, 147; "Introduction: Race Is the Prism," 5.

84 Lee Bridges and Paul Gilroy, "Striking Back," *Marxism Today*, June 1982: 34–35.

85 Lee Bridges, "Review of *The Empire Strikes Back*," *Race & Class* 25, no. 1 (1983): 99–100.

86 Lee Bridges, "Review of *The Empire Strikes Back*," *Race & Class* 25, no. 2 (1983): 94–95.

87 Paul Gilroy, "Police and Thieves," in *The Empire Strikes Back*, ed. CCCS, 174.

88 Paul Gilroy, *There Ain't No Black in the Union Jack*, 51; "Not Yet Humanism or the Non-Jewish Jew Becomes the Non-Humanistic Humanist," in *Conflicting Humanities*, ed. Rosi Braidotti and Paul Gilroy (London: Bloomsbury, 2016), 96.

89 Colin Prescod, "Review of *There Ain't No Black in the Union Jack*," *Race & Class* 29, no. 4 (1988): 97–100.

90 Ambalavaner Sivanandan, "All That Melts into Air Is Solid: The Hokum of New Times," *Race & Class* 31, no. 3 (1989): 1–30.

91 Gilroy, *There Ain't No Black in the Union Jack*, xxx.

92 Gilroy, "Steppin' out of Babylon," 302.

93 Gilroy, *The Black Atlantic*, 69; *Darker than Blue*, 2.

3. A Movie-Struck Kid from Detroit

1   Suzanne E. Smith, *Dancing in the Street: Motown and the Cultural Politics of Detroit* (Cambridge, MA: Harvard University Press, 2001), 10–11.

2   Stephen M. Ward, "An Ending and a Beginning: James Boggs, C.L.R. James, and *The American Revolution*," *Souls* 13, no. 3 (2011): 279–302.

3   James Boggs, John Williams, and Charles Johnson, "The Myth and Irrationality of Black Capitalism," James and Grace Lee Boggs Papers, Box 4, Folder 15, Walter P. Reuther Library, Wayne State University. Also see Mark Jay and Philip Conklin, *A People's History of Detroit* (Durham, NC: Duke University Press, 2020); Austin, *Dread Poetry and Freedom*, 212–14.

4   See, for example, John Cosby Jr., "How U Sound Motown," *Inner City Voice* 1, no. 3 (December 15, 1967): 11.

5   Iton, *In Search of the Black Fantastic*, 98.

6   For more on *Finally Got the News* see Dan Georgakas and Marvin Surkin, *Detroit, I Do Mind Dying: A Study in Urban Revolution* (New York: St. Martin's Press, 1975); Frederic Jameson, "Cognitive Mapping," in *Marxism and the Interpretation of Culture*, ed. Cary Nelson and Lawrence Grossberg (Chicago: University of Illinois Press, 1988), 347–57; Fred Moten, *In the Break: The Aesthetics of the Black Radical Tradition* (Minneapolis: University of Minnesota Press, 2003); Flatley, *Affective Mapping*.

7   Armond White, "Hollywood Meets the CAB [Coalition Against Blaxploitation]," *South End*, November 9, 1972. Many Black DJs would boycott Motown songs, with the exception of Stevie Wonder's, after rumors that Berry Gordy, the owner of Motown, had claimed that he wouldn't "give a damn" if Black DJs never played any of his records.

8   Glieberman, "Why Armond White Got Kicked Out of the Critics Circle."

9   Georgakas and Surkin, *Detroit, I Do Mind Dying*.

10   John Watson, "Black Editor: An Interview," *Radical America* 2, no. 4 (July–August 1968): 30–38; Herb Boyd, *Black Detroit: A People's History of Self-Determination* (New York: HarperCollins, 2017), 207. These militant organizations were systematically infiltrated and placed under surveillance by the Detroit Police Department's Red Squad, which increased from six members in 1958 to seventy in 1968.

11   Georgakas and Surkin, *Detroit, I Do Mind Dying*, 28.

12   "Soul Power or Workers Power?: The Rise and Fall of the League of Revolutionary Black Workers," *Workers Vanguard* 36 (January 18, 1974), transcribed by Paul Saba, Encyclopedia of Anti-Revisionism On-Line, marxists.org.

13   Dan Georgakas, "Letter from America," May 9, 1969 [republished in *Viewpoint Magazine*, November 20, 2018].

14   Editorial, *South End*, September 21, 1967.

15   Georgakas and Surkin, *Detroit, I Do Mind Dying*, 71.

16   Heather Ann Thompson, *Whose Detroit?: Politics, Labor, and Race in a Modern American City* (Ithaca, NY: Cornell University Press, 2017), 129.

17   Thompson, *Whose Detroit?*, 168, 195–96.

18   Jacobson, "No Kiss Kiss, All Bang Bang."

19   Pauline Kael, "Trash, Art, and the Movies," *Harper's*, February 1969. Also see Leo Charney, "Common People with Common Feelings: Pauline Kael, James Agee, and the Public Sphere of Popular Film Criticism," *Cinémas: Revue d'études cinématographiques / Journal of Film Studies* 6, no. 2–3 (1996): 113–26; Sanford Schwartz, "Introduction," in *The Age of Movies: Selected Writings of Pauline Kael* (Library of America, 2011); Jonathan Kirshner, "When Critics Mattered," *Boston Review*, March 1, 2012.

20   Ray Sawhill and Polly Frost, "Kaeleidoscope," *Interview Magazine*, April 1989.

21   Pauline Kael, "Why Are Movies So Bad?: Or, the Numbers," *New Yorker*, June 23, 1980.

22   Pauline Kael, *Reeling: Film Writings, 1972–1975* (Boston: Little, Brown, 1976), 329.

23   Pauline Kael, *The Citizen Kane Book: Raising Kane* (Boston: Little, Brown 1971), 15.

24   Sawhill and Frost, "Kaeleidoscope."

25   Pauline Kael, *I Lost It at the Movies: Film Writing, 1954–1965* (Boston: Little, Brown, 1965), 78. Also see Michał Oleszczyk, "Hooked & Gridlocked: Notes on Pauline Kael's Provincialism," *Cineaste*, Summer 2015; Ed Sikov, "Circles, Squares, and Pick Triangles: Confessions of a Gay Cultist," in Andrew Sarris and Emanuel Levy, *Citizen Sarris, American Film Critic: Essays in Honor of Andrew Sarris* (Scarecrow Press, 2001).

26   Editorial, *South End*, September 28, 1972.

27   Sweet T Williams, "White, Liberal Press Dangerous Says Critic," *South End*, September 1, 1977.

28   Armond White, "Hester Street; Honest Effort," *South End*, January 20, 1976.

29   Armond White, "Political View of a Mafia King," *South End*, February 7, 1975.

30   Armond White, "Jeremy Is Tolerable," *South End*, October 3, 1973; "Weekend Film Clips," *South End*, November 9, 1973; "Summer Wishes Winter Dreams," *South End*, March 6, 1974; "Year of Good Acting in Films of 1976," *South End*, January 11, 1977; "Movie Follies," *South End*, May 31, 1977.

31   Armond White, "Providence: Cultural Fraud at the DFT [Detroit Film Festival]," *South End*, July 28, 1977.

32   Armond White, "The Nelson Affair," *South End*, April 19, 1973; "A Bridge Too Far; Tactical Blunder," July 5, 1977.

33   Armond White, "Sheila Levine Is a Living Joke," *South End*, February

18, 1975; "Nouveaumania: New Look at American Culture," *South End*, November 6, 1975.

34 Armond White, "Badlands," *South End*, May 28, 1974.

35 In the opening scenes of *Nashville* (dir. Robert Altman, 1975), Opal, a reporter from the BBC, observes a Black choir from Fisk University singing "Do you believe in Jesus?" in a recording studio, and remarks:

> Look at that. That rhythm is fantastic.
> It's funny . . . You can tell it's come down in the genes . . . through ages and ages and hundreds of years, but it's there. I mean, take off those robes and one is in . . . darkest Africa. I can just see their naked, frenzied bodies . . . dancing to the beat of . . .
> Do they carry on like that in church?

36 Armond White, "Film Retrospect 1975," *South End*, January 12, 1976.

37 Armond White, "The Day of the Dolphin," *South End*, January 24, 1974; "Gone Is Back," *South End*, May 7, 1973; "Two Older Films in Town," *South End*, August 1, 1974; "Burn! Bravura and Brilliant," *South End*, November 7, 1974.

38 Armond White, "3 Women: Altman Atrocity," *South End*, May 5, 1977.

39 Pauline Kael, "The Current Cinema," *New Yorker*, September 30, 1972.

40 Pauline Kael, "The Current Cinema," *New Yorker*, November 4, 1972.

41 White, "Hollywood Meets the CAB."

42 Armond White, "Shape of Things (Black) to Come," *South End*, November 21, 1972; "Sold/Soul Brother," *South End*, December 6, 1972.

43 Armond White, "Sounder: Above and Beyond," *South End*, January 12, 1973.

44 W.E.B. Du Bois, *The Souls of Black Folk* (Chicago: A C McClurg & Co., 1903), 3.

45 Justin Desmangles, "Interview with Armond White," *New Day Jazz*, KDVS 90.3 FM, March 16, 2014; Armond White, "Kanye West's Musical Rebellion," *National Review Online*, April 30, 2018.

46 Armond White, "Ali, the Greatest," *South End*, May 25, 1977.

47 Armond White, "Greased Lightning, Pryor's Predicament," *South End*, August 8, 1977.

48 Armond White, "Sold/Soul Brother"; "Movies from Other Media," *South End*, January 26, 1973.

49 Armond White, "Great Expectations," *South End*, February 26, 1973.

50 Armond White, "Hilberry and Aaron Loves Angela," *South End*, February 2, 1976.

51 Armond White, "The Passenger: Tale of Psychological Suspense," *South End*, June 4, 1975.

52 Armond White, "Taxi Driver: Seeing the City as Hell," *South End*, February 25, 1975.

53 Armond White, "Cries and Whispers," *South End*, April 27, 1973; "The Gambler," *South End*, October 17, 1974; "Use and Abuse of Movie Power," *South End*, September 1, 1977.

54 Armond White, "Amarcord Is Awesome," *South End*, November 19, 1974.

55 Armond White, "Movie Masterpiece Returns to DIA [Detroit Institute of Arts]," *South End*, May 29, 1975.

56 Armond White, "Failing to Find an Image," *South End*, August 29, 1974; "Failing to Find an Image, pt 2," *South End*, September 26, 1974.

57 Armond White, "Class of 44," *South End*, April 12, 1973; "Paper Moon Doesn't Cut It," *South End*, August 28, 1973; "The Urban 'Westerns,'" *South End*, January 7, 1974; "The Last Detail," *South End*, February 27, 1974.

58 Jacobson, "No Kiss Kiss, All Bang Bang." The interview describes White covering the film for the *South End*, but he had left the paper shortly before the release of *Close Encounters of the Third Kind* and was reporting on it for WDET, a public radio station broadcast from Wayne State University.

59 Only 10.8 million out of 18.1 million Black people over fourteen years of age could find legal employment in Michigan in 1978. Campbell Gibson and Kay Jung, Historical Census Statistics on Population Totals, "Table 23. Michigan—Race and Hispanic Origin for Selected Large Cities and Other Places: Earliest Census to 1990." The number of state prisoners in Michigan increased from 7,000 in 1967 to more than 41,000 in 2016, and the state increased spending on corrections by 219 percent between 1979 and 2013 (during the same period it increased spending on schools by 18 percent). Lori Higgins, "Michigan Spending on Prisons Far Outpaces Schools," *Detroit Free Press*, July 7, 2016. Since the U.S. census data counted prisoners as residents of the areas where they were locked up rather than where they previously lived, "a full four state senate districts in Michigan drawn after the 2000 Census . . . would not even have met federal minimum population requirements to be a district if they didn't count prisoners—who themselves couldn't vote—as their constituents." Thompson, *Whose Detroit?*, 14, 19. Also see James Forman Jr., *Locking Up Our Own* (New York: Farrar, Straus and Giroux, 2020).

60 Gilroy, *Small Acts*, 12.

61 Gilroy, *The Black Atlantic*, 40.

4. Slave-Descendants, Diaspora Subjects, and World Citizens

1 "Black Writers in Praise of Toni Morrison," *New York Times Book Review*, January 24, 1988.

2 Gilroy, *Small Acts*, 175.

3 Gilroy, *Small Acts*, 180.

4 Gilroy, *Small Acts*, 5.

5 Gilroy, *Small Acts*, 185, 190–91.

6   Race Today Review, "Talking to Two Black American Women Writers: Toni Morrison and Ntozake Shange," in *Here to Stay, Here to Fight: A "Race Today" Anthology*, ed. Paul Field, Robin Bunce, Leila Hassan, and Margaret Peacock (London: Pluto Press), 97.

7   Gilroy, *Small Acts*, 205.

8   Isaac Julien, Colin MacCabe, and Paul Hallam, *Diary of a Young Soul Rebel* (London, British Film Institute, 1991), 15.

9   Gilroy, *The Black Atlantic*, 142, 171.

10 Barbara Korte and Claudia Sternberg, *Bidding for the Mainstream?: Black and Asian British Film since the 1990s* (Amsterdam: Rodopi, 2004), 96–97.

11 Gilroy, *Small Acts*, 86–94.

12 In contrast to left-wing publications such as *New Socialist* and *City Limits*, Rushdie considered the film to be a clumsy, jargonistic, and unoriginal rejoinder to the superficiality and sensationalism of media reports about looting, riots, and arson. He reproached the film for using language that overemphasized structural forces and left little room to tell the stories of how the people of Handsworth responded to state violence as individuals, families, and members of religious communities. Salman Rushdie, "Agenda," *Guardian*, January 12, 1987. Hall's response defended the film's struggle to find a new language to attend to the racial tensions and social unrest in Birmingham and London in 1985, and suggested that Rushdie may not have been able to perceive its interweaving of politics and experience, as well Blackness and Englishness, because of his lofty and secure position in the British literary firmament. Stuart Hall, "Songs of Handsworth Praise," *Guardian*, January 15, 1987.

13 Homi Bhabha, Paul Gilroy, and Stuart Hall, "Threatening Pleasures," *Sight and Sound*, August 1, 1991.

14 Serpent's Tail would later publish *Voices of the Crossing: The Impact of Britain on Writers from Asia, the Caribbean and Africa*, a collection of essays edited by Ferdinand Dennis that included Beryl Gilroy's hopes and aspirations for her children's generation.

15 Gilroy, *Small Acts*, 21.

16 Gilroy, *Small Acts*, 245.

17 King, "Traditions, Genealogies, and Influences," 11, 26n29.

18 Gilroy, *Small Acts*, 100. Gilroy's thinking on this moribund social order was influenced by Patrick Wright, *On Living in an Old Country: The National Past in Contemporary Britain* (London: Verso, 1985). Wright was one of the people thanked in the acknowledgments of *There Ain't No Black in the Union Jack* for encouraging and challenging Gilroy in the most productive way possible by their disagreements. He is described as a "most acute observer of the morbidity of heritage" in *Postcolonial Melancholia*. Paul Gilroy, *There Ain't No Black in the Union Jack*, ix; *Postcolonial Melancholia* (New York: Columbia University Press, 2005), 100.

19 Gilroy, *Small Acts*, 9, 12.

20 Gilroy, *Small Acts*, 81–84.

21 Gilroy, *Small Acts*, 79, 221–22.

22 Gilroy, *Small Acts*, 211.

23 Gilroy, *Small Acts*, 74, 113–14n3, 213.

24 Gilroy, *Small Acts*, 233.

25 Gilroy, *Small Acts*, 157.

26 Gilroy, *Small Acts*, 199. Emphasis added.

27 Gilroy, *The Black Atlantic*, 3; Chrisman, "Journeying to Death," 51.

28 Amiri Baraka, "The Changing Same (R&B and New Black Music)," *The LeRoi Jones / Amiri Baraka Reader* (New York: De Capo Press, 1968), 186–209.

29 Gilroy, *The Black Atlantic*, 217.

30 Gilroy, *The Black Atlantic*, 96.

31 Gilroy, *The Black Atlantic*, 188.

32 Gilroy, *The Black Atlantic*, 100.

33 Chrisman, "Journeying to Death." There is a danger of overstating this argument and failing to acknowledge passages in *The Black Atlantic* in which Gilroy talks about the lived, profane realities of Black Atlantic cultures amid the debris of deindustrialization. It is notable, however, that *The Black Atlantic* does not substantively engage with Black, bitter humor in a similar manner to Armond White's writing for alternative media in Detroit and New York, or Gilroy's cultural criticism for alternative arts magazines in London in the 1980s.

34 Gilroy, *The Black Atlantic*, 203

35 Gilroy, *The Black Atlantic*, 69. Emphasis added.

36 Gilroy, *The Black Atlantic*, 181. Emphasis added.

37 Gilroy, *The Black Atlantic*, 127.

38 Gilroy, *The Black Atlantic*, 115.

39 Gilroy, *The Black Atlantic*, 125.

40 Gilroy, *The Black Atlantic*, 41.

41 Gilroy, *The Black Atlantic*, 42, 45, 171.

42 Gilroy, *Small Acts*, 113–14n3.

43 Gilroy, *The Black Atlantic*, 4.

44 Chrisman, "Journeying to Death," 51–65; Neil Lazarus, "Is a Counterculture of Modernity a Theory of Modernity?," *Diaspora: A Journal of Transnational Studies* 4, no. 3 (1995): 323–39.

45 Eric Lott, "Review of *The Black Atlantic: Modernity and the Double Consciousness*," *Nation*, May 2, 1994.

46 Chrisman, "Journeying to Death."

47 Lazarus, "Is a Counterculture of Modernity a Theory of Modernity?"

48 Robin Kelley, "Foreword," in Cedric Robinson, *Black Marxism: The*

Making of the Black Radical Tradition (University of North Carolina Press, 2000), xviii.

49 Robinson, *Black Marxism*, 5. Also see McNeil and Russill, "'Multicultural Snake Oil' and Black Cultural Criticism."

50 Art galleries and museums in the twenty-first century have also erroneously claimed that Gilroy coined the concept of the Black Atlantic rather than put it into wider academic circulation. See, for example, Tanya Barson, Peter Gorschlüter, and Petrine Archer, *Afro Modern: Journeys through the Black Atlantic* (London: Tate Publishing, 2010).

51 Gilroy, "A Dialogue on the Human," 208.

52 Gilroy, *The Black Atlantic*, 3, 4, 19, 218.

53 Gilroy, "A Dialogue on the Human," 209.

54 Paul Gilroy, "Travelling Theorist," *New Statesman & Society*, February 12, 1993.

55 Raymond Williams and Edward Said, "Media, Margins and Modernity," in Raymond Williams, *The Politics of Modernism: Against the New Conformists* (London: Verso, 1989): 196–97.

56 Gilroy, *The Black Atlantic*, 164–65, 202.

57 Gilroy, *The Black Atlantic*, 85.

58 Gilroy, "A Dialogue on the Human," 208.

59 White would also contribute an essay to *Birth of a Nation'hood: Gaze, Script, and Spectacle in the O.J. Simpson Case*, ed. Toni Morrison and Claudia Brodsky Lacour (New York: Random House, 1997).

60 Gilroy, *Small Acts*, 189.

61 Gilroy, *Black Britain*, 236; *The Black Atlantic*, 69.

62 Armond White, "On-Time Pop Culture: 1989's Best Images in Film and Video," *Emerge*, January 1990; "Videos Change the Style of Black Film," *City Sun*, August 18, 1993; "Camera Ready: Hip Hop and the Moving Image," in *DEFinition: The Art and Design of Hip Hop*, ed. Cey Adams and Bill Adler (New York: HarperCollins, 2008), 108.

63 Armond White, "Blade Cuts Open Race, Sex and Showbiz," *City Sun*, November 9, 1984; "Life on the Fringe," *City Sun*, July 9, 1986; "Beyond Malcolm X: African-American Cinema in the 90's," panel discussion at *Speaking Out: The Performing Arts Forum*, New York Public Library for the Performing Arts, 1993, Performing Arts Research Collection NCOW 126.

5. Enlarging *The American Cinema*

1 Nick James, "Print the Legend," *Sight and Sound* 20, no. 6 (June 2010).

2 John Lingan, "Interview: Armond White," *Moving Pictures*, May 15, 2008.

3 Andrew Sarris, "Pauline and Me: Farewell, My Lovely," *New York Observer*, September 17, 2001.

4 Renata Adler, "The Perils of Pauline," *New York Review of Books*, August

14, 1980; Phillip Lopate, *American Movie Critics: An Anthology from the Silents until Now* (Library of America, 2006), 330.

5   Armond White, "Chair's Speech," New York Film Critics Circle Awards, January 11, 2010.

6   See, for example, William Julius Wilson, "The Declining Significance of Race," *Society* 15, no. 2 (1978): 56–62; Trey Ellis, "The New Black Aesthetic," *Callaloo* 38 (1989): 233–43; Gina Dent, ed., *Black Popular Culture* (Seattle: Bay Press, 1992); Stuart Hall, "What Is This 'Black' in Black Popular Culture?," *Social Justice* 20, no. 1/2 (51–52) (1993): 104–14; Black Public Sphere Collective, ed., *The Black Public Sphere: A Public Culture Book* (Chicago: University of Chicago Press, 1995).

7   White, *The Resistance*, 80.

8   *New York Daily News* reporter Dave Hardy, for example, noted that his paper's readership was 50 percent Black or Latino while only 5 percent of its editorial staff were Black.

9   Wayne Dawkins, *City Son: Andrew W. Cooper's Impact on Modern-Day Brooklyn* (Jackson: University Press of Mississippi, 2012), 106.

10 Dawkins, *City Son*, 112–13.

11 Dawkins, *City Son*, 116–17.

12 *City Sun*, September 24, 1988.

13 White would return to Columbia and complete all of the course requirements to receive an MFA in 1997.

14 Andrew Sarris, *The American Cinema: Directors and Directions, 1929–1968* (New York: E.P. Dutton & Co, 1968). Also see Sarris and Levy, *Citizen Sarris*; James Naremore, *An Invention without a Future: Essays on Cinema* (Berkeley: University of California Press, 2013).

15 Armond White, "Fade to Black: 20 Years of Movie History," *City Sun*, July 1, 1987.

16 Andrew Sarris, "Notes of an Accidental Auteurist," *Film History* 7, no. 4 (1995): 358–61.

17 White also wrote record reviews under the noms de guerre Harry Allen and Allen and William Bonney.

18 Armond White, "A Jawful 'Black Christmas,'" *South End*, November 10, 1975.

19 Armond White, "The Color Purple: A Rethinking of Archetypes," *City Sun*, January 15, 1986; "Spielberg Strikes Again," *City Sun*, December 16, 1987.

20 Armond White, "The Color Purple."

21 Armond White, "Hook Gives Serious Happiness Its Due," *City Sun*, February 5, 1992.

22 Armond White, "Apartheid Chic," *Film Comment*, November/December 1987.

23 White, "Hook Gives Serious Happiness Its Due."

24 Armond White, "Keeping Up with the Joneses," *Film Comment*, July 1989.

25 Armond White, "Keeping Up with the Joneses"; "Rob Reiner's WASP Fantasy," *City Sun*, December 3, 1986.

26 Armond White, "My Schindler's List Problems—and Yours," *City Sun*, March 16, 1994.

27 Armond White, "Toward a Theory of Spielberg History," *Film Comment*, March 1994.

28 White, *The Resistance*, 237–38.

29 Armond White, "Michael Jackson Screams to Be Heard," *City Sun*, June 28, 1996; *The Resistance*, 236.

30 White, *The Resistance*, 236–43; Chicago Cultural Studies Group, "Critical Multiculturalism," *Critical Inquiry* 18 (Spring 1992): 530–55; Hall, "What Is This 'Black' in Black Popular Culture?"

31 White, *The Resistance*, 54.

32 Armond White, "Television: Prince of the City," *Film Comment*, November 1989. Emphasis added.

33 Ian Penman, "The Question of U," *London Review of Books*, 41, no. 12 (2019).

34 Penman, "The Question of U," 12.

35 White, *The Resistance*, 353–55.

36 White, *The Resistance*, 52–54.

37 Armond White, "Rock's Rebellion," *Film Comment*, November 1988.

38 White, *The Resistance*, 90–93. Emphasis added. Also see Armond White, "Lists and Prizes for the Arts in 88," *City Sun*, January 11, 1989.

39 White, "Television: Prince of the City."

40 White, "On-Time Pop Culture"; "Videos Change the Style of Black Film"; "Camera Ready."

41 Armond White, "De Niro Examines the Folklore of Racism," *City Sun*, October 13, 1993.

42 Armond White, "Bertolucci Saves Cinema with Little Buddha," *City Sun*, May 25, 1994.

43 Armond White, "Brian DePalma, Political Filmmaker," *Film Comment*, May 1991.

44 White, "Brian DePalma, Political Filmmaker."

45 Armond White, "The Good Guys and the Bad Guys," *City Sun*, June 17, 1987.

46 Armond White, "Weekend Film Check Up and Down," *South End*, July 18, 1977.

47 Armond White, "Movie Confusions: Women and Film," *South End*, May 9, 1975; "Satirizing Satanic Rock," *South End*, January 15, 1975; "Tommy: Senseless Surrealism," *South End*, April 9, 1975.

48 Armond White, "The Child's the Image of the Man?," *City Sun*, November 13, 1985; "Wilson and Goodie Mob Serve Up Soul Food," *City Sun*, August 28, 1994.

49   Armond White, "Looking at the Underside," *City Sun*, October 15, 1986.

50   White, *The Resistance*, 18–19.

51   Armond White, "Humor Surreal, They Didn't Get the Punchline," *City Sun*, August 5, 1987.

52   Morrissey, *Autobiography* (London: Penguin Classic, 2013), 198.

53   Armond White, "Morrissey Hooks Power with a Left," *City Sun*, October 25, 1991; "Culture Pruning," *City Sun*, July 30, 1986.

54   Armond White, "RPM—Kirsty MacColl," *City Sun*, March 9 1994.

55   Armond White, "Borrowed Images: Music—Celluloid Songs," *Film Comment*, March 1989; "Flipper Purify and Furious Styles," *Monthly Film Bulletin*, August 1991; "Des'ree Sings Her Gotta-beatitudes," *City Sun*, March 29, 1995.

56   Armond White, "Morrissey Says No to Narcissism in Movie Life," *City Sun*, January 15, 1992; "Morrissey Offers an Emotional World Tour," *City Sun*, March 15, 1995.

57   Armond White, "Rappin' It Up," *City Sun*, August 27, 1986; "Bought Can I Get a Witness?," *City Sun*, June 28, 1988.

58   Armond White, "Fear of Language: American Media and Public Enemy," *City Sun*, December 12, 1990.

59   Armond White, "Morrissey Joins the Love Struggle," *City Sun*, May 10, 1995.

60   Armond White, "Morrissey's Interesting Drug," *City Sun*, July 19, 1989. White worked on a manuscript called *Knee Deep in Great Experiences: A Critical Survey of Morrissey and Public Enemy* in the late 1980s and early '90s. Armond White, "Murray Puts the Sting in Scrooged," *City Sun*, December 14, 1988; "Ethnophobia or Ethnocentrism," *City Sun*, February 10, 1988; "Looking for Langston," *Looking for Langston* (Criterion DVD, 2007).

61   Armond White, "Lists and Prizes for the Arts in 88," *City Sun*, January 11, 1989.

62   White, *The Resistance*, 103.

63   See, for example, Hider Rizi, "Elections in Pakistan Are for Men; Most Women Stay at Home," *City Sun*, September 15, 1993; William Anthony and Karen Mahy, "Eastern Caribbean Experiences Increase in Number of AIDS Cases," *City Sun*, September 29, 1993; Gumisai Mutume, "Zimbabwe's Agricultural Sector Needs 3 Years to Recover," *City Sun*, October 6, 1993.

64   Armond White, "Salaam Cinema Redefines Peoples' Movies," *City Sun*, July 24, 1996.

65   Armond White, "Basque to the Future," *Film Comment* 24, no. 1 (January 1988).

66   Armond White, "They Were Expendable," *City Sun*, July 22, 1987.

67   White, *The Resistance*, 66.

68 McNeil, "The Last Honest Film Critic in America"; "Ethnicity, Ethicalness, Excellence." Baldwin was, for example, willing to deploy anecdotal evidence from African American GIs that Liverpool-born Blacks were poor dancers (and lacked "soul") because they happened to have "white lower-class mothers." James Baldwin and Margaret Mead, *Rap on Race* (Philadelphia: J.B. Lippincott, 1971), 18. While esteeming Frantz Fanon, the well-known French wartime hero, Martinican psychiatrist, and Algerian freedom fighter (whose *Wretched of the Earth* had sold approximately 750,000 copies in the United States by 1970), Baldwin also argued that he would never be as relevant to African Americans as Malcolm X. Baldwin, *Collected Essays*, 302, 404; Malcolm X, *The End of White World Supremacy*, 137; William Van Deburg, *New Day in Babylon: The Black Power Movement and American Culture, 1965–1975* (Chicago: University of Chicago Press, 1992), 60–61.

69 John E. Drabinski, "Affect and Revolution: On Baldwin and Fanon," *PhaenEx* 7, no. 2 (2012), 124–58.

70 White, "Looking for Langston."

71 White, "Young Soul Rebels."

72 Armond White, "Journals: Young Guns and Old Masters," *Film Comment*, July 1988. Also see Daniel McNeil, *Sex and Race in the Black Atlantic*; "Slimy Subjects and Neoliberal Goods: Obama and the Children of Fanon," *Journal of Critical Mixed Race Studies* 1, no. 1 (2014), 203–18.

73 Homi Bhabha, Paul Gilroy, and Stuart Hall, "Threatening Pleasures," *Sight and Sound*, August 1, 1991.

74 Armond White, "Looking for Langston"; "Boomerang Challenges Nothing," *City Sun*, July 1, 1992; "Snipes and Hooks Make Anything-for-a-Buck Flick," *City Sun*, November 18, 1992; "Probing Mariah's Music Box," *City Sun*, September 21, 1994; "And Now, the Dawning of a New Rae," *City Sun*, November 21, 1984; "An Australian 'Don't Believe the Hype,'" *City Sun*, November 23, 1988; "Haile Gerima Puts Faith in Sankofa," *City Sun*, April 13, 1994; "A Soldier's Story: Pro and Con," *City Sun*, September 19, 1984.

75 Cruse, *The Crisis of the Negro Intellectual*, 84–85.

76 Malcolm X and Alex Haley, *The Autobiography of Malcolm X* (New York: Ballantine Books, 1973), 277, 286. Also see McNeil, *Sex and Race in the Black Atlantic*, 93.

77 Frantz Fanon, *The Wretched of the Earth*, trans. Constance Farrington (New York: Grove Press, 1963), 154.

78 Lewis Gordon, *Existentia Africana: Understanding Africana Thought* (London: Routledge, 2000).

79 Armond White, "Spike Lee and His Coloured Element," *City Sun*, February 17, 1988.

80 Armond White, "Echobelly Shows Britpop the Fire This Time," *City Sun*, March 20, 1996.

81 Armond White, "The Empire Strikes Out," *City Sun*, February 4, 1986.

82 Armond White, "To the Best, Their Due," *City Sun*, December 17, 1986; "A Lesson in Ethnic Ethics," *City Sun*, April 9, 1986.

83 White, "Echobelly Shows Britpop the Fire This Time." Emphasis added.

84 Armond White, "Drab Realism," *City Sun*, April 22, 1992; "Mike Leigh's Films Remain in Progress," *City Sun*, January 15, 1992.

85 Armond White, "Geto Boys Resurrect Hiphop with Great Voices," *City Sun*, April 24, 1996.

86 Armond White, "De La Soul Beat Hip Hop's Mind Game," *City Sun*, November 10, 1994.

87 Armond White, "Creative Anarchy in the USA," *City Sun*, October 26, 1988.

88 Armond White, "Exiles on Catfish Row," *City Sun*, July 12, 1989; "White Dog: A Moral Metaphor Causes Uproar," *City Sun*, July 24, 1991.

89 Armond White, "Tim Burton Honors Eccentricity in Ed Wood," *City Sun*, December 7, 1994.

90 Armond White, "Strange Gifts: *André Téchiné* Remakes the Melodrama," *Film Comment* 31, no. 4 (1995): 70–75.

91 Armond White, "Remembrance of Songs Past," *Film Comment*, May 1993.

92 Lott, "Public Image Limited," 65.

93 Armond White, *The Resistance*, 269; "East Surpasses West," *City Sun*, April 1, 1986.

94 White, *The Resistance*, 149, 270, 273.

95 White, *The Resistance*, 268–70, 278–79. Also see White's commentary on *Sankofa*, which acknowledged that the director Haile Gerima had accomplished "the basic work of enlightening a debased audience" even though he "took a torch to Christianity" and did not move past "the superficialities of Afrocentricity." White, *The Resistance*, 421–24.

96 Armond White, "Jane Campion's Piano Hits the Wrong Notes," *City Sun*, November 17, 1993.

97 Armond White, "Underground Man," *Film Comment*, May 1991; "Zwick on His Feet: Fighting Black," *Film Comment*, January 1990.

98 Baldwin, *Collected Essays*, 11, 175, 320, 412.

99 Armond White, *The Resistance*, 179, 182, 199, 266; "Looking at the Underside," *City Sun*, October 15, 1986; Steven Boone, "In a World That Has the Darjeeling Limited, Sidney Lumet Should Be Imprisoned!: A Conversation with Armond White, Part I," *Big Media Vandalism*, December 10, 2007.

100 Armond White, "White on Black," *Film Comment*, November 1984; "Two Films That Make Slice of Life Seem Real," *City Sun*, July 31, 1985.

101 Armond White, "Bopha! Pulls an Arsenio," *City Sun*, September 29,

1993; "Sidney Poitier Goes on Parole," *City Sun*, March 2, 1988; "Morgan Freeman Eats Crow for Hollywood," *City Sun*, April 1, 1992.

102 Armond White, "Bugsy Sells Lies as Fantasy," *City Sun*, February 26, 1992; "Hagiography and Robeson," *City Sun*, August 24, 1988.

103 Armond White, "Diana Ross in the Gray Area of Pop," *City Sun*, June 21, 1989.

104 Armond White, "Washington and Hackman Make an American Mutiny," *City Sun*, May 10, 1995.

105 Armond White, "Denzel Plays Chump in Hollywood's Game," *City Sun*, January 12, 1994.

106 Armond White, "Good Golly Miss Molly or, Deeper than Oedipus," *City Sun*, April 19, 1989.

107 Armond White, *The Resistance*, 26; "Denzel Plays Chump in Hollywood's Game."

108 Armond White, "Tell Miramax: Save Burnett's Movie," *City Sun*, February 8, 1995.

109 Black Public Sphere Collective, *The Black Public Sphere* (Chicago: University of Chicago Press, 1995), 1–3.

110 "Critical Perspectives on The Culture Wars," *City Sun*, October 12, 1994.

111 White, *The Resistance*, 310.

112 White, "Whose Black Cinema Is it Anyway?" Also see White, "History Gets Lost in The Matrix."

113 Armond White, *The Resistance*, 255, 419–20, 429–30; "Yes, and it Counts," *City Sun*, February 15, 1994.

114 Henry Louis Gates Jr., "2 Live Crew Decoded," *New York Times*, June 19, 1990.

115 White's desire to contest a rigid, hard, stoic stereotype of masculine identity is also evident in, for example, his appreciation for *Point Break* and "the greatest male bonding scene ever put in a commercial Hollywood film," the willingness of male actors in *To Wong Foo, Thanks for Everything! Julie Newmar* to play against macho stereotypes, and his dismissal of many "hip hop exploitation" films. Armond White, "Point Break," *City Sun*, August 21, 1991; "Snipes Relaxes Winningly in To Wong Foo," *City Sun*, October 4, 1996; "Singleton Dramatizes How Boys Will Be Boyz," *City Sun*, July 1, 1991.

116 White, *The Resistance*, 309–15; Henry Louis Gates Jr., "The White Negro," *New Yorker*, May 11, 1998; Armond White, "Kanye West's Musical Rebellion," *National Review*, April 30, 2018.

117 Phillip Lopate, "Armond White," in *American Movie Critics: An Anthology*. Also see Robert Fulford, "The Man Who Hated Almost Everything: Armond White Is Just the Latest in a Long Line of Poison-Penned Critics," *National Post*, January 4, 2011.

118 Armond White, "Rebirth of a Nation," in *American Movie Critics:*

An Anthology, ed. Lopate; "De Palma on the Burden of Memory and Conscience," *City Sun*, August 16, 1989.

119   Armond White, "Spike Lee's Pornograffiti in Jungle Fever," *City Sun*, June 5, 1991.

120   Armond White, "Malcolm X'd Again," *City Sun*, December 2, 1992.

121   Armond White, "'Spite' Lee Puts the Brakes on Unity," *City Sun*, October 2, 1996.

122   White, "Beyond Malcolm X"; "Camera Ready," 104.

123   Armond White, "Burnett Supplies Pop Culture's Missing Link," *City Sun*, January 11, 1995.

124   Armond White, "40 Acres and Bull: Spike Lee Worships White Cops in Clockers," *City Sun*, September 20, 1996.

125   Armond White, "Chris Rock Makes Comedy Painful," "Paul Mooney Exposes the Joke of Politics," *City Sun*, June 19, 1996.

126   Armond White, "Self-Destruction for Money's Sake," *City Sun*, December 12, 1984.

127   Armond White, "The Agony and the Ebony," *City Sun*, January 7, 1987.

128   Armond White, "Betrayed by Hollywood—Again," *City Sun*, October 12, 1988.

129   Moten, *In the Break*, 5–6; Iton, *In Search of the Black Fantastic*, 104, 110, 175, 203.

130   White, *The Resistance*, 95–96.

131   Dawkins, *City Son*, 152–56.

132   Eddie Murphy, "Open Letter," *City Sun*, August 3, 1988.

133   "Armond White Responds," *City Sun*, August 3, 1988.

134   "Armond White Responds."

135   Armond White, "The Notorious E.D.D.I.E. Charms Professor," *City Sun*, July 17, 1996.

136   White, *The Resistance*, 109.

137   Armond White, "The New Wave Stereotype," *City Sun*, July 16, 1986; "White on Black"; "Only the Nose Knows," *City Sun*, June 24, 1987.

138   Armond White, "Eye, the Jury," in *Birth of a Nation'hood*, ed. Morrison and Brodsky Lacour, 350. On the "hellish cycle" of anti-Black racism that attributes eruptions of anger against white racism to Black immaturity rather than dreadful objectivity, and uses such manifestations of anger to justify ongoing white supervision and supremacy, see, for example, Fanon, *Black Skin, White Masks*; Kara Keeling, "'In the Interval': Frantz Fanon and the 'Problems' of Visual Representation," *Qui Parle* 13, no. 2 (2003): 91–117.

139   Armond White, "Two Thumbs Down," *Film Comment*, January 1989.

140   Armond White, *The Resistance*, 439–43; "RPM: Pimps, Players and Private Eyes," *City Sun*, November 2, 1994.

141   White, "Dead Presidents," *City Sun*, October 11, 1995.

142 White, "Singleton Dramatizes How Boys Will Be Boyz."

143 Armond White, "Poetic Justice," *City Sun*, August 21, 1993.

144 Armond White, "Doggystyle Crosses Over and Undermines Hip Hop," *City Sun*, December 22, 1994; "Beyond Malcolm X"; "Keenen Ivory Wayans Panders and Promotes Shame," *City Sun*, November 30, 1994; "Kiss of Death Revives Film Noir Bias," *City Sun*, May 3, 1995.

145 Lynda Richardson, "A Firm New Boss at an Old Voice of the Left," *New York Times*, January 17, 2001. In October 1992, the paper's media kit and accounts stated that its circulation was 53,000. However, the newspaper's ownership statement in November claimed that its paid circulation was just over 11,000. Even if one accepts the claim that there may have been an unpaid readership of around 14,000, this would still produce a circulation figure less than half the size advertised in the paper's media kit and accounts. Dawkins, *City Son*, 248.

146 Dawkins, *City Son*, 264.

147 Benj DeMott on behalf of First of the Month Writers Collective (Stanley Aronowitz, Benj Demott, Charles O'Brien, Armond White), "Mission Statement," firstofthemonth.org.

148 Gilroy, *The Black Atlantic*, 253.

6. Middle-aged, Gifted, and Black

1 *High Fidelity* did make it into some of the top ten lists concocted by critics, and was one of the ten winners of the American Film Institute's Movie of the Year Award in 2001.

2 Simon Reynolds, "Hybrid Fidelity," *Village Voice*, April 25, 2000.

3 For a summary of the critical response to *Against Race* see, for example, Laura Chrisman, "The Vanishing Body of Frantz Fanon in Paul Gilroy's *Against Race* and *After Empire*," *Black Scholar* 41, no. 4 (2011). Chrisman's review includes references to Patricia Hill Collins et al., "Review Symposium: *Between Camps / Against Race*," *Ethnicities* 2, no. 4 (2002): 539–60; Don Robotham, "Cosmopolitanism and Planetary Humanism: The Strategic Universalism of Paul Gilroy," *South Atlantic Quarterly* 104, no. 3 (2005): 5561–82; Simon Gikandi, "Race and Cosmopolitanism," *American Literary History* 14, no. 3 (2002): 593–615; Carol Boyce Davies, "Against Race or the Politics of Self-ethnography," *JENdA: A Journal of Culture and African Women Studies* 2, no. 1 (2002): 1–9.

4 Armond White, "On Guard," *New York Press*, September 2001.

5 Jim Knipfel, "Introduction," in *The Press Gang: Writings on Cinema from the New York Press, 1991–2011*, ed. Jim Colvill (New York: Seven Stories Press, 2020).

6 Christopher Flaherty, Letter to the Editor, *New York Press*, July 9, 1997; Sean Burns, Letter to the Editor, *New York Press*, July 23, 1997.

7   Georgia Brown, "For Queen and Country," *Village Voice*, May 23, 1989; White, "Keeping up with the Joneses," 9.

8   Armond White, "Mr. Jealousy," *New York Press*, June 3, 1998.

9   Andrew O'Hehir, "Banned from the Screening Room!," *Salon*, March 11, 2010. Also see the following tweet from Dana Stevens, a writer who admires Hoberman as one of the greatest film critics of all time: "When you suggest that someone should've been aborted (didn't he say that abt Baumbach?) banning seems appropriate," Dana Stevens (@thehighsign), Twitter, January 7, 2014.

10 Armond White, "Blade Cuts Open Race, Sex and Showbiz"; "Beyond Malcolm X"; "Symphonies for the Bedeviled," *New York Press*, November 1999.

11 Armond White, "3 Women: Female Reversions," *New York Press*, May 7, 1997; "3 Women: Altman Atrocity," *South End*, May 5, 1977.

12 Armond White, "Titanic," *New York Press*, December 1997.

13 Robert W. Welcos, "Debating an Icon's Genius, Racism," *Los Angeles Times*, February 1, 2000.

14 Armond White, "Christopher Nolan Pursues Hollywood's New Tenets," *National Review*, December 23, 2020.

15 Armond White, "Things Done Changed," *First of the Month*, 1999, firstofthemonth.org; "Intelligence Quotient," *New York Press*, July 2001.

16 Armond White, "Spielberg's A.I. Dares Viewers to Remember and Accept the Part of Themselves That Is Capable of Feeling," *New York Press*, July 4, 2001; "Iron Giant," *New York Press*, August 25, 1999; "Ready, Set, Cinema," *New York Press,* October 1999; John Lingan, "Interview: Armond White," *Moving Pictures*, May 15, 2008.

17 Gilroy, "Analogs of Mourning, Mourning the Analog," 262.

18 Gilroy, *Against Race*, 2, 214, 157, 237.

19 Gilroy, *Against Race*, 259.

20 Gilroy, *Against Race*, 201.

21 Gilroy, *Against Race*, 203, 259.

22 Gilroy, *Against Race*, 274.

23 Gilroy, *Against Race*, 356.

24 Gilroy, *Against Race*, 251.

25 Gilroy, *Against Race*, 131.

26 Gilroy, *Against Race*, 252.

27 Chrisman, "Journeying to Death"; "The Vanishing Body of Frantz Fanon."

28 Armond White, "Divine Intervention," *New York Press*, February 4, 2003.

29 Armond White, "xXx," *New York Press*, August 20, 2002.

30 Steven Boone, "Sweet Lime and Sour Grapes: Armond White Conversation, Part III," *Big Media Vandalism*, December 10, 2007.

31 Armond White, "Songs from the Second Floor," *New York Press*, July 2002; "Paranoia for President," *New York Press*, August 2004; "Freedom Cry,"

New York Press, March 16, 2005; "They Call Me Jackie," *New York Press*, April 13, 2005; "The Politics of Mopery," *New York Press*, May 2, 2006.

32 Gilroy, *Postcolonial Melancholia*, xii.

33 Gilroy, *Postcolonial Melancholia*, xiv.

34 Fred Moten, *Black and Blur* (Durham, NC: Duke University Press, 2017), 293–95n3.

35 Gilroy, *Postcolonial Melancholia*, 137, 108.

36 Gilroy, *Postcolonial Melancholia*, 117. Emphasis added.

37 Gilroy, *Postcolonial Melancholia*, 80.

38 Gilroy, *Postcolonial Melancholia*, 5, 25.

39 Gilroy, *Postcolonial Melancholia*, 17.

40 Gilroy, *Postcolonial Melancholia*, 50, 80.

41 James, *Notes on Dialectics*; David Graeber, *Fragments of an Anarchist Anthropology* (Chicago: Prickly Paradigm Press, 2004).

42 Gilroy, *Postcolonial Melancholia*, xiv.

43 Gilroy, *Postcolonial Melancholia*, 67, 151.

44 Gilroy, *Postcolonial Melancholia*, 25, 150.

45 Gilroy, *Postcolonial Melancholia*, 115.

46 Gilroy, Sandset, Bangstad, and Høibjerg, "A Diagnosis of Contemporary Forms of Racism, Race and Nationalism," 176.

47 Gilroy, "A Dialogue on the Human," 221, 226. Emphasis added.

48 Shelby and Gilroy, "Cosmopolitanism, Blackness, and Utopia," 128.

49 Although he may feel hesitant about repeating ideas, Gilroy also acknowledges that "it is often through repetition that the possibility of a political response can be generated." Paul Gilroy, "'Where Every Breeze Speaks of Courage and Liberty': Offshore Humanism and Marine Xenology, or, Racism and the Problem of Critique at Sea Level," The Antipode RGS-IBG Lecture, September 2, 2015.

50 Gilroy, *Postcolonial Melancholia*, 141. Emphasis added.

51 Catherine Wheatley, *Michael Haneke's Cinema: The Ethic of the Image* (New York: Berghahn Books, 2009), 171. To be fair to Wheatley, the book also includes a short sentence that notes that shame of a specific and limited sort can be constructive (and guilt can be excessive and oppressive). Also see Grada Kilomba, *Plantation Memories: Episodes of Everyday Racism* (Toronto: Between the Lines, 2021 [2008]), 20–21, which builds on what Kilomba perceives to be an all-too-brief allusion to shame and guilt in a presentation Gilroy delivered, to describe shame as an emotion closely connected to the sense of insight because it occurs when one fails to achieve an ideal of behavior one has set out for oneself (in contrast to guilt, which occurs if one transgresses an injunction derived from outside oneself).

52 Paul Gilroy, "Shooting Crabs in a Barrel," *Screen* 48, no. 2 (2007): 235.

53 Gilroy, *Postcolonial Melancholia*, 99. Emphasis added.

54   Armond White, "The Expendable Other," *New York Press*, January 1, 2006; Gilroy, "Shooting Crabs in a Barrel."

55   Roger Ebert, "Not in Defense of Armond White," *Roger Ebert's Journal*, August 14, 2009.

56   Armond White, "Terminator Salvation," *New York Press*, May 21, 2009.

57   Armond White, "Reel War Is Hell," *New York Press*, August 20, 2008.

58   Armond White, in David Chen, Devindra Hardawar, and Adam Quigley, *The /Filmcast: After Dark*, July 26, 2010.

59   Gilroy, *Black Britain*, 257.

60   Gilroy, *Black Britain*, 257.

61   Gilroy, *Black Britain*, 252.

62   Gilroy, *Black Britain*, 18.

63   Gilroy, *Black Britain*, 236.

64   Gilroy, *Black Britain*, 308.

65   Gilroy, *Black Britain*, 257; Paul Gilroy, "Free Thinking," BBC Radio 3, September 4, 2017.

66   Gilroy, *Black Britain*, 306.

67   Gilroy, *Darker than Blue*, 121.

68   Gilroy, *Darker than Blue*, 122.

69   Gilroy, *Darker than Blue*, 40, 54.

70   Gilroy, *Darker than Blue*, 90, 116, 127, 148.

71   Gilroy, *Darker than Blue*, 66, 73, 151, 168.

72   Gilroy, *Darker than Blue*, 173. Also see Gilroy, "Shameful History," 26.

73   Gilroy, *Darker than Blue*, 154.

74   Gilroy, "Introduction: Race Is the Prism," 9.

75   Gilroy, "A Dialogue on the Human," 210.

76   Barack Obama, "Address by the President to the Nation," July 25, 2011.

Coda

1   Jared Sexton, *Amalgamation Schemes: Antiblackness and the Critique of Multiracialism* (Minneapolis: University of Minnesota Press, 2008), 158–59.

2   Semley, "Armond White Is the Kanye West of Film Criticism."

3   Bell, "Historical Memory, Global Movements and Violence," 23–24; MacCabe, "Paul Gilroy: Against the Grain."

4   Armond White, "Can't Trust It," *City Arts*, October 16, 2013.

5   Gilroy, "12 Years a Slave."

6   Gilroy, *Black Britain*, 173, 236. Also see Gilroy, "Shameful History," 26.

7   Barack Obama, "Keynote Address," Democratic National Convention, Boston, July 27, 2004.

8   Armond White, "The Year the Culture Broke," *National Review Online*, August 25, 2014.

9 Armond White, *The Resistance*, xiv, 90; "The Cheap Route Costs," *City Sun*, March 6, 1984; "Blade Cuts Open Race, Sex and Showbiz."

10 William Finnegan, "The Candidate," *New Yorker*, May 31, 2004.

11 White, "Pursuit of Crappyness."

12 White, "Pursuit of Crappyness." Also see McNeil, "Slimy Subjects and Neoliberal Goods"; Daniel McNeil and Leanne Taylor, "Radical Love: A Transatlantic Dialogue about Race and Mixed-Race," *Asian American Literary Review* 4, no. 2 (2013): 15–27; Daniel McNeil, "'Mixture Is a Neoliberal Good': Mixed-Race Metaphors and Post-racial Masks," *Dark Matter* 9, no. 1 (2012).

13 Barbara Walters, *The View*, November 22, 2004. Also see Tom Wolfe, "Radical Chic: That Party at Lenny's," *New York Magazine*, June 8, 1970; McNeil, *Sex and Race in the Black Atlantic*, 100–101; "Slimy Subjects and Neoliberal Goods."

14 Adam Nagourney, "Biden Unwraps '08 Bid with an Oops!," *New York Times*, February 1, 2007.

15 Adrian Martin, "Superbad Critic," *De Filmkrant*, June 2008.

16 See, for example, Fred Goldberg, Vice President of United Artists, who sought to target *The Landlord* (Hal Ashby, 1970) to "downtown Chicago and other downtown areas, [where] the black audience is 70% of the toal [sic] downtown audience." Fred Goldberg to Norman Jewison, August 19, 1970, Norman Jewison Papers, Victoria University in the University of Toronto, 38-4-9. In 1991, African Americans comprised approximately 12.5 percent of the American population and around 25 percent of the commercial audience. Judith Mayne, *Cinema and Spectatorship* (London: Routledge, 1993), 154. Also see Daniel McNeil, "Nostalgia for the Liberal Hour: Talkin' 'bout the Horizons of Norman Jewison's Generation," *Canadian Journal of Film Studies* 21, no. 2 (2012): 115–39.

17 Robin Winks, *The Blacks in Canada* (Montreal: McGill-Queen's University Press, 1971), 403, 478. Also see McNeil, "Even Canadians Find It a Bit Boring."

18 Armond White, "Do Movie Critics Matter?," *First Things*, April 2010; "Why Kael Is Good for You," *Columbia Journalism Review* 50, no. 6 (2012): 53–54.

19 Armond White, "Discourteous Discourse," *New York Press*, September 28, 2010.

20 Ramin Setoodeh, "New York Critics Met for Hours to Oust Armond White," *Variety*, January 14, 2014. Emphasis added.

21 Mark Kermode, *Hatchet Job: Love Movies, Hate Critics* (London: Picador, 2013), 89, 109. Emphasis added.

22 Armond White, "Grace under Fire," *New York Press*, February 22, 2007; "Superpathology," *National Review Online*, May 2, 2014.

23 Gilroy, "12 Years a Slave."

24 Armond White, "Revolution Movies Then and Now," *National Review Online*, July 18, 2018.

25 Chrisman, "Journeying to Death," 63–64.

26 White, *New Position*, 111.

27 Armond White, "Heroes Debunked," *National Review Online*, February 3, 2017.

28 Armond White, "At the Oscars: Revenge of the Hollywood Crybullies," *National Review Online*, March 3, 2017.

29 "Interview with Armond White," *MeatBone Express Filmmaking Podcast*, January 16, 2018. Also see White, "Revolution Movies Then and Now."

30 Justin Desmangles, "Armond White Interview," *New Day Jazz*, January 25, 2015.

31 Justin Desmangles, "Armond White Interview," *New Day Jazz*, March 16, 2014.

32 Glieberman, "Why Armond White Got Kicked Out of the Critics Circle."

33 Ishmael Reed, "Exclusive Interview with Armond White about the Oscars," *Konch Magazine*, February 2016, ishmaelreedpub.com.

34 White, "Movies from Other Media"; McNeil, "Ethnicity, Ethicalness, Excellence."

35 Armond White, "Roots: Subversive History Lesson," *City Sun*, December 7, 1988.

36 Armond White, "The 13th via the Un-talented Tenth," *National Review Online*, October 5, 2018. Revealingly, White notes DuVernay's reliance on Black public intellectuals that he associates with the superficiality and hustling of white guilt in a liberal public sphere, such as Henry Louis Gates Jr., and elides the fact that *13th* also engages with civil rights activists that he respects for their principled radicalism, such as Angela Davis.

37 Armond White, "'This Is America' Is the New Minstrel Show," *National Review Online*, May 7, 2018.

38 Armond White, *The Resistance*, 95–96; "Black Panther's Circle of Hype," *National Review Online*, February 16, 2018.

39 Armond White, "After the Debate: Fact-Checking Hollywood Propaganda," *National Review Online*, October 10, 2016.

40 Armond White, "Kanye Goes Back to the Old Landmark," *First Things*, October 29, 2018.

41 Armond White, "Kanye West's Musical Rebellion," *National Review Online*, April 30, 2018.

42 Tara Burton, "The Insidious Cultural History of Kanye West's Slavery Comments," *Vox*, August 30, 2018.

43 David Olusoga, "Kanye West's Infantile Views on Slavery Have Worrying Echoes of the Alt-Right," *Observer*, May 6, 2018.

44 Sara Cascone, "Is Kanye West's Meltdown a Joseph Beuys–Inspired Work of Performance Art?: One Theorist Has It All Figured Out," *Artnet*

news, May 4, 2018; Sean Nelson, "The 'Kanye West's Pro-Trump Stance Is Performance Art' Theory Has Emerged," *Portland Mercury*, May 4, 2018; Ta-Nehisi Coates, "I'm Not Black, I'm Kanye," *Atlantic*, May 7, 2018; Andrew Sullivan, "Kanye West and the Question of Freedom," *New York Magazine*, May 11, 2018.

45   Steven Boone, "Phonies, Cronies, American Ironies, American Gangsters: Armond White Conversation, Part II," *Big Media Vandalism*, December 10, 2007; Armond White, "Pursuit of Crappyness"; "Kanye Goes Back to the Old Landmark," *First Things*, October 29, 2018.

46   Gilroy, *Darker than Blue*, 124–26.

47   White, "Whose Black Cinema Is it Anyway?"; Gilroy, *The Black Atlantic*, 254; Michael Eric Dyson, "Book Offers Tongue-in-Cheek Awards to Black Public Intellectuals," *Chronicle Review*, September 6, 1996.

48   Moten, *Black and Blur*, 293–95n3. Moten had earlier felt compelled to respond to the praise bestowed on *12 Years a Slave* by Gilroy and Tavia Nyong'o (an academic who studied with Gilroy at Yale and a cousin of Lupita Nyong'o, the recipient of an Oscar for her portrayal of Patsey in the film) in public lectures. Fred Moten, "Black Studies: Grammars of the Fugitive," Goldsmiths, December 6, 2013.

49   Gilroy, "Diaspora," 211-12.

50   Gordon, "Black Intellectual Tradition."

51   Paul Gilroy, "A New Cosmopolitanism," *Interventions* 7, no. 3 (2005): 290.

52   Paul Gilroy, "In Search of a Not Necessarily Safe Starting Point . . .," *open-Democracy*, May 1, 2016.

53   Paul Gilroy, "An Audience with Paul Gilroy: In Conversation with Tony Herrington," Off the Page Literary Festival for Sound and Music, September 27, 2014.

ACKNOWLEDGMENTS

This book would not have been possible without Karl Shaw, Monica Robinson, John Duffy, John Lally, Philip Waller, and many other coaches, teachers, and tutors who took the time to help a diffident young man in England perceive the discreet charms of eccentric souls, figure out how it was possible to appear 100 percent sincere and 100 percent ironic at the same time, and imagine and build an intellectual life.

This intellectual history of a rebel generation is also indebted to two critics who I would have benefited from reading as a young Black teenager. I am grateful to have eventually found my way to the work of Paul Gilroy and Armond White and, over the past twenty years, had the opportunity to read and reread their books, access their articles hidden behind academic paywalls, and travel to archives that house their attempts to change the terms of discussion about racism and culture in the United Kingdom and the United States. I would also like to extend warm appreciation to Paul and Armond for their patience, openness, and generosity in talking about the people, ideas, and events that have informed, inspired, and provoked their writing. Although this is not a conventional biography or duography about their personal lives, friends, families, partners, and break-ups—or their professional colleagues, challenges, rivalries, setbacks, disappointments, and accomplishments—our wide-ranging conversations helped me to think more deeply about their principled commitments to humanistic praxis and independent journalism, dissatisfaction with the blandishments of official and corporate multiculturalism, and distaste for the totalizing schemes of macro-political narratives. I learned and continue to learn a lot from their thoughts on Black cultures and planetary humanism, and I am grateful that they were willing to work through any understandable feelings of shyness, guardedness, and modesty to provide some formative context about the historical circumstances that have shaped their structures of feeling.

The research for *Thinking While Black* was supported by Carleton University, DePaul University, and the Jackman Humanities Institute at the University of Toronto. I am thankful for the research funds that made it possible to visit the manuscripts and archives of Northwestern University, Harvard University, Cambridge University, Wayne State University, and the New York Public Library, and the fellowships and teaching releases that granted me time to think more deeply about disseminating humanities research across disciplinary boundaries and into the broader public realm for discussion, debate, and examination. I also owe a deep debt of gratitude to the librarians, archivists, and photographers on both sides of the Atlantic who provided practical help and permission to reproduce the revolutionary and counterrevolutionary images that enrich this book.

Amanda Crocker supported the book's initial vision and, alongside Tilman Lewis, offered thoughtful prompts, questions, guidance, and editorial finesse to bring clarity to its translation of Armond White, Paul Gilroy, and the politics and popular culture of a rebel generation. It was a pleasure to work with Amanda, Tilman, and the staff at Between the Lines as well as Nicole Solano and the editorial team at Rutgers University Press. Feedback from anonymous reviewers nurtured the ideas in the book and helped clarify my thinking, as did the sage and balsamic comments on earlier iterations of the book shared by Jay Garcia, Zélie Asava, Malini Guha, David Austin, and Sam Sahlu. Mattias Frey, Cecilia Sayad, and Sharrell D. Luckett also provided invaluable editorial assistance on my essays on Armond White's contributions to the study of American culture and film criticism in *Film Criticism in the Digital Age* and *African American Arts: Activism, Aesthetics, and Futurity*, which are revised and expanded in this book.

I am grateful to have had the opportunity to share my work in progress with audiences at the University of Kent, the University of Winnipeg, the University of Toronto, the University of Ottawa, and the College of Charleston as well as Harvard University, Birmingham City University, Brown University, Leeds University, Bucknell University, Freie Universität Berlin / Humboldt-Universität Berlin, Newcastle University, York University, New York University, and Elmhurst College. Thanks to everyone who arranged and attended these talks and workshops. I would also like to express deep and sincere gratitude to Sara Salih, Karen Dubinsky, Sofia Noori, Yinka Alli-Balogun, Mezeker Ghide, Mugoli Samba, Sarah Mayangi, Nadine Powell, Sally El Sayed, Emily Hersey, Franny Nudelman, Sarah Brouillette, Sandra Jackson, Fassil Demissie, Julie Moody Freeman, Francesca Royster, Aboubakar Sanogo, Chris Russill, Kamari Clarke, Roger Connah, Ozayr Saloojee, David Dean, Victoria Bisnauth, Liliane Braga, Jenn Ko, Ayaan Ismail, Diane Roberts, Stéphane Martelly, Angelique Willkie, Dhanveer Brar, Lewis Gordon, Tony Purvis, Bruno Cornellier, Christian Jacobs, Ben Miller, Paget Henry, Francesca D'Amico-Cuthbert, Michele Johnson, Alison Keith, Kim Yates, Ben Akrigg, Bhavani Raman, Katherine McKittrick, Yana Meerzon, William Felepchuk, Taylor Cenac, Susan Lord, and many other colleagues and students who have pushed academic climates on both sides of the Atlantic, which sometimes appear irony-free and burdened by strained seriousness, into livelier and more radical dimensions.

The work and ideas of many artists and keen observers of media, culture, and society have also helped me to wrestle with the soulful style of critics who strive to emulate the complexity and control of creative artists, and are always a little dissatisfied by dry, academic reports and journalism that confuse accessibility with literal-mindedness. Thanks to Marvin Gaye, Gil Scott-Heron, Milan Kundera, Mike Leigh, Lubaina Himid, Roy Andersson, Jean-Pierre Dardenne, Luc Dardenne, Ken Loach, Edwidge Dandicat,

Duncan MacMillan, August Wilson, Éric Rochant, Assia Djebar, Colm Tóibín, Richard Iton, Roland Clark, James Richardson, Adam Hurrey, Barney Ronay, David Lean, Denis Villeneuve, Claire Denis, Jephté Guillaume, Joe Claussell, MJ Cole, Roni Size & Reprazent, Alison Crockett, Kaytranada, Jamie Woon, Goapale, Vusi Mahalasela, Terence Nance, Benji B, Gilles Peterson, Danny Krivit, Mansur Brown, Little Simz, Stewart Lee, Timmy Regisford, DJ Spinna, Sade, Change, Osunlade, Monique Bingham, Joi Cardwell, Quentin Harris, Larry David, Martin Carter, the Blaze, and many others for their seriously soulful work. I am also grateful for public events, platforms, services, and places that bring reality into focus and inspire people to imagine new forms of belonging with time, space, and each other: Blockorama, BBC Sounds, Rideau Park, Mount Royal Park, Roxy Blu, Alto Basso, 718 Sessions, Central Tech Stadium, Academy of Lions, Apex Training Centre, NuYorican Poets Café, Art Gallery of Ontario, Walker Art Gallery, V&A Museum, Radcliffe Camera, Toronto Public Library, Toronto Transit Commission, Bluecoat Arts Centre, Art House Café, Harbourfront Centre, Kay Gardner Nature Trail, Chicago Lakefront Trail, and the Museum of Contemporary Art Chicago.

Many friends and family members have helped me to take this project seriously but not too seriously. Special thanks to Sam Sahlu (reminding me, as always, that there can be joy in repetition), Anjhela Salonga, Joel McIlven, Anand Verma, and Richard Mullan for keeping me plugged into the real world and sending me funny and enlightening posts from social media sites and platforms I studiously avoid. I also owe an unquantifiable debt to Leanne Taylor for sharing holidays that included trips to archives and historical sites, and co-parenting our curious, wise, and witty daughter. The book is dedicated to Alex Taylor-McNeil and her great-grandmother, Sheila McNeil, whose ambitions, achievements, regrets, vulnerabilities, fears, desires, eccentricities, keen powers of observation, tenacity, tenderness, and love, have taught me to think and feel my way through abstract concepts like the changing same as well as the politics and popular cultures of generations that never quite speak the same language.

INDEX

Note: Numbers in italics refer to images.

Abdul-Jabbar, Kareem, 137
abjection, 4, 141
Academy Awards, 84, 97, 133, 141; diversification of, 141
action-adventure films: deleterious impact of, 121
activism: African American, 4; political, 7, 124
Adler, Renata, 78
Adorno, Theodor, 53
advertisements, 74, 87; Benetton, 85; Nike, 74; political, 29–31; Primitive, 109
aesthetes: exclusionary acts of, 68
aesthetic(s): African American, 4; of Black Atlantic cultures, 3; diaspora, 74; iconoclastic, ironic, and scatological, 141; new Black, xvii, 78; of rebel cultures and creative artists, 11; resistance, 4, 78, 145; of silent films, 117

African American culture, 4, 55, 114, 129; totems and taboos of, 93
African American letters, 70
African Americans, 19; closing ranks, 130; color caste divisions among, 62; discrimination against, 58; disengagement of from African and Black diaspora, 130; filmmakers, 95; first radio station of, 43; global, 92; history, creativity, and resistance of, 130; and homophobia, 62; intellectuals, 11, 21, 70, 92–94; and masculinity, 109; men, 73; and misogyny, 62; narratives of, 130; policing and incarceration of, 58; political aspirations and achievements of, 43; racial slavery as exclusive property of, 140; social and political thought of, 2, 12, 136, 140; as violent threats, 40; and war in Iraq, 123; women, 73, 83, 96
African American Studies, xix, 6, 93; Global, 4–6, 8, 93
Afro-Caribbean people, 31–32

Afrocentricity, 69, 96, 97, 109, 171n95
Afro-pessimism, 134, 146
AIDS epidemic, 10
Ali, Muhammad, 12, 55
Almodóvar, Pedro, 51
alternative media, 66
Altman, Robert, 53, 56, 87, 95, 103, 104, 117–18; *Nashville*, 53; *3 Women*, 53, 117
alt-right: contemporary, 143
Amazing Grace, 140
American American concept, 46, 53, 56, 95; and film, 49–51, 53; and identity, 50; and jazz, 53; multiracial / "mulatto-minded," 83; Spielberg and, 143
American Beauty, 113
The American Cinema: enlargement of by White, 77–110. *See also under* Sarris, Andrew
American Cultural Studies, xiv
Americanism, 62
American melting pot, 51
American Society of Composers, Authors and Publishers, 85
American Studies: deprovincialization of, 114
Amsterdam News, 80
Anderson, Jim, 20
Anderson, Wes, 118
Andersson, Roy, 122
Anglophilia, xiii
anti-anti-essentialism, 68
anti-capitalism, 8, 12; resistance in Black expressive cultures, 35–37
anti-Caribbean rhetoric, 149n1
anti-colonialism, 47, 120
anti-essentialism, 68; premature, 68
anti-fascism, 31, 36, 38
anti-homophobia, 33
anti-imperialism, 33
Anti-Nazi League, 25
anti-racism, 24, 25, 31, 33, 34, 36, 38, 150n10
anti-sexism, 33
anti–Vietnam War protests, 20
Arendt, Hannah, 35; *The Origins of Totalitarianism*, 114
Armond Dangerous blog, 116

Armstrong, Louis, 21
Ashby, Hal: *The Landlord*, 178n16
assimilation, 18
Attille, Martina, 63, 93
autodidacticism, 3, 13; cultural, 23
autopoiesis, 40
Avalon Equity Partners, 126

baby boomers: male, 114
Babylon, 64
Babymother, 63
Bailey, David, 67
Baldwin, James, 4, 90, 92, 98
Bambaataa, Afrika, 34
Baraka, Amiri, 8, 23, 69, 103
barbarism: bourgeois, 114
Baron Cohen, Sacha, 125
Batson, Brendon, 27–28
Baumbach, Noah, 116–17; *Greenberg*, 117; *Mr. Jealousy*, 116
Beasts of the Southern Wild, 136
Before Columbus Foundation, 4
Belle, 140
Bertolucci, Bernardo, 87
Between Camps. See High Fidelity
Beyoncé, 144
Bhabha, Homi, 65; "Threatening Pleasures," 66
Biden, Joe, 138
Biko, Steve, 10, 80–81
Biko Lives Festival, 80
Bird, Brad, 118
Black art: possibilities of, 8; therapeutic and nostalgic approaches to, 62
Black Arts Conventions, 43, 44
Black Arts Movement: British, 71; US, 8
Black athletes, 119; eroticization of, 119
Black Atlantic: coinage of term, 72; mapping of, 73
Black Atlantic cultures, 3, 71, 145–46; dynamic potency of, 145; modernity and double consciousness in, 33, 69–73; network of, 71; political aspirations and achievements of, 58; politics and poetics of, 146; structures of feeling in, 113–30

Black Atlantic exchange, 39; in the digital age, 141–47; White's contributions to, 74
Black Atlantic musicians, 34
Black Audio Film Collective, 9, 71, 93
Black belonging, 16
Black bodies: as sites of pleasure and autonomy, 35
Black bourgeoisie: alienation from, 61; contradictions of, 74; White vs., 77–110
Black Canada, xiv
Black Consciousness, 3, 10, 46, 54, 81, 83
Black criminality: stereotype of, 30
Black cultural expression, 101
Black cultural groups: stereotypes of, 66
Black cultural history, 39
Black culture(s): affirmation of, 44; commercial and conservative views of, 74; commodified, 119; explanation of, 4; white America's guilt and loathing toward, 101
Black disillusionment, 64
Black excellence, 9, 55
Black expressive cultures, 11–13, 35, 62, 81
Black film, 54–55, 63
Black filmmakers, 55, 99
Black identity, 31, 55, 62
Black Liberator, 39
Black Lives Matter, 141, 146
Black music, 7, 16, 26, 34, 64–65, 67; anti-capitalism in, 35–37; "deskilling" of, xix; exploitation of, 33; jazz as, 33
Blackness, 94, 128; commodification of, 74; 1,001 shades of, 94; political definition of, 32; repressed, denied, and disavowed, 125
Black on Black, 32
Black Panther, 143, 144
Black popular cultures, 13, 69, 129; colonization and commodification of rebel spirit of, 119
Black popular modernism, 8–9, 68
Black postmodernist intellectual "tradition," 145

Black Power, 156n16
Black press: independent, 11, 100, 106
Black public intellectuals, xvii–xviii, 2, 4, 65, 79, 101, 104, 179n36
Black public sphere, xvii–xviii, 65, 67, 74, 81, 100–101; decline or diversification of, 79
Black radicalism, xvii, 26, 45, 48, 72, 138, 144; US Senate surveillance of, 47
Black rage, 93, 108
Black representation and inclusion, 58
Black self-reliance/survival, 34
Black struggle, 44
Black subject, 66; essential, end of innocent notion of, 79
Black vernacular cultures, 17
Black women, 30, 73
Blackwood, Maureen, 63, 93
Black youth, 26, 105
Blair, Tony, 123
Blaxploitation, 99; coalition against, 54; films, 107, 108
B-movies, 82, 84, 95
Boateng, Paul, 29
Boggs, Grace Lee, 43–44
Boggs, James, 44
Bond, Julian, 137
Booker T. Washington Trade Association, 43
Boorman, John, 122
Bowie, David, 88
Boyce, Sonia, 11; Talking Presence, 67
Bridges, Lee, 38–39
British Cultural Studies, 6, 73
British Empire, 5, 123, 125; allegory of, 65
British Film Institute (BFI), 63
British Sociology, 2
Brixton riots, 32
Broadside Press, 43
Brooks, Avery, 149n1
Brown, Georgia, 116
Bruno, Frank, 65
Bruno, Pete, 23
Bulworth, 102
Burnett, Charles, 99; Glass Shield, 99
Bush, George H.W., 78

Cabral, Amílcar, 39, 47
Callaghan, James, 28
Campion, Jane: *The Piano*, 97
Canada, xiv, 123
"cancel culture," 146
Cannes Film Festival, 65, 125
capitalism, 8, 27; American, 106;
    commodified, xix; consumer, 129,
    146; contradictions of, 75; critique
    of, 32–37; indoctrination, 74, 91;
    racial, xiii, 75; suppression of his-
    torical and temporal consciousness
    under, 37; white supremacist, 75
Captain Phillips, 136
careerism, 82, 100, 104, 138
Caribbean political and social
    thought, 8, 22–23
Carmichael, Stokely, 156n16
Castro, Fidel, 47
celebrity culture, 13
Centre for Contemporary Cultural
    Studies (CCCS), 7, 16, 26; disjunc-
    tures between IRR and, 39; *The
    Empire Strikes Back*, 31–32, 38–39;
    Mugging Group, 26; Race and
    Politics Group, 17, 22, 32, 36, 38
Chambers, Iain, 26
"changing same," 9, 69
Channel 4, 63
Cheshire, Godfrey, 116, 120–21, 127
child-rearing: male contempt for, 34
Chisholm, Shirley, 80
choreopoems: African diasporic, 83
Chow, Stephen, 122
Chrisman, Laura, 141
Churchill, Winston, xiii
cinema: American, 50, 88, 98;
    art-house, 53; Black, xviii, 101, 103;
    Iranian, 121
cinema authorship, 81
City Arts, 127
City Limits, xvi, 17, 34, 164n12
City Sun, xvii, 6, 74, 78, 79–82, 92, 99,
    101, 102, 104–6, 109, 116; folding
    of, 110
City Sun Employees Inc., 110
civil rights movement, 91, 98, 105,
    138; opposition to, 141; wake of,
    8–13

Clapton, Eric, 23
Clarke, John, 7, 26–27
the Clash, 25
class: and Black Americans, 79;
    experiential fault lines of, 91;
    fracturing of reading publics by, 27;
    masculinist and heteronormative
    approaches to, 40; privilege, 97;
    and racism, 29
classism, xiii, 13, 82, 99
Clinton, Bill, 78
collective protest, 26
collective resistance, 141
colonialism, xiv, 94; opposition to,
    104; white, xiv
Columbia University, 122
commodification, xviii, 82; of
    Blackness, 74
Congress of Racial Equality, 46
consumer culture, 128
consumption: conspicuous, 129;
    passive, 119
Cooper, Andrew, 79–80
Cooper, Anna Julia, 73
Coppola, Francis Ford, 87
Corrie, Rachel, 123
Corrigan, Paul, 27
cosmopolitanism, 119–20
countercultural journalism, 7
countercultural politics, 13
counterculture, 17, 20, 40; extin-
    guishment of, 88–89, 100
Cox, Alex, 88–89; *Straight to Hell*, 89
crack epidemic, 10, 35, 69
crime: race and, 38–39; violent, 26
critical theory: European, 46
Crouch, Stanley, 4
Cruse, Harold, 4, 93, 149n1
Crusz, Robert, 63, 93
Cry Freedom, 83
cultural criticism, 45, 62, 71; by
    Gilroy, 62; reduction of, 136–37;
    by White, 5, 40, 45, 74, 78, 81, 84;
    working-class, 5
cultural formation, 69
cultural history: Black, 39; writing of,
    68, 69, 128, 146
cultural inferiority: Blacks compared
    to whites, 141

culturalism, 39
cultural politics, xix, 3, 29, 33, 44, 62, 64, 86; Black, 23, 40, 46, 71, 74; of "race" and nation, 93
cultural production, xvi, 9, 13, 53; Black, 3, 62, 67, 103; and radical politics, xiv, 34
cultural protectionism, 69
Cultural Studies, 27, 38; American, xiv; British, 6, 73; institutionalization of, xvii
cultural theory, 30, 72
culture industry, 100, 119; neo-Marxist critique of, 46, 52–53
Cunningham, Gene, 51–52
Cunningham, Laurie, 27–28

Daily Collegian, xvii, 47. See also South End
dance floor, 45, 79; Black control of, 36–37; British, 70
D'Arby, Terence Trent, 92
"dark-skinnedness," 94
Dash, Julie, 96; Daughters of the Dust, 96
Davies, Terence, 5, 96, 97, 122; The Long Day Closes, 96
Davis, Angela, 10, 137, 179n36
Dead Presidents, 108
death drive, 70, 141
deconstruction, 39
De La Soul, 95
democracy, xiv; American, 87; multiracial, 81
De Niro, Robert, 87
Denning, Michael, 10
Dennis, Felix, 20
Dennis, Ferdinand: Voices of the Crossing, 164n14
De Palma, Brian, 88, 104
De Sica, Vittorio, 49
Destiny's Child, 113
Detroit, 40; African American political aspirations in, 43; Black community in, 56; Black population of, 57; Black radical tradition in, 45; Central High School, 49, 51, 52; collective struggle for liberation in, 62; Concept East Theater, 43;

first African American mayor of, 79; Great Rebellion in, xvii, 44; as "Murder city," 57; Police Department Red Squad, 160n10; political authority in, 45; radio stations in, 88; underground media in, 45; urban revolution in, 46; WCHB, 43; white flight from, 57
diaspora, 32–37; African, xvi, 17, 31, 40, 62, 69–70, 83, 92, 130, 149; Asian, 17, 31, 40, 62; Black, xii, 67, 73, 130; Caribbean, 17, 31, 40, 62
diaspora subjects, 61–75
diasporic artists, 22, 62
diasporic contexts: comparative 67
diasporic criticism, 92
diasporic cultures, 145
diasporic identities/aesthetics, 74, 119
diasporic intellectuals, 5, 94, 136
Diasporic Studies, 5
diasporic theory, 5, 8
Dienes, Paul, 15
Diesel, Vin: xXx, 121
difference: engagement with, 105; mundane encounters with, 124; pleasure of encountering, 36; racialized, 128
Directors Guild of America, 117
discourse: acceptable, 79, 101, 139, 146; "discourteous," xix; liberal, xv; new right, 30; patronizing, xv; Powellite, 36
discourse analysis, 39; visual, 30
diversity, 117, 124, 128, 130, 145; American, 88; lack of in Oscars, 141
DJs: removal of record labels by, 35–36
Dodge, 44, 47
Dodge Revolutionary Union Movement (DRUM), 44, 45, 46, 48
Do the Right Thing. See under Lee, Spike
double consciousness, xv, 33, 55, 69–73
Douglas, Aaron: Building More Stately Mansions, 69
Douglass, Frederick, 71, 103, 107
Dover, Cedric, 132
Dr. Dre, 109

Du Bois, W.E.B., xix, 23, 24, 46, 55, 72, 107; *Souls of Black Folk*, 21, 70–71, 134
DuVernay, Ava: *Selma*, 141; *13th*, 142
Dyer, Geoff, 60
Dyer, Richard: *Heavenly Bodies*, 77
Dyson, Michael Eric, 101, 144

Eagleton, Terry, 94
Eastern Eye, 32
Ebert, Roger, 108, 126–27, 139, 140
eccentrics: experiences of, 118
Elba, Idris, 149n1
Elder, Lonne, III, 55
Ellison, Ralph, 4, 23; *Invisible Man*, 21, 98
Emerge, 78
Emergency, xvi, 17, 33, 36, 38
England: London-centric approach to, 68–69; morbid celebrations of, 70; moribund cultural order of, 67; northern, 5
Englishness: morbid celebrations of, 70
equity, 124, 145
essentialism: nationalist, 11; pitfalls of, 66; therapeutic, 68
ethicalness, 55, 142
ethnicity, 32, 55, 84, 142; Afro-Caribbean, 31; Asian, 32
ethnic minorities, 18, 29, 84, 87; films about, 56
Euro-American academic establishment: disruption of, 71
Eurocentric beauty standards, 86
excellence, 55, 135, 142; Black, 9, 55
existentialism, 8, 96; American, 54–57, 98, 118; European, 56, 71

Fanon, Frantz, xviii, xx, 8, 10, 47, 76, 94, 107, 119, 135, 170n68; *The Wretched of the Earth*, 22–23, 25–26, 170n68
Farrar, Max, 33; "Love and Dread in Modern Times," 33
fascism, 36
fatalism, 70, 141
Fellini, Federico, 49

female auteurs: Afrocentric vision of, 96
feminism/feminist theory, 5, 73, 74, 96; white, 97
Fetchit, Stepin, 105
50 Cent, 144
Film Comment, 6, 78
film criticism: dignity of, 115, 139; integrity of, 2, 12, 139; significance of, 2, 12, 115, 139; reputation of, 127; by White, xvi, 2, 12, 49, 115, 122, 127, 135, 139
film culture, 53; balance between art and commerce in, 50; and Black consciousness, 54; consumption of, 49; decolonization of, 6; independent Black, 63; and whiteness, 108
film festival circuit, 9; international, 6, 71, 92
Film Quarterly, 49
First of the Month, 9, 110
Fishbone, 95
Fishbourne, Laurence, 109
folk historicism, 35
footnotes: fetishization of, 72
FOX News, 145
Freedom Now Party, 43–44
Free South Africa / Free the South Bronx Network, 80
Frith, Simon, 27
Fuller, Samuel, 95
fusion: as explanatory tool for analysis of cultural formation, 69

Gambino, Childish: "This Is America," 142
Garber, Jenny, 27
Garner, Eric, 141
Garvey, Marcus, 103, 107
Gates, Henry Louis, Jr., 11, 100–102, 104, 179n36
Gaye, Marvin, 137; *What's Going On?* 56
gender, 46, 63, 90; experiential fault lines of, 91; fracturing of reading publics by, 27; as modality in which race is lived, 73; race taking precedence over, 74
gender politics, 24, 73

General Motors, xvii, 48
generation: fracturing of reading
  publics by, 27
Georgakas, Dan, 46
George, Nelson, 109
Gerima, Haile: *Sankofa*, 171n95
Geto Boys, 95, 102, 142
Get Out, 135
Gilroy, Beryl, 14, 15, 164n14
Gilroy, Darla, 15
Gilroy, Patrick, 15
Gilroy, Paul, xii, xv–xix, xx, 5, 6,
  9, 20, 31–32, 58, *66*, 74, 93, 110,
  132, 135–36, 140–41, 144–46; and
  advertisements, 74; *Against Race*,
  114, 118–20, 149n1; and ambiv-
  alence of community, 6–8; and
  belonging, 9–10; birth and childhood of, 15–16; *The Black Atlantic*,
  xvii, 7, 33, 63, 69–73, 141; *Black
  Britain*, 127–29; and Caribbean
  intellectuals, 8, 22; children of,
  123; as critic of police brutality, 37;
  and cultural criticism, 62; *Darker
  than Blue*, 128–29; denounced as
  heretic, 37–39; as "domesticated
  foe" of British Sociology, 2; and
  double consciousness, 33, 69–73;
  "generational affliction" of, 118–19;
  and Greater London Council, 33;
  as G-Roy, 25; on guilt and shame,
  125–26; and Hall, 6–7, 38, 65–66,
  67, 127; and hip hop, 35; historical
  sensibility of, 61–75; Holberg
  Award, 1; and hybridity, 114, 120;
  inspirations to, 11–12; late style
  of, 13, 144; and McQueen, 136,
  140–41; and media, culture, and
  sport, 25–28; and militancy, 22–25;
  and modernity, 33, 69–73; and
  Morrison, 7–8, 40, 61–62, 69, 73,
  74; as "most influential intellectual
  writer" in UK, 135, 139–41; and
  music, 16, 21–24, 34–37, 40, 65, 114,
  124, 119; and music journalism, 34;
  "Police and Thieves," 38; and "policy," 124; *Postcolonial Melancholia*,
  122–26, 164n18; as protégé of Hall,
6–7; rationale for comparing with
  White, 1–3; relationships with
  African American intellectuals, 11,
  70; and Said, 72–73; *Small Acts*,
  33, 62, 67–69, 70, 72; and soccer,
  27–28; and *Temporary Hoarding*,
  25, 36; *There Ain't No Black in
  the Union Jack*, 29–30, 35–36,
  39, 62, 93, 164n18; "Threatening
  Pleasures," 66; as university
  student, 22–23, 25; as utopian, 38,
  120, 124; and Wilmer, 33–34; and
  Young Soul Rebels, 65
Giuliani, Rudy, 122
Global South, 92
Godard, Jean-Luc, 7, 118
Goldsmiths College, 115
Gordon, Lewis, 94
Gordy, Berry, 44, 160n7
government: oppressive or dis-
  criminatory, 68; and policing, 37;
  political machinery of, 48
Graeber, David, 124
Gramsci, Antonio, 26
Greater London Council, 17, 32–33,
  37, 63; police committee, 29
Green, David Gordon, 118
Griffith, D.W., 83, 103, 117–18; racism
  of, 117
Grimes, Carol, 23
Guess Who, 135
Guess Who's Coming to Dinner, 133, 135
Guevara, Che, 47
guilt: paralyzing, 126; of Powellite
  discourse, 36; and shame, 125–26;
  of white America toward Black
  culture, 101; white feelings of, 104
Gunn, Bill, 99

Habermas, Jürgen: *The Structural
  Transformation of the Public
  Sphere*, 100
Hackman, Gene, 108
Hall, Stuart, x, xiii, xiv, 5, 8, 20, 26,
  65, 67, 73, 127, 164n12; and Gilroy,
  6–7, 38, 65–66, 67, 127; New
  Times project, 39; "Threatening
  Pleasures," 66

Hallam, Paul, 64
Handsworth Songs, 66
Haneke, Michael: *Caché*, 125
Hare-Brown, Nikki, 27
Harris, Wendell B., Jr., 97–98;
    Chameleon Street, 97
Hartman, Saidiya, 134
Harvard University Press, 70
Healey, Denis, 28
Heath, Edward, 18, 19
Hebdige, Dick: "Reggae, Rastas and
    Rudies," 26
hegemony, 26; disruption of, 130
The Help, 136
Hendrix, Jimi, 21
Henry, Frances, 150n10
Hernández, Julián, 122
heteronormativity, 35, 40
High Fidelity, 113–14
Hillsborough stadium disaster, xiii
Himid, Lubaina, 11
hip hop, 35, 81, 95, 102, 104, 109, 142–
    43; cultural and political expression
    of, 78; exploitation era, 99, 107,
    109; impudent integrity of, 103,
    172n115; and juvenile posturing, 91;
    populist candor of, 93
"hippyism," 24
Hoberman, J., 116–17
Holiday, Billie, 54
Hollywood, 83, 104, 107, 109;
    challenge to, 87; clichés and values
    of, 95; colonization of taste by, 92;
    deep distrust of, 140; "flash" of, 82,
    117; hype of, 139
homelessness: demonization of, 87
homoeroticism, 120
homophilia, 120
homophobia, 62, 106, 120
hooks, bell, 11, 73, 75, 101
Hooks, Benjamin, 80
Hornby, Nick, 114
Howe, Darcus, 17
HRUM, 44
Huddle, Roger, 23
Hudson, Peter James, xv
Hughes, Albert, 108
Hughes, Allen, 108
Hughes, Langston, 92

humanism: all-American, 40;
    Marxist, 6; planetary, 124–25,
    149n1; redemptive, soulful, 129;
    spurious, 84
humanist community: sustaining
    sense of, xix, 110, 118
Hundall, Thomas, 123
hybridity, xv; defense of, 114; as
    explanatory tool for analysis of cul-
    tural formation, 69; and mixture,
    120; and regression, 69

Ice Cube, 119
identity: all-American, 107–8;
    American American, 50; beige,
    137; Black British political, 17,
    31, 32, 62, 70, 115; boomer, 114;
    complexities of, xiv; diaspora, 73,
    119; diasporic approaches to, 93;
    ethnic, 86; gay, 96, 138; national,
    39, 130; racial, 137
identity politics, 12; white male
    middle-class, 50
immigrants/immigration, xiv;
    construction of, 16; policy on, 135;
    suspicion of, 123; to the UK, 16–20,
    24, 40, 70, 123
imperialism, 7; American, 6; British,
    5; of past, 126
inclusion, 58, 124, 130, 145
independent Black press, 11, 100, 106
independent film, 74, 95, 100, 108;
    American, end of golden era of, 88;
    Black, 63
individualism: exaggerated, 88
Inner City Voice, 44–45, 47
Institute of Race Relations (IRR), 38;
    disjunctures between CCCS and,
    39; *Race & Class*, 38–39
integration, 18
"Internet hordes," 107, 139
interracial marriage, 134
Iranian cinema: New Wave of, 121
Iraq: war in, 115, 121, 123, 128
Islamophobia, 121
Isle of Wight Festival, 21
Iton, Richard, 9–10

Jackson, Jesse, 55, 79

Jackson, Michael, 85; "Black or White," 85
Jackson, Samuel L., 109
Jacques, Martin: New Times project, 39
Jagger, Mick, 88
James, C.L.R., 8, 17, 24, 33, 44, 47, 94, 124; *The Black Jacobins*, 22–23, 25–26
Jay-Z, 144
jazz, 5, 8–9, 21, 33, 54; *American American*, 53; as Black music, 33; precarity of Black male artists, 33
Jefferson, Tony, 26
Jim Crow segregation, 140, 142
Johnson, Linton Kwesi, xi–xii, 14, 17, 94; "Five Nights of Bleeding," 23
Jones, Claudia: "The Caribbean Community in Britain," 23
Jordan, June, 40, 73
Judkins, Nacretia, 52
Julien, Isaac, 62, 63–64, 67, 92–94, 122; *Looking for Langston*, 62, 92, 93; *Territories*, 63; *Who Killed Colin Roach?* 63; *Young Soul Rebels*, 62, 63–66, 93

Kael, Pauline, 4, 5, 7, 49–51, 53–55, 78, 122, 139, 141; death of, 121; *Deeper into Movies*, 50; *Kiss Kiss Bang Bang*, 49, 77; *Reeling*, 77; White and, 46, 49, 52–53
Kamugisha, Aaron, xv
Kelly, R., 119, 149n1
Kermode, Mark, 139–40
Khomeini, Ayatollah Ruhollah, 65
Kierkegaard, Søren, 71
Kilomba, Grada, 176n51
King, Martin Luther, Jr., xix, 18, 133
Koch, Ed, 80
Kundera, Milan, 51
Kureishi, Hanif, 5, 94

Lady Sings the Blues, 54, 55–56
Landis, John, 85
LA Weekly, 78
League of Revolutionary Black Workers (LRBW), 45, 46; *Finally Got the News*, 45

Lee, Spike, 62, 69, 74, 102–4; *Clockers*, 103; *Do the Right Thing*, 91, 102–4; *Jungle Fever*, 103; *Malcolm X*, 102–4
Left: British, 9, 17, 38
"leftist cynics," 118
leftist/left-wing publications, 9, 17, 164n12
left-wing politics, 13
Leid, Utrice, 80, 110
Leigh, Mike, 95, 122; *Naked*, 95
Lenin, V.I., 47
liberalism: anemic, 133, 135; Black, 47; "kneejerk," 138; white, 4, 52, 93, 98, 101, 103, 134–37
liberation: anti-colonial, 138; Black, 12, 17, 38, 46, 146; collective, xi, 36–37; collective struggles for, 5, 40, 62; minority groups and, xiv; national, 120; Third World, 17, 38, 75, 89
liberation theology, 138
libertarianism, xv, 8, 145
Life, 49
"light-skinnedness," 94
Limbacher, James L., 42
Lincoln Center (New York), 9
live music/concerts, 16, 115, 119, 124, 129
Liverpool (UK), xii–xiii
Livingstone, Ken, 32
livity, 22, 68
London School of Economics, 115, 127
Lopate, Philip: *American Movie Critics*, 102
Lordi, Emily J., 10
Lott, Eric, 153n18
lynching, 73

MacCabe, Colin, 64
Madan, Sonya, 5, 94
Mahal, Taj, 55
Malcolm X. See under Lee, Spike
Manhattan Media, 126–27
Mao Zedong, 39
March on Washington, 149n1
marginalized communities: politics and poetics of, xiv; reporting relevant to, 80

market deregulation, 10
Marley, Bob, 8, 21–22, 114, 119–20, 136; "Get Up, Stand Up," 22, 25; "I Shot the Sheriff," 23; spiritual connection to Africa, 120
Marriott, David, 134
Marsh-Edwards, Nadine, 63, 93
Martin, Adrian, 138
Martin, Lionel, 91
Marvel Studios, 142
Marx, Karl, 47
Marxism, 6, 24–25, 72, 141, 142; cultural, 145; European, 26
Marxism-Leninism, 45–46, 47
Marxism Today, 32, 38
masculinism, 27, 35, 40, 91
masculinity, 96; American, 109; Black, demeaning stereotypes about, 86; modes of, 22; stereotype of, 172n115
The Matrix, 109
Mayfield, Curtis, 21
McCron, Robin, 27
McKittrick, Katherine, xv
McLintock, Derrick Saldaan, 64
McQueen, Steve, 130, 136, 139, 144, 146; 12 Years a Slave, xviii, 130, 136, 139, 141
McRobbie, Angela, 27
media, 25–28; gatekeepers, 91, 95; white liberal, 101, 138, 146
Mehmood, Tariq, 31; Hand on the Sun, 31
Melody Maker, 23
meritocracy, 12
"message movies," 86
"metropolitan academic climate," 69
Michaels, Lorne, 122
middle class: African American, 7; Black, 97, 101, 103; proto-Black, 61; straight white, 77–110, 143
Middle East: injustice in, 124
militancy, 22–25
militarism, 13, 21
military-industrial complex, 128
military spending: increases in, 10
Millennial generation, 107
Miller, Marcus, 34
minorities, 105; experiences of, 118; non-mainstream, 90; oppressed, 51; racial, 24, 74, 80, 138; sexual, 138; social, 53; in urban cultures, 97. See also ethnic minorities
minority citizenship, 16
Miramax, 99
misogyny, 62, 106
Mississippi Burning. See under Parker, Alan
mixed-race individuals, 65, 66, 93
mixing: racial, 94, 108; regression and, 69
modern consciousness, 81, 88
modernism: Black popular, 8–9, 68; British African, Caribbean, and Asian, 67
modernity, xv, 33, 69–73; Black, 70, 141
modern values: post-sacral, 71
Modood, Tariq, 32
Mods, 27
Mooney, Paul, 105
Morrison, Toni, 5, 7–8, 17, 40, 61, 69, 73, 74, 137; as diasporic artist, 62; Gilroy and, 7–8, 40, 61–62, 69, 73–74; Pulitzer Prize for Fiction, 61; White and, 69, 74
Morrissey, 5, 89–90, 122
Moten, Fred, 144–45; Black and Blur, 144
Motown, 7, 43, 44, 55, 99; Motown Record Company, 45, 160n7
mugging, 26
"mulattoes," 94
multiculturalism, 36, 85, 124, 126; corporate, 9, 119–20, 124, 128, 129, 144; "ordinary," 124
multinationals, 120; artists working "inside and against," 68
multiracial collaboration, 23
multiracial democracy, 81
multiracial culture, 83
multiracial people, xii, 28, 44, 55, 114; legitimization of, 134
Murdoch, Rupert, xiii
Murdock, Graham, 27
Murphy, Eddie, 104–7; Boomerang, 107; Coming to America, 106, 143; The Nutty Professor, 107
Murray, Albert, 4

music, 75; of African America and the
  Caribbean, 32, 34; Afro-American,
  22; and collective protest, 26;
  commercialization of white pop
  world, 35; Gilroy and, 16, 21–24,
  34–37, 40, 65, 114, 119, 124; and
  modern existence, 33; political,
  25; pop, 33; pop, deskilling of,
  114; soul, 64; underground spaces
  of, 35–37; White and, 10, 45, 51,
  56, 77–79, 81, 85–89, 91–92, 99,
  102; working-class, 5; in *Young
  Soul Rebels*, 64–65. *See also* Black
  music; hip hop; jazz; punk
music videos, 74, 87, 125
Muslims: representation of in
  Western media, 65

nation: cultural politics of race and,
  29, 33, 93
National Association for the
  Advancement of Colored People,
  80
nationalism, 21, 56, 97;
  Americocentric Millennial, 119;
  British, 20; sclerotic forms of, 129;
  unwholesome power of, 16
National Negro Business League, 43
National Review, 141, 142
Nation of Islam, 43; *Muhammad
  Speaks*, 47
Neal, Mark Anthony: *Looking for
  Leroy*, 149n1; *Soul Babies*, 149n1
neocolonialism, 10, 94; sickness of,
  94; struggle of oppressed peoples
  against, 52; working-class struggles
  against, 39
neoliberalism, 4, 10, 110, 120, 145;
  progressive, 12, 136
Neville, Richard, 20
New Black Aesthetic: birth of, 78
New Black Realism, 109
"New Colossus," 51
New Haven (Connecticut), 70
"New Jim Crow," 140
New Left, 10
New Musical Express, 23
new right discourse, 30
NEWRUM, 44

New Socialist, 164n12
New Statesman, 72
New York, 57
New Yorker, 49–50, 54
New York Film Critics Circle, 2, 4, 78,
  107, 116–17, 139
New York Press, xv, 110, 115–18,
  120–22, 126–27; discontinuation of,
  127; sale of, 126
New York Times, 9, 101; *Book Review*,
  61, 65
Nietzsche, Friedrich, 71
nostalgia, 51, 62, 68, 83, 89, 95–98,
  119–20, 129
Notting Hill Carnival, 63
Nugent, Frank S., 139
Nyong'o, Lupita, 180n48
Nyong'o, Tavia, 180n48

Obama, Barack, xix, 12, 13, 129–30,
  134, 135–36, 143, 144; "Obama
  effect," 130, 137–38; re-election of,
  xviii; "sad legacy" of, 4
Observer, 140
Occupy movement, 141
Orientalism, 121
Osborne, Cyril, 17
Oscars. *See* Academy Awards
The Other Story exhibition, 67
Out, 96
Oz, 7, 20, 24

pain, 70, 105, 141
Parker, Alan, 107–8; *Mississippi
  Burning*, 83, 107–8
parochialism, 21, 51, 93; challenge to,
  92; rejection of, 6
patriarchy, 102
patriotism, 64; cheap, 124
Perez, Rosie, 92
periodization, 73
personal history, 70
Point Break, 172n115
Poitier, Sidney, 98–99, 137
police: and African Americans, 58;
  brutality and machismo of, 37;
  collective defeat of, 37; dissociation
  of law from, 68; harassment by, 47;

racist aggression by, xi, 32, 35, 63, 68, 141
Policing the Crisis, 26
political correctness, 117–18, 145
political oppression: European, 94
"politricksters," 68
poor: depiction of, 37
populism: authoritarian, 119
post–civil rights generation, 78–79, 82, 86, 100, 105–6, 137–38, 149n1
postcolonialism, xiv, 5, 31, 65, 70, 75
Postcolonial Studies, 73
postmodernism, 39, 70, 145
Powell, Colin, 123
Powell, Enoch, 16, 18–19, 27, 36, 39; sacking of, 19; victimization of, 20
Precious, 136
Prescod, Colin, 39; "Revolution of the Caribbean Peoples," 23
Prince, 85–87; *Purple Rain*, 86; *Under the Cherry Moon*, 86; video for *Batman*, 87
Prismatic Images, 98
privatization, 145
profiteerism, 138
propaganda, 24; militarized and nationalized, 119; political, 33
protest ethic, 1970s, 138, 146; wake of, 8–13
provincialism, 6; European, 94
Pryor, Richard, 55, 105
pseudo-performances, 119
Public Enemy, 91–92, 142; "Fight the Power," 91–92; *It Takes a Nation of Millions to Hold Us Back*, 91; "Night of the Living Baseheads," 91
public sphere, 100; American, 108, 134–36; authentic, 36; Black, 65, 67, 74, 79, 81, 100–101; bourgeois, 100; Canadian, xv; countercultural, xvii; liberal, 100; literary, 100; refeudalized, 100
punk, 24–25, 27, 64, 74, 81, 89, 99, 143; do-it-yourself ethos of, xvi, 5, 24, 138; impact of on suburban consumers, 114; intransigence and independence of, 138; and mainstream film, 89; revolutionary zeal of, 89; and rock, 90

Pursey, Jimmy, 25

race: Black Americans and, 79; Black Britons and, 69; and crime, 39; cultural politics of nation and, 33, 93; diasporic approaches to, 93; disruption of dramatic storytelling conventions about, 86; experiential fault lines of, 91; fracturing of reading publics by, 27; masculinist and heteronormative approaches to, 40; as modality in which class is lived, 73; national conversations about, 101; privilege, 97; scripts and statecraft of, 123; taking precedence over class and gender, 74
"race hustlers," 140
race-mixing, 108
race relations, xiv, 17, 18, 38, 115
race thinking, 94; therapeutic approaches to, 145
Race Today, xvi, 17, 31, 40, 62
racial discrimination, xviii; opposition to, 134
racial domination: law and, 35–36
racial hierarchy, 91
racial intermediaries, 93
racialization, 123
racialized ways of seeing, 93
racial stereotypes: dismantling of, 82; recycling of, 106
racial violence, xiv, 19, 40
raciology, 69
racism, xiii, xv, 29, 36, 56, 67, 97, 99, 107, 116, 117, 123, 147, 150n10; American, 95; American, sickness of, 94; anti-Black, 146, 173n138; antidote to, 25; challenges to, 145; cultural or new right, 30; fight against, xi; institutional, 104; and jazz, 33; police, 63; resistance to, 27; romantic, 138; settler-colonial, xiv; sickness of, 135; systemic, 146; violent, 24; white, 16, 173n138; white British left indifference to, 38; working-class struggles against, 39
racist hierarchy, 74
radicalism: Black, 26, 45, 47–48,

72; cultural, 24; masculine sexual, 24; principled, 179n36; of soul musicians, 143

Rage, 63

rap, 91, 99

Rastafarianism, 34, 67–68

raves: underground, 35, 37, 66, 124

Reagan, Ronald, 78

Reaganomics, 35

record sleeves: visual pleasure of, 67–68

Redford, Robert, 108

Reed, Adolph, Jr., 4

Reed, Ishmael, 4

Regis, Cyrille, 27–28

regression: mixing and hybridity and, 69

religion, 67, 138, 146

resentment, 142

Resistance through Rituals, 25–26

review aggregator sites, 139

Rice, Condoleezza, 123

Ritt, Martin, 55, 83

Robinson, Cedric: *Black Marxism*, 72

Rock, Chris, 105; *Bring the Pain*, 105

Rock Against Racism (RAR), 7, 16, 23, 25, 114

Rolling Stone, 20

Roots, 142

Rotten Tomatoes, 139, 140

Rushdie, Salman, 65–66, 94, 164n12

Ruskin, John, 68

Said, Edward, x, 72–73, 74, 101; *Culture and Imperialism*, 72; *Orientalism*, 72

Sankofa Film and Video Collective, 63, 93

Sarris, Andrew, 78, 81, 122, 139; *The American Cinema*, 77, 79–82; White and, 77–110

Saturday Evening Post, 49

Saturday Night Live, 122

Saunders, Red, 23

scholasticism: "timid" and "selfish," 129

Schuyler, George, 4

Scorsese, Martin, 56, 87, 103, 104; *Mean Streets*, 56; *Taxi Driver*, 56, 98

Scott, Dred, 121

Scott, Ridley, 122; *Black Hawk Down*, 122

"screenies," 125

Searchlight, 38

Seitz, Matt Zoller, 116, 120, 126, 127

self-activity: working-class, 13

self-discipline: narcissistic, 36

self-fashioning, individual, 26

September 11 attacks, 115, 121, 122

Serpent's Tail publishing house, 67, 70

sex: disruption of dramatic storytelling conventions about, 86

sexism, 99; and jazz, 33

Sex Pistols, 64

Sexton, Jared: *Amalgamation Schemes*, 134–35

sexual assault: Black settlement and, 39; young men of color and, 87

sexual politics, 24

shame, 125, 141

Shange, Ntozake, 83

Shrine of the Black Madonna, 43

Sight and Sound, 66, 77, 78

Singleton, John, 109; *Boyz n the Hood*, 109

Siskel & Ebert at the Movies, 126

Sivanandan, A., 38, 39

skinheads, 27

Skinner, Mike, 124

slave-descendants, 61–75

slavery, xiv, 121, 142, 143; identification with, 140–41; opposition to, 104; racial, 140

slave suicide, 70, 141

Smith, Russ, 115

Smith, Suzanne E., 43

Smith, Will, 137; *Hancock*, 137

Snoop Dogg, 109, 119

soccer: racism in, 27–28, 120

social desolation, 86

Socialist Worker, 23

"social justice warriors," 118

social spending: decreases in, 10

solidarity: non-national, 123

The Sopranos, 113

soul musicians: radicalism and conservatism of, 143

Sounder, 54–55, 83
Sounds, 23
sound system culture, 63
South End, xvii, 40, 45–48, 51–52, 54, 56, 79, 82, 99, 145
Sowell, Thomas, 80
Spielberg, Steven, 82–84, 117–18; *Close Encounters of the Third Kind*, 57, 85, 88; *The Color Purple*, 83, 85; *Hook*, 84; *Indiana Jones and the Last Crusade*, 84; *Jaws*, 82, 84, 117; *Lincoln*, 143; Presidential Medal of Freedom, 143; *Raiders of the Lost Ark*, 84; *Schindler's List*, 84
sport, 25–28
Springsteen, Bruce, 114
Stalinism, 142
Star Wars, 83
state brutality, 36, 104
Steel Pulse, 25
Stevens, 175n9
Strachan, Michael, 156n16
"straight middle-class white world," 84, 87; White vs., 77–110
the Streets, 124
Student Nonviolent Coordinating Committee, 46–47
subcultural affiliation, 25
subculture consciousness, 89
subcultures: experiences of, 118; in urban cultures, 97
suffering, 4, 128, 130, 141; Black, xviii
Sundance Film Festival, 96, 97
Sun newspaper, xiii
Surkin, Marvin, 46
surrealism, French, 24
suspicion: hermeneutics of, 140
syncretism: as explanatory tool for analysis of cultural formation, 69

Tarantino, Quentin, 108, 110
Tator, Carol, 150n10
Tatum, Wilbert, 80
Téchiné, André, 95, 122
technocratic expertise, 12
Teds, 27
television, 32, 53, 117, 119; "golden era" of, 113

Temporary Hoarding, xvi, 7, 23, 24–25, 36, 38
Terminator Salvation, 127
Thatcher, Margaret, xii–xiii, 25; "Caesarist regime" of, 34
Thatcherism: "in drag," 39
Third World Liberation, 17, 38, 75, 89
Thompson, E.P., 39
Thompson, Heather, 48
Thompson, Robert Farris, 72; *Flash of the Spirit*, 72
"Threatening Pleasures," 66
Tim Dog, 69
Time, 49
Time Out, 9, 17
TMZ, 143
Toronto: collective struggle for liberation in, 40, 62
totalitarianism, 142
To Wong Foo, Thanks for Everything! Julie Newmar, 172n115
trade union movement, 24, 48, 52
transatlantic dialogue, 12, 40, 136
transatlantic rebels: multiracial cohort of, 114
Trans-Urban News Service, 80
Tropic Thunder, 127
Trotsky, Leon, 142
Turner, J.M.W.: *Slavers Throwing Overboard the Dead and Dying*, 68
12 Years a Slave. See under McQueen, Steve
2 Live Crew, 102

underground raves, 35, 37, 66, 124
unionization, 52
United Auto Workers, 47, 56
United Black Youth League, 31
United Kingdom, xvi; Americanization of politics in, 28; analysis of race in, 32; "androgynous rock stars" from, 88; Black, history of, 129; Black artists in, 67; Black Britons, 69; Black cultural production in, 62, 71; Black identity in, 62, 115; Black political identity in, 17, 70; Black political imagination in, 68; Black popular culture in, 129; commodified Black

cultures in, 119; Conservative Party, xiii, 17–18, 25, 28–31, 37; diasporic communities in, 17; diasporic intellectuals in, 5; disruption of dominant political language in, 40; dominant sociology of race relations in, 38; exclusion of Blacks in, 32; Gilroy as "most influential intellectual writer" in, 135, 139–41; House of Commons Sub-committee on Race Relations and Immigration (1981), 29; immigrants in, 16–20, 24, 40, 70, 123; Immigration Act (1962), 17–18; industrial decline in, xii; Labour Party, 25, 28–31, 37; mainstreaming of Black culture in, 37; monarchy in, 5; Monday Club, 17; "moribund cultural order" of, 67, 70; multi-cultures in, 124; National Front, 23, 24–25, 30, 64, 157n36; nationalism in, 20; New Labour, 123; political advertisements in, 29–31; political culture of, 16; postcolonial, 65; postcolonial/diasporic intellectuals in, 5; proto-Black middle class in, 61; Race Relations Act (1965), 18–19; race riots in, 29; radical Black politics in, 17; radical politics and cultural production in, xvi; Socialist Workers Party, 25; SUS law, 29; Thatcher era in, xii–xiii; unemployment in, xii; and US, 19, 114; Vagrancy Act, 29; white left in, 38; working class in, 27; young people's response to racism in, 31
United Nations: Universal Declaration of Human Rights, xii, 22, 128
United States: Black bourgeoisie in, 61; Black cultural production in, 62; Black popular culture in, 129; civil disturbances in, 18; commodified Black cultures in, 119; decentering/deprovincializing of, 93; Democratic National Convention (1968), 20–21, (2004), 137; diasporic criticism as decentering, 92; extreme crime in, 26; imperial adventures of, 6; lived experiences of Black people in, 33; New York–centric view of, 68–69; parochialism of whites in, 92; racial capitalism in, xiii; racial problem in, 18–19; racial violence in, 40; Senate surveillance of Black radicals in, 47; and UK, 19, 114; white liberals in, 93
University of Birmingham, 16, 26
University of Sussex, 22, 25, 65
UPRUM, 44
utopia, 32–37

Van Peebles, Melvin, 99, 107
Verso, 70
video-based simulations, 119
video games: deleterious impact of, 121
video installation artists, 87
Village Voice, 4, 7, 78, 114–16
violence, 130; colonial, 124; domestic, 34; exclusionary, 101; gun, xiv; of isolated figures, 56; lack of assimilation/integration and, 18; racial, xiv, 19, 40; racist, 24, 68; state, 36, 135, 164n12
Visconti, Luchino, 49
Voices of East Harlem, 21

Walker, Alice: *The Color Purple*, 83
Walker, William, 89
Waller, Fats, 21
Walt Disney Studios, 142–44
Walters, Barbara, 138
Ware, Vron, 38
Washington, Booker T., xix
Washington, Denzel, 99
WASP ideal, 87
Watson, John, 45, 46–48, 51–52; as "hardcore revolutionary," 46
Wayans, Keenen Ivory, 109
Wayne State University, xvii, 45, 47–48, 51
Weinstein, Harvey, xviii, 99
Welles, Orson, 104
Wells-Barnett, Ida B., 73
West, Cornel, xix, 4, 101
West, Kanye, 12, 135, 139–41, 143–44, 146

West Bromwich Albion, 27
Wheatley, Catherine, 176n51
White, Armond, xii, xv–xix, xx, 9,
　40, 42, 52, 74–75, 76, 112, 126,
　135–36, 141–46; and adolescent
　films, 53; and advertisements, 74;
　as aesthete, 2, 46, 75, 142; and
　African American "race men," 4;
　American Book Award, 4; and
　art-house films, 83; and belonging,
　10; "better than lists," 126–27;
　birth and childhood of, 49; and
　Black Consciousness, 3, 10, 46,
　54, 83; "chauvinist pride" of, 6,
　92; and "childish" mainstream
　films, 83; and City Sun, xvii, 74,
　78, 79–82, 92, 99, 101, 102, 104–6,
　109, 110, 116; cultural criticism by,
　5, 40, 45, 74, 78, 81, 84; Deems
　Taylor Award, 85; dissidence and
　defiance of, 57; and Ebert, 108,
　127, 140; and enlargement of The
　American Cinema, 77–110; entry
　of into New York Film Critics
　Circle, 78; and European films,
　53; expulsion of from New York
　Film Critics Circle, 2, 4, 135, 139;
　and feminism, 5, 96; and film
　criticism, 49; and Gilroy, 114–15;
　and Global African American
　Studies, 4–6, 8; and hip hop, 81,
　91, 93, 102, 1-3, 142–43; inspirations
　to, 11–12; journalistic integrity of,
　103; and Kael, 46, 49, 52–53; as
　"Kanye West of film criticism,"
　12, 135, 139–41; Knee Deep in Great
　Experiences, 169n60; late style of,
　12–13, 142; as lone, dogged figure,
　57; and McQueen, 136, 139–41; and
　Morrison, 69, 74; and music, 10,
　45, 51, 56, 77–79, 81, 85–89, 91–92,
　99, 102; at New York Press, 115–18,
　120–22, 126–27; and nostalgia,
　83, 89, 95–98, 143; and Obama,
　137–38; and objectivity, 50; and
　political correctness, 117–18, 145;
　rationale for comparing with
　Gilroy, 1–3; and resentment, 142;
　The Resistance, 77–78; resistance
　aesthetics of, 4; reviews by, 45,
　51, 54–55, 78–110; and South End,
　45, 51–52, 54, 56; spats with film
　critics, 116–17; as "troll," 127; vs.
　straight middle-class white world/
　Black bourgeoisie, 77–110; as
　young critic, 51–53
whiteness, 108
white privilege, 48, 118
white supremacy, 32, 55, 75, 91,
　173n138; authentic resistance
　against, 142
Whitman, Walt, 118
Whodini: Funky Beat, 91
Widgery, David, 7–8, 23–24
Wilderson, Frank, 134
Williams, Raymond, 6–7, 39
Williams, Sweet T, 52
Wilmer, Val, 7–8, 33–34; As Serious as
　Your Life, 7, 67
Wilson, August, 137
Winks, Robin, 60, 138
The Wire, 149n1
wokeness, 142
Wonder, Stevie, 160n7; "Living for
　the City," 56
Wood, Donald, 22
work: dispiriting/alienating, 35;
　intersection of race, class, gender,
　and sexuality at, 63; and its
　overcoming, 35
working class: American, 44, 51;
　Black, 35, 37, 39, 103; British,
　27; and cultural radicalism, 24;
　cultures, 74; disenfranchised/
　disenchanted, 24; self-activity, 13;
　white, 114, 120
world citizens, 61–75
world-systems theory, 72
Wreford, Jo, 23
Wright, Patrick: On Living in an Old
　Country, 164n18
Wright, Richard, 33, 71, 72
Wynter, Sylvia, 8, 15, 101

X, Malcolm, xix, 4, 10, 47, 94, 103,
　170n68
xenophobia, 93, 146; rejection of, 6
X-Ray Spex, 25

Yale University, 115, 119, 123, 127
Young, Coleman, 56, 57
Young Soul Rebels. See under Julien,
    Isaac
youth cultures, 26–27

 **DANIEL MCNEIL** is a professor in the department of gender studies at Queen's University and the Queen's national scholar chair in Black studies. His scholarship and teaching in Black Atlantic studies explore how movement, travel, and relocation have transformed and boosted creative development, the writing of cultural history, and the calculation of political choices. He is the author of *Sex and Race in the Black Atlantic* and, with Yana Meerzon and David Dean, a co-editor of *Migration and Stereotypes in Performance and Culture*. He lives in Tkaronto/Toronto.